DEBATING THE ORIGINS OF THE COLD WAR

Debating Twentieth-Century America
Series Editor: James T. Patterson, Brown University

Debating American Immigration, 1882–Present
  by Roger Daniels and Otis L. Graham
Debating Southern History: Ideas and Action in the Twentieth Century
  by Bruce Clayton and John Salmond
Debating the Civil Rights Movement, 1945–1968
  by Steven F. Lawson and Charles Payne
Debating the Origins of the Cold War: American and Russian Perspectives
  by Ralph B. Levering, Vladimir O. Pechatnov, Verena Botzenhart-Viehe,
  and C. Earl Edmondson

Forthcoming in the series:

Debating the American Welfare State, 1945–Present
  by Nelson Lichtenstein, Sonya Michel, and Jennifer Klein
Debating FDR's Foreign Policy, 1932–1945
  by Justus Doenecke and Mark Stoler
Debating the New Deal
  by Robert McElvaine and Anthony Badger
Debating the Kennedy Presidency
  by James Giglio and Stephen Rabe
Debating the "Negro Problem"
  by Barbara J. Ballard and Marcus C. Bruce

DEBATING THE ORIGINS OF THE COLD WAR

American and Russian Perspectives

RALPH B. LEVERING, VLADIMIR O. PECHATNOV,
VERENA BOTZENHART-VIEHE,
AND C. EARL EDMONDSON

ROWMAN & LITTLEFIELD PUBLISHERS, INC.
Lanham • Boulder • New York • Oxford

ROWMAN & LITTLEFIELD PUBLISHERS, INC.

Published in the United States of America
by Rowman & Littlefield Publishers, Inc.
4720 Boston Way, Lanham, Maryland 20706
www.rowmanlittlefield.com

12 Hid's Copse Road
Cumnor Hill, Oxford OX2 9JJ, England

Map on page vii from *American Foreign Policy Since World War II*, 15th ed., by Steven W. Hook and John Spanier (CQ Press, 2000).

British Library Cataloguing in Publication Information Available

Library of Congress Cataloging-in-Publication Data

Debating the origins of the Cold War : American and Russian perspectives / Ralph B. Levering ... [et al.].
      p. cm.—(Debating twentieth-century America)
   Includes bibliographical references and index.
   ISBN 0-8476-9407-0 (alk. paper)—ISBN 0-8476-9408-9 (pbk. : alk. paper)
      1. United States—Foreign relations—Soviet Union—Sources. 2. Soviet Union—Foreign relations—United States—Sources. 3. Cold War—Sources. 4. World politics—1945—Sources. 5. United States—Foreign relations—1945–1989—Sources. I. Levering, Ralph B. II. Series.

E183.8.S65 D43 2002
327.73047—dc21   2001048522

Printed in the United States of America

♾™The paper used in this publication meets the minimum requirements of American National Standard for Information Sciences—Permanence of Paper for Printed Library Materials, ANSI/NISO Z39.48-1992.

CONTENTS

The American Perspective   1
Ralph B. Levering and Verena Botzenhart-Viehe

Documents

1. *The Atlantic Charter, August 14, 1941*   65

2. *"Comment on the Results of the Decisions Made at the Yalta
   Conference"*   67

3. *George F. Kennan's "Long Telegram," February 1946*   69

4. *Secretary of State James Byrnes's Speech in Stuttgart on Germany's
   Future, September 6, 1946*   74

5. *Speech by J. Edgar Hoover, Director, Federal Bureau of Investigation,
   at the Annual Convention of the American Legion in San Francisco,
   September 30, 1946*   76

6. *Henry A. Wallace's Speech in New York City, September 12, 1946*   78

7. *President Harry S. Truman's Speech to Congress, March 12, 1947*   81

The Russian Perspective   85
Vladimir O. Pechatnov and C. Earl Edmondson

Documents

1. *Stalin to "Politburo Four" ([Vyacheslav] Molotov, [Lavrenti] Beria,
   [Anastas] Mikoyan, and [Georgy] Malenkov), Ciphered [Coded]
   Telegram, December 9, 1945*   155

2. *A Compilation of [Written] Comments on Draft Treaties Regarding Demilitarization and Disarmament of Germany and Japan Proposed by [U.S. Secretary of State James] Byrnes, June 8, 1946*   *157*

3. *The [Nikolai] Novikov Report ["Telegram"]*   *160*

4. *The Minister of State Security Appeals for Measures to Close Down British Propaganda in the U.S.S.R.*   *165*

5. *Instructions for the Soviet Delegation to the Meeting of Foreign Ministers in Paris, June 25, 1947*   *167*

6. *Record of I[osef] V[issarionivich] Stalin's Conversation with the Czechoslovak Government Delegation on the Issue of Their Position Regarding the Marshall Plan and the Prospects for Economic Cooperation with the U.S.S.R.*   *169*

7. *Record of the Meeting of Comrade I[osef] V[issarionivich] Stalin with the Secretary of the Central Committee of the French Communist Party [Maurice] Thorez*   *173*

8. *Report by L. P. Beria and I. V. Kurchatov to I. V. Stalin on Preliminary Data Received during the Atomic Bomb Test*   *176*

Acknowledgments   179

Selected Readings   183

Index   187

About the Authors   199

Soviet expansion in Europe, 1939–1948

THE AMERICAN PERSPECTIVE

Ralph B. Levering and Verena Botzenhart-Viehe

UNEASY U.S.–SOVIET RELATIONS: 1917–1944

On March 8, 1943, the U.S. ambassador to the Soviet Union, retired Admiral William C. Standley, spoke with a group of American reporters in the embassy. Ever since he had arrived in Moscow early in 1942, Standley commented, "I've been looking for recognition in the Russian press of the fact that they are getting material help not only through Lend-Lease but through Red Cross and Russian–American Relief, but I've yet to find any acknowledgment of that."

Surprised that the ambassador was criticizing America's most powerful ally in the war against Nazi Germany, a reporter asked whether the statement could be quoted. After saying, "Yes," Standley continued: "The [Soviet] authorities seem to want to cover up the fact that they are receiving outside help. Apparently they want their people to believe that the Red Army is fighting this war alone. . . . It's not fair—the American people are giving millions to help the Russian people and yet the Russian people do not know where the supplies are coming from."

Within hours, stories reporting Standley's criticisms were appearing in radio news reports and on the front pages of America's newspapers. The story resonated for several days as administration officials, members of Congress, radio commentators, and editorial writers offered opinions. President Franklin Delano Roosevelt (FDR) said nothing publicly about the ambassador's truthful but undiplomatic remarks. Privately, however, FDR soon made it clear to Standley that he no longer had his confidence and should resign.

Viewed from the perspective of normal U.S. foreign relations, Standley's statement was highly unusual. American ambassadors normally do not criticize an allied nation in which they are serving, and certainly not—as in this case—when they have failed to seek prior approval for their remarks from higher-ranking officials in Washington. In fact, however, U.S. relations with the Union of Soviet Socialist Republics (commonly abbreviated to U.S.S.R., also known as the Soviet Union) had been abnormal in varying degrees ever since Vladimir Lenin had proclaimed the Soviet state in November 1917, and so they would remain until shortly before the U.S.S.R. ceased to exist in 1991.

Some scholars argue that the Cold War began in 1917–1920 with the first ideological, political, and military clashes between the U.S.S.R. and the West. But most scholars (ourselves included) believe that it makes more sense to place the start of the Cold War in the mid-1940s when, as a result of victory in World War II, American and Soviet leaders had the military power, the economic resources, and the determination to engage in a far-flung and intense ideological, political, military, economic, and cultural struggle for influence. Deeply affecting the domestic politics and foreign affairs of most of the world's nations, this multifaceted competition between the United States and its allies and the U.S.S.R. and its allies was one of the major phenomena in modern history.

Regardless of when one thinks the Cold War began, it is necessary to take into account major developments in world affairs and in American life from 1917 through 1944 in order to understand why it developed so quickly after the end of World War II in 1945. From the outset, U.S.–Soviet relations combined international and domestic components. The latter feature is often ignored or given short shrift; we will give it the attention we think it deserves. Itself multifaceted, the domestic component involved primarily the role of the Soviet-directed Communist party and opposition to it, as well as the way in which various segments of both the Democratic and Republican parties responded to it. The animosity that the overwhelming majority of Americans felt toward domestic communists and their sympathizers between 1917 and 1944—an attitude that typically was more intense and more consistent than the public's generally distrustful but varying views of the U.S.S.R.—helps to explain why America's international/domestic Cold War developed so swiftly after the wartime alliance with Russia ended.

U.S.–Soviet relations also involved a second combination: government officials and private citizens. Because of the ongoing political process, public opinion was of vital importance to officials. Both elected and appointed officials knew that leaders in the mass media, in labor unions, in business and farm organizations, and in religious and civic organizations often had as much or more influence than they had on many Americans' attitudes toward the U.S.S.R. and toward domestic communists. An example is Henry Luce, the moderate Republican publisher of *Time*, *Life*, and other magazines and of newsreels shown in movie theaters, who probably influenced American public opinion on foreign affairs in the 1930s and 1940s more than anyone other than President Roosevelt.

In stark contrast to the Soviet government's total domination of the news media and harsh suppression of dissent, the American people vigorously discussed issues with the confidence that government officials and fellow voters would pay attention. What the public thought about foreign policy issues and about America's Communist party mattered greatly to officials in Washington both before and during the Cold War.

A third combination that helps to explain the uneasiness in U.S.–Soviet relations is the two-pronged approach that America characteristically takes in conducting its foreign relations. This approach combines a careful calculation of interests (often called "realism") with a strong appeal to core principles (often called "idealism"). Like those of other nations, U.S. interests included such considerations as wanting to have allies to deter potential enemies and desiring trading partners to increase domestic prosperity. America's core principles—belief in a wide range of individual freedoms and in limited government with democratically elected leaders—contrasted sharply with the politically dictatorial, economically collectivist, and atheistic ideology of the U.S.S.R. As John Fousek has noted, "American nationalism has always been rooted in universal values—freedom, equality, and justice under law—that the United States claimed to stand for." Another historian, M. J. Heale, is equally perceptive: "The vigor of anticommunism has owed much to its capacity to tap the dominant values of American life."

In the first half of the twentieth century, the world effectively became smaller and more closely tied together due to rapid advances in the means of transportation and communication and in the potency and striking range of weapons of war. Realistic and idealistic motives—and the "foreign" and the "domestic"—were inextricably intertwined as America joined Great Britain, Canada, and other democratic nations in opposing imperial Germany in World War I, in fighting Nazi Germany and imperial Japan in World War II, and in combating Soviet and communist expansion after World War II.

Having outlined broad combinations that help to explain the background of the Cold War from America's perspective, we now look briefly at three significant periods between 1914 and 1945 that contributed greatly to animosity between the United States and the U.S.S.R.: the era of World War I (1914–1920), the Great Depression of the 1930s, and especially World War II

(1939–1945). In light of their consistently contrasting ideologies and often diverging interests, it is not surprising that the two countries found their relations strained or uneasy during each of these periods. And because the long-range goal of the Soviet-directed U.S. Communist party was to overthrow the nation's political and economic system, it also is not surprising that most Americans disliked communism and communists—including U.S. communists—just as intensely during these years as they did after World War II.

THE IMPACT OF WORLD WAR I AND ITS AFTERMATH

In order to understand the coming of the Cold War roughly thirty years later, one needs to be aware of several important developments of the era of World War I: (1) America's entry into the war and its vigorous participation in the postwar settlement under the leadership of President Woodrow Wilson; (2) the communist revolution in Russia under the leadership of Lenin, including its implications for Russia's domestic life and for world affairs; (3) the widespread animosity in Britain, France, Japan, and the United States toward Lenin's government, whose decision to make a separate peace with Germany in early 1918 increased Western anger toward the seemingly pro-German Bolsheviks and contributed to limited Allied military interventions in Russia; and (4) the birth of communist and anticommunist movements in the United States and other nations.

As numerous scholars have noted, Wilson chose to ask Congress for a declaration of war against Germany in April 1917 not only because he wanted to protect concrete U.S. interests, but also because he wanted America to have a prominent place at the peace table in order to help to make the world better. His reformist ideals were summed up in the most famous passage of his eloquent speech to Congress: "We are glad . . . to fight thus for the ultimate peace of the world and for the liberation of the peoples, the German peoples included; for the rights of nations great and small and the privilege of men everywhere to choose their way of life and of obedience. The world must be made safe for democracy. Its peace must be planted upon the tested foundations of political liberty."

Wilson's proposals for peace based on democratic self-determination and a League of Nations attracted widespread backing, especially among liberals and noncommunist, moderate socialists in America and western Europe. But they also encountered opposition. At home, many Republicans in Congress, who already felt disdain for the president's idealism and presumed arrogance, expressed skepticism about his proposals. Abroad, conservative

European leaders, especially in France and Italy, opposed Wilson's plan to treat Germany leniently and were dubious about the value of the League of Nations and about applying the concept of self-determination too broadly.

By far the most comprehensive challenge to Wilson's vision of a liberal, democratic peace came from the Bolshevik (communist) revolutionaries, led by Lenin and Leon Trotsky, who seized power in Petrograd on November 7, 1917, only months after a democratic government had replaced the tsar. Although the Bolshevik leaders sometimes were friendly in private talks with U.S. visitors, most of their words and deeds challenged Western liberal values and practices. Trotsky, for example, said that his country's fragile democracy had to be "trampled underfoot" for the "sake of the loftier principles of a social revolution"; not surprisingly, the Bolsheviks dissolved Russia's freely elected Constituent Assembly in January 1918. Similarly, religious institutions were suppressed because, in the Bolsheviks' view, they were dangerous relics of earlier feudal and capitalist eras. And because the Bolsheviks did not recognize individual rights or the rule of law, people who criticized the new government risked their lives. Lenin described the situation clearly: "The dictatorship means—learn this once and for all—unrestrained power based on force, not on law."

To Bolshevik leaders, harsh means were justified because their "scientific" goal—a harmonious, peaceful worldwide society lacking class distinctions and class conflict—was so desirable. But to Wilson and most other Western leaders, Lenin's dictatorial regime was an illegitimate abomination that they hoped the Russian people would overthrow. Secretary of State Robert Lansing called Bolshevism "the most hideous and monstrous thing that the human mind has ever conceived." Lansing and most other members of America's fervently capitalist, largely Protestant, and overwhelmingly pro-British elite hated and feared Lenin's communistic, atheistic, and pro-German regime.

In Lenin's and Trotsky's view, anticapitalist radicals in other countries should emulate the Bolsheviks' achievement and seek to overthrow their existing governments. To provide direction and encouragement to fledgling communist parties in other nations, the Bolsheviks established the Communist International (Comintern) in March 1919. Inspired both by the Soviet example and by the Comintern, radicals in Germany, Hungary, and Finland sought to seize power in those countries.

In America, too, communists and other radicals led general strikes, sent bombs through the mail addressed to high officials, and talked and wrote hopefully about seizing power. During this first Red Scare, which peaked in 1919 and early 1920, angry and fearful U.S. law-enforcement officials at all levels, often joined by probusiness activists who detested leftist labor unions, acted forcefully and often with little concern for civil liberties to quash what they saw as a serious communist and anarchist threat to American institutions. Because many of the radicals admired the hated Bolsheviks, most Americans supported the antiradical actions.

Disappointed by the Bolsheviks' behavior inside Russia and their calls for revolution abroad, and hopeful that anti-Bolshevik forces might be able to win the civil war of 1918–1920, Wilson and his closest advisers did not seriously consider recognizing Lenin's government. Wilson's last secretary of state, Bainbridge Colby, cited three main reasons in a statement in August 1920: (1) the Soviet government did not represent the will of the Russian people; (2) it violated fundamental principles of international relations by repudiating the tsarist government's debts and refusing to honor contracts; and (3) it used the Communist Information (Cominform) Bureau to foment revolution abroad.

By the time Wilson left office in March 1921, the struggle between the capitalist, largely democratic West and the communist, increasingly totalitarian Russia had reached something of a standoff. Although the anti-German powers dispatched troops to Russia from 1918 to 1920, partly to weaken the Soviet government, they had not sent sufficient forces to tip the balance of power from the communist "Reds" to the anticommunist "Whites" in Russia's civil war. The main results were enduring anger among many Russians toward the intervening powers and some justification for the communists' use of the word "imperialists" to describe them. At the same time, Soviet support for communist uprisings in Western nations backfired. By frightening and infuriating most people in the affected countries, the failed uprisings strengthened anticommunist sentiment in the West.

Having been gravely weakened by Russia's involvement in World War I and then by costly civil war, needing Western assistance to rebuild and modernize its economy, and counting as allies only small communist parties in other countries, the U.S.S.R. was too weak in the 1920s and early 1930s to conduct a substantial contest against the major capitalist powers. For their part, the American people, as demonstrated in the overwhelming victory for Republicans and "normalcy" in the 1920 election, had no desire for additional crusades anytime soon. Despite ongoing ideological antagonism reflected in the continuation of the nonrecognition policy and most Americans' animosity toward the Soviet-controlled U.S. Communist party, the challenges posed by the U.S.S.R. largely receded from public attention during the 1920s.

THE DEPRESSION'S MANY CHANGES

The Great Depression of the 1930s brought sweeping changes both in world affairs and in the role of the federal government, labor unions, and the Communist party in America. The largely peaceful world order of the postwar decade was threatened in the early 1930s by Japan's conquest of Manchuria, and in the middle 1930s by Italy's conquest of Ethiopia and by the militarism, racism, and expansionism of Adolf Hitler, Germany's new National Socialist (Nazi) ruler. In the same year, 1933, Hitler came to power in Germany and Roosevelt became the first Democratic president since Wilson.

Domestically, the early Roosevelt years are best known for the many innovative New Deal programs that sought to alleviate the worst effects of the Depression and to reform American capitalism by giving the federal government a major role in shaping the nation's economic and social life. In foreign affairs, the dominant attitude among the American people and Congress was isolationist or, more accurately, noninterventionist. Most Americans at the time had no desire for cultural or economic isolation. Largely because of the obvious failure of America's involvement in World War I to ensure lasting peace, however, they strongly believed that the United States should not send troops again to fight in European or Asian wars. For the majority, this belief lasted until Japan's attack on Pearl Harbor in 1941.

Although Roosevelt privately thought that noninterventionism represented a shortsighted, overly rigid approach to U.S. foreign policy in a dangerous and interdependent world, he yielded to public and congressional sentiment and signed a series of neutrality acts in the mid-1930s. Even after war began in Europe in 1939, FDR insisted that his successful effort to have Congress revise the neutrality acts and his other pro-Allied policies were intended to keep the United States out of the conflict. After Pearl Harbor, most Americans—including most former noninterventionists—endorsed FDR's now openly internationalist (i.e., interventionist) views. The America that Soviet leaders dealt with for fifty years after Pearl Harbor was overwhelmingly internationalist.

Ever optimistic, typically shrewd, and occasionally naïve, Roosevelt during his early years in office was much more positive than most Americans were about working with the U.S.S.R. and accepting the U.S. Communist party. He established diplomatic relations with the Soviet government in November 1933; as the decade progressed, he tacitly accepted communists' aspirations to play a significant, growing role in the nation's public life. In short, FDR deeply influenced both U.S.–Soviet relations and the domestic politics of the communist issue.

In Wilson's time and during the 1920s, virtually all Democratic and Republican leaders had opposed both recognizing the U.S.S.R. and granting any legitimacy to America's small Communist party. During the Roosevelt years, however, lively debates took place within and outside the administration on the proper policy to follow toward Russia's dictatorial government headed by Josef Stalin, as well as on the proper treatment of the growing communist and procommunist (fellow traveler) movement within the United States. These debates, during both the Depression and World War II, foreshadowed the similar but more decisive debates on these issues in the middle and late 1940s.

FDR had several reasons for establishing diplomatic relations with the U.S.S.R. in late 1933. He wanted to be able to work with Russia to counter Japanese expansion in East Asia and German ambitions in Europe. He sought increased trade between the two countries, a goal that many U.S. businessmen shared. Aware that nonrecognition had changed Russia's behavior neither at home nor abroad, he hoped that recognition might contribute to a mellowing of Soviet policy and thus to a gradual shift from a revolutionary state to a status quo power. Viewing the U.S.S.R. as inherently progressive and potentially democratic despite Stalin's ruthless dictatorship, FDR hoped throughout his presidency that Russia and America eventually would evolve into similar democratic nations that combined the best features of capitalism and socialism.

Most of Roosevelt's hopes were disappointed. Congress and the American people were too opposed to foreign commitments at the time to permit effective strategic cooperation against Japan and Germany; U.S.–Soviet trade remained meager; and Soviet leaders continued to direct U.S. communists' activities, despite a pledge not to do so. Moreover, Stalin's highly repressive policies disturbed most U.S. diplomats and journalists in Moscow, as did the rudeness and dishonesty of Soviet officials, their conspicuous spying on foreign diplomats, and their frequent refusal to respond positively even to minor requests. As diplomat George F. Kennan later commented, partly to emphasize his profound disagreement with FDR's largely conciliatory policy: "Never—neither then nor at any later date—did I consider the Soviet Union a fit ally or associate . . . for this country."

In Roosevelt's defense, it should be noted that his decision to recognize the U.S.S.R. gave America a listening post and a way to raise concerns and conduct negotiations with Stalin's government. Most important, it facilitated the U.S.–Soviet collaboration during World War II that contributed so greatly to victory over Hitler's Germany.

Three other developments of the 1930s that are essential to under-standing the Cold War merit brief discussion. The first was the rapid rise, both in numbers and in prominence, of the American Communist party— a development that occurred on a larger scale in France, China, and else-where. In 1930, the U.S. party had fewer than 10,000 members and very lit-tle political, economic, or cultural influence. The Depression's devastating impact on ordinary people, the widespread belief that the New Deal was too timid in addressing economic and social problems, respect for the So-viet stand against fascism in Europe, remarkably large financial support from the U.S.S.R. and from wealthy left-leaning Americans—these and other factors led to a rapid rise in the Communist party's membership and influ-ence. After Soviet leaders decided in 1935 that the communist parties in the United States and elsewhere should shift course and work with noncom-munists in "popular fronts" to oppose fascism, U.S. communist leader Earl Browder portrayed himself as an ally of FDR and other liberal Democrats and insisted—boldly but inaccurately—that "Communism is twentieth-century Americanism."

During the heyday of the Popular Front in the middle and late 1930s, communists were especially active in the Congress of Industrial Organiza-tions (CIO), which was founded in 1936 and quickly challenged the fer-vently anticommunist American Federation of Labor (AFL) for leadership in the labor movement. U.S. communists also worked actively in organiza-tions seeking equality for black Americans; in creative arts communities, es-pecially in New York and Hollywood; on the campuses of major universi-ties; and in the federal government. By 1939, communists held dominant leadership positions in eighteen CIO unions that together contained roughly 25 percent of all CIO members. At that time, Harvey Klehr and John Earl Haynes have noted, the party "had 66,000 registered members and perhaps ten times as many sympathizers." Because of their frequently high levels of education and fervent commitment to the anticapitalist cause, communists and fellow travelers had greater influence on American life than their numbers alone would have suggested.

The second phenomenon, related closely to the first, was the large-scale recruiting of American citizens to spy for Russia. One consequence of the U.S. decision to recognize the U.S.S.R. was the arrival of Soviet agents, attached to the embassy in Washington and consulates in New York and San Francisco, who avidly recruited spies, mainly among Communist party members and others who sympathized with the Left. By the mid-to-late 1930s, numerous officials in such agencies as the State Department and the

Treasury Department had been recruited as spies or informal sources, and large quantities of confidential documents were being made available to Soviet agents. At least one spy, Lauchlin Currie, worked in the White House, and many others stole secrets from U.S. industries. Because the communist spy network was well developed by the late 1930s, it was relatively easy for the Russians to place spies in the atomic bomb project during World War II and thus obtain information that speeded up their own work on atomic weapons.

Lack of concern among high administration officials also contributed to the extensive Soviet espionage. In September 1939, after Whittaker Chambers stopped spying for Russia, he went to see Assistant Secretary of State Adolf A. Berle Jr. Chambers named eight communist agents in the government and several others outside it. Berle later spoke with presidential aide Marvin McIntyre, who talked with Roosevelt. The latter dismissed the information McIntyre presented as "paranoid fantasy." To journalist Walter Winchell, who also spoke with the president about the communist penetration of the federal government, FDR responded angrily: "I don't want to hear another thing about it! It's not true!" During World War II, the Federal Bureau of Investigation (FBI) and other agencies focused on limiting spying by enemy nations, thus in effect permitting large-scale Soviet spying to continue. Contemporary critics were right to point out that the administration's typically cavalier attitude toward concerns about communist penetration of the federal government and labor unions threatened both the nation's security and the impartiality of such agencies as the communist-influenced National Labor Relations Board.

The final Depression-era root of the Cold War was the growing strength of the American anticommunist movement in the late 1930s, partly in reaction to the growth of communist influence in the labor movement and in the government and partly in reaction to the New Deal's prolabor, pro–civil rights, and "big government" stands. Two organizations that had been strongly anticommunist since the U.S.S.R.'s early years—the AFL and the Roman Catholic Church—played important roles. In an encyclical issued in March 1937, Pope Pius XI stated a view of communism that the overwhelming majority of American Catholics shared: "Communism is intrinsically evil, and therefore no one who desires to save Christian civilization from extinction should render it assistance in any enterprise whatsoever." Other organizations vocally opposed to communism included the two large veterans' groups, the American Legion and Veterans of Foreign Wars, the Daughters of the American Revolution and other patriotic societies, and such business groups as the U.S. Chamber of Commerce and the National Association of Manufacturers, some of whose member industries were fighting vigorous efforts by communist-influenced CIO affiliates to unionize them.

Seeking a legitimate issue on which to attack the Roosevelt administration and the labor movement, conservative Republicans and Democrats in Congress seized on the communist issue in the late 1930s. In 1938, liberals concerned about Nazi activities in America and conservatives worried about communist influence came together in the House of Representatives to create the House Committee on Un-American Activities (HUAC).

Under the leadership of conservative Texas Democrat Martin Dies, HUAC focused primarily on uncovering communist activities. Although Gallup polls consistently showed that most Americans supported HUAC's work, Dies himself was too anti–New Deal and too careless in lumping together liberals and communists to be an effective anticommunist leader. Nevertheless, HUAC lasted into the post–World War II era and played a prominent role in the early Cold War.

UNEVEN RELATIONS DURING WORLD WAR II

During most of World War II, America's government and public had uneven, often uneasy relations with the U.S.S.R. and domestic communists. From August 1939 until June 1941, the dominant emotion was anger, especially among the public and members of Congress, over the German–Russian pact. Then the period from the German invasion of Russia on June 22, 1941, through the first "Big Three" meeting at Teheran, Iran, in late 1943 was a generally hopeful time for both the government and the public. Appreciating the Russians' sacrifices and successes in their brave fight against Hitler's huge invading force, most Americans shared FDR's optimism that Stalin and his Western allies would be able to work together in winning both the war and the peace. As Russian armies moved into eastern Europe in 1944, however, concerns grew about Stalin's behavior and postwar goals, about FDR's commitment to Wilsonian principles in his dealings with the U.S.S.R., and about the influence of U.S. communists and fellow travelers.

Americans' widespread, intense anger toward the U.S.S.R. and toward domestic communists began when the two archenemies, Hitler and Stalin, signed a nonaggression pact on August 23, 1939. Having long and loudly proclaimed itself to be the leading opponent of Nazi Germany, Russia changed course and became Hitler's ally. *Collier's* magazine noted that the pact removed "all doubt, except in the minds of incurable dreamers, that there is any real difference between Communism and Fascism."

Having long been upset that Roosevelt had worked with Stalin and had supported many of the Popular Front's goals, Republican newspapers seized the opportunity to criticize FDR, Stalin, and the Popular Front. "Mr. Roosevelt's great Russian liberal democratic friend [Stalin] has turned despot," the *Chicago Tribune* editorialized. "The New Deal gets the busy signal on the Moscow line." The editors of the *New York Herald-Tribune* balanced anger at the pact with satisfaction that American communists' "'popular front' strategy is doomed, and they stand forth for what they have always been, the tools of a dictator whose principles and objectives differ only in nomenclature from those of [Hitler]."

Things only got worse for Stalin's government and U.S. communists after German troops invaded Poland on September 1, 1939, thus triggering World War II in Europe. Two weeks later, in accordance with the pact's secret provisions, Russia invaded Poland from the east and seized almost half the country. The next month, it demanded and received base rights in the small Baltic nations of Latvia, Lithuania, and Estonia that had broken off from the Russian empire during World War I. This was the first step toward incorporating these nations into the U.S.S.R., despite Western protests, the following summer. Then on November 30, 1939, after Finland had rejected Soviet demands for bases and territory, Russian forces invaded the lightly populated country. Although all of these moves could be justified as defensive measures to protect against the possibility that Germany might attack its new ally in the future, most Americans saw no reason to condone these Soviet actions.

The Soviet attack on "poor little Finland" outraged Americans of all political persuasions except for the dwindling number of communists and fellow travelers. "In the smoking ruins of the damage wrought in Finland lies what remained of the world's respect for the Government of Russia," the *New York Times*, the nation's leading newspaper, editorialized on December 1.

Roosevelt and other political leaders also condemned the Soviet invasion. Urging U.S. aircraft manufacturers to stop selling supplies to Russia, FDR invoked a "moral embargo" against the U.S.S.R. And in a move that had the effect of shoring up support among Catholic and other anticommunist supporters prior to the 1940 election, FDR asserted in a well-publicized speech that the Soviet Union "is run by a dictatorship as absolute as any other dictatorship in the world." The president condemned the "regimentation," the "indiscriminate killing," and the "banishment of religion" in Russia. But he resisted congressional pressure to break diplomatic relations. In his response to Soviet actions, Roosevelt skillfully combined the strands of idealism and realism—and of the domestic and the international—that long had characterized U.S. foreign policy.

During this period, American communists added to their unpopularity by defending Stalin's actions. They also triggered strikes in the unions they controlled against industries making defense materials that were being sold to Britain and France. Reflecting majority opinion, officials at all levels responded by arresting communists—including Browder on charges of using a falsified passport—and by passing laws limiting communist and fascist activities. Directed primarily against communists, the Smith Act of 1940 made it illegal to establish or belong to organizations that would "teach and advocate the overthrow of the United States government by force and violence." The public agreed: In a Gallup poll conducted in May 1941, 71 percent of the respondents favored making it a crime to belong to the Communist party.

Anticommunist labor leaders tried to expel communists from leadership positions in the CIO. This effort failed, but the United Auto Workers and other CIO unions passed resolutions criticizing the communist-led strikes in defense plants and condemning "the brutal dictatorships, and wars of aggression of the totalitarian governments in Germany, Italy, Russia, and Japan." Because of these and many other anticommunist/anti-Russian statements and actions by governmental and private bodies, the period from late August 1939 through mid-June 1941 is often called the "little Red Scare."

Despite the widespread animosity toward Russia and domestic communists, Roosevelt worked to improve U.S.–Soviet relations, especially after France surrendered to Germany in June 1940. FDR correctly viewed Germany and Japan as serious threats to U.S. interests and Russia as a potential ally against them. Lengthy talks in Washington between U.S. and Soviet officials bore fruit when America lifted the "moral embargo" early in 1941. Having learned that Hitler intended to attack Russia, Roosevelt also successfully resisted congressional efforts to prevent Russia from receiving future U.S. aid under the Lend–Lease Act that FDR signed on March 11, 1941.

In June and December 1941, Hitler made two dramatic moves that changed the course of twentieth-century history. Although Britain was far from defeated, he ordered German forces to invade Russia, seeking to conquer that huge, populous country. Then, only days after Japan's surprise attack at Pearl Harbor, he declared war on the United States, another industrialized country with a population more than twice the size of Germany's. Through these actions, Hitler brought into being the Grand Alliance—led by Russia, Britain, and America—that totally defeated Germany and its relatively weak European allies by May 1945.

In the months before and immediately after America became fully involved in the war, FDR established two central goals for the nation: first, to keep the Allied nations working together effectively until victory was ensured; and second, to establish the basis for a lasting peace. To Roosevelt, one key to a lasting peace was continued cooperation among the Big Three powers plus China, which he sometimes called the "Four Policemen" in conversations about the postwar world.

Another key to the peace, FDR and the vast majority of his fellow citizens believed, was strong U.S. leadership in world affairs. Blaming World War II largely on America's withdrawal from world leadership after World War I, most politically aware Americans thought that their country should take the lead in shaping and ensuring the peace. Never again would a dictator be permitted to divide the democracies and win an easy victory over them, as Hitler had at the Munich Conference in 1938. Between the wars, the U.S. military had been weak; after the war, it would be as strong as was necessary to defend freedom and preserve the peace. The humiliating defeat at Pearl Harbor must never be allowed to happen again. Americans also agreed overwhelmingly that the peace should be based on such Wilsonian principles as national self-determination, religious and other personal freedoms protected by law, growing freedom in international trade and investment, and increasingly effective international institutions.

Because of the broad consensus on goals in world affairs, very few Americans raised objections to the Allies' two great statements of purpose, the Atlantic Charter announced by Roosevelt and British prime minister Winston Churchill in August 1941 and the Declaration of the United Nations signed by America and twenty-five other nations—including Britain and Russia—in January 1942.

Among other things, the Atlantic Charter asserted "the right of all peoples to choose the form of government under which they live"; ruled out "territorial changes that do not accord with the freely expressed wishes of the peoples concerned"; and, in the first official reference to what in 1945 became the United Nations organization, advocated "a wider and more permanent system of general security" (see document 1). Pledging not to make a separate peace with any of the Axis powers until "complete victory" was achieved, the signatories of the Declaration of the United Nations agreed "to defend life, liberty, independence and religious freedom, and to preserve human rights and justice in their own lands as well as in other lands."

U.S. leaders in government and in private life enthusiastically endorsed both statements, but Soviet officials raised objections. When a Russian

diplomat expressed concern about the clause guaranteeing religious freedom, FDR blithely assured him that Russia could develop its own defini-
tion. After reading the Atlantic Charter, another Soviet official, Ivan Maisky,
commented that it sounded "as if England and the USA fancied themselves
as Almighty God, with a mission to judge the remainder of the sinful world,
including my own country." Maisky was half right: Although few if any
Britons or Americans saw themselves as God, most readily criticized behavior abroad that did not conform to their sense of right and wrong.

To argue that Americans were largely united on goals is not to suggest
that they supported all the specific actions that Roosevelt undertook in pursuit either of Allied unity during the war or a Wilsonian peace thereafter.
On the contrary, FDR faced significant constraints and dilemmas resulting
both from domestic political realities and from Churchill's and especially
Stalin's wartime and postwar goals. Perhaps he himself was not certain about
whether the peace really could be built from Wilsonian materials (a mixture of ideals and interests), or whether it would have to be based on the
more traditional "realist" constructs of balances of power and spheres of influence.

Aware of the conflicting pressures and the immense challenges that he
faced, Roosevelt made one of his most self-revelatory comments to trusted
aides in May 1942: "You know I am a juggler, and I never let my right hand
know what my left hand does. . . . I may be entirely inconsistent, and furthermore I am perfectly willing to mislead and tell untruths if it will help
win the war."

During the war, FDR had to try to be an even more accomplished
juggler than he had been in leading America during the Depression. With
regard only to issues involving U.S.–Soviet relations, he had to keep in the
air such domestic political balls as Americans' desire for a Wilsonian peace,
the fears of Polish Americans and other Catholics and Americans of east
European descent that Stalin would try to dominate and communize eastern Europe, and the need from his standpoint to have Democratic candidates for president and Congress (himself included) win the 1944 election.

Simultaneously, FDR had to keep aloft such international balls as
Stalin's desire for an early large-scale invasion of western Europe by British
and American forces—a massive second front—to relieve German pressure
on Soviet forces and Churchill's contrary insistence that the Western allies
should concentrate their efforts in the Mediterranean area and in southeastern Europe. If Roosevelt occasionally chose to "mislead and tell untruths" in order to keep these and other balls in the air, he clearly was doing so for what he saw as the greater good for America and the world,

whose fates—especially after the United States entered the war—appeared inextricably intertwined.

FDR's efforts to juggle conflicting realities were evident in a series of diplomatic meetings in 1942 and 1943. In meetings with Soviet foreign minister V. M. Molotov in late May and early June 1942, Molotov urged Roosevelt to agree to create "a second front in Europe in 1942." Recognizing both British reluctance to risk such a gamble and the difficulties of assembling sufficient men and supplies in England to undertake such a large-scale operation, America's top military leader, General George C. Marshall, urged the president to delete "in 1942" from the joint statement. FDR refused, thus creating difficulties with Churchill and especially with Stalin, who was disappointed with his Western allies when Churchill informed him a couple months later that the second front had been postponed to 1943.

Not surprisingly, Stalin became truly angry when, in June 1943, Roosevelt and Churchill put off the second front until 1944, thus in effect forcing Russian soldiers and civilians to continue doing more than 90 percent of the fighting and dying against German forces for yet another year. Yet, as Ambassador Standley noted, Stalin also should have shown more appreciation for the huge quantities of Lend–Lease aid (e.g., 400,000 trucks) and private assistance (e.g., through Russian War Relief) that Americans were sending to Russia during the war. He also should have acknowledged that America and Britain were also fighting Japan at the time and thus could not join the U.S.S.R. in devoting their full energies to the war against Germany. Nevertheless, Stalin's expectation of territorial and other rewards for Russia in the peace settlement, regardless of the principles proclaimed in the Atlantic Charter and similar statements, is easily understood.

A believer in his ability to establish trust and overcome differences in face-to-face meetings, FDR was disappointed when Stalin, angry about the further postponement of the second front, rebuffed his efforts in mid-1943 to set up a meeting between the two leaders. But Stalin finally agreed to a foreign ministers' meeting in Moscow in October and to a Big Three meeting in Teheran late in the year.

Soviet leaders were more cooperative at the Moscow Conference than they had been a few months earlier. They agreed not only to join the war against Japan after Germany was defeated, but also to support Secretary of State Cordell Hull's—and millions of other Americans'—virtual panacea for peace, a new international organization to replace the ineffective, discredited League of Nations.

FDR had three main goals when he departed in November 1943 on his long and arduous trip to Teheran: (1) to establish a positive personal relationship with Stalin that might last well into the postwar era; (2) to enable the three leaders to develop a fuller understanding of each other's positions on major issues, thus limiting misunderstandings and hopefully smoothing the path toward agreement on solutions; and (3) to persuade Congress and the American public, after the end of the conference, that his plans for continuing Big Three cooperation in war and peace were realistic and achievable.

At Teheran, Roosevelt worked hard to develop a warm and trusting relationship with Stalin. He did so partly by slighting and criticizing his good friend and distant relative, Churchill. Refusing to meet alone with the prime minister either before or during the conference, he set up private sessions with Stalin and criticized Churchill and British foreign policy both in these conversations and in meetings at which Churchill was present. FDR later told Labor Secretary Frances Perkins that he felt he finally established a warm relationship with Stalin when, on the last morning of the conference, he teased Churchill "about his Britishness, . . . about his cigars, about his habits. . . . Winston got red and scowled, and the more he did so, the more Stalin smiled. . . . I kept it up until Stalin was laughing with me, and it was then that I called him 'Uncle Joe'. . . . The ice was broken and we talked like men and brothers."

More important from the standpoint of policy, FDR sought Stalin's friendship and cooperation by repeatedly telling him that he largely agreed with him on such major issues as the future of eastern Europe and Germany. Only domestic political considerations, Roosevelt implied, kept him from fully endorsing Stalin's views.

On the important questions of Poland's postwar boundaries, FDR agreed with Stalin in principle that Russia should be allowed to have much of eastern Poland, with Poland being compensated with land taken from its western neighbor, Germany, at war's end. But Roosevelt also told Stalin, a U.S. aide recorded, that "there were in the United States from six to seven million Americans of Polish extraction, and, as a practical man, he did not wish to lose their vote" in the upcoming election. He thus hoped that Stalin would understand that "he could not publicly take part in any . . . arrangement [to redefine Poland's borders] at the present time."

Explaining to the skeptical Stalin and Churchill why he supported a powerful new international security organization, FDR noted that the U.S. public and Congress would oppose regional arrangements as creating spheres of influence and would support only a worldwide approach. Roosevelt did not need to cite public opinion in regard to Germany: He rightly believed that most Americans, like most Britons and Russians, desired a harsh peace. The Big Three largely agreed on this issue at Teheran.

There is now substantial evidence from Soviet sources that Stalin never understood how the U.S. political system worked. He apparently thought either along Marxist–Leninist lines that the wealthiest capitalists controlled the country or that, during wartime, FDR had the same unquestioned power in America that he wielded in Russia. Stalin commented to aides privately that Roosevelt was raising concerns about public opinion and Congress as "an excuse." "He's [America's] military leader and commander in chief," Stalin told Molotov. "Who would dare object to him?"

In his upbeat radio address to the American people on Christmas Eve, 1943, FDR said that he had established "fine" personal relations with Stalin and that "we are going to get along very well with him and the Russian people." FDR assured his listeners that they "could look forward into the future with real, substantial confidence that . . . 'peace on earth, good will toward men' can and will be realized and insured." "The rights of every Nation, large or small, must be respected and guarded as jealously as the rights of every individual within our own Republic," FDR asserted in Wilsonian language. "The doctrine that the strong shall dominate the weak is the doctrine of our enemies—and we reject it."

In traveling to Teheran and then communicating directly with the public, FDR recognized that the Big Three had a dual task: to negotiate with each other and also to persuade a broad range of leaders and ordinary voters in the two powerful Western democracies that their words and actions were likely to lead to what a group of prominent mainstream Protestants, headed by New York lawyer John Foster Dulles, called "a just and durable peace."

From the U.S. public's perspective, prospects for a lasting peace generally looked good in 1943. From the great Russian victory at Stalingrad early in the year to the conferences at Moscow and Teheran near the end, the major media—newspapers, magazines, books, radio, newsreels, and movies—repeatedly praised Russia's contributions in the war against Hitler and predicted continued Allied cooperation in the postwar world. Communist party membership and influence were growing again, and pro-Russian organizations like the National Congress of American–Soviet Friendship reached the height of their popularity. Seen in retrospect, 1943 marked the apogee of American goodwill toward the U.S.S.R.

Cooperation, most Americans assumed, would largely be based on their nation's ideals, which were thought to be both just and universally applicable. These assumptions were evident in the wording of the question about U.S.–Soviet relations that the Gallup poll asked most frequently during the war: "Do you think Russia can be trusted to co-operate with us after the war is over?" Judged by today's standards, this question seems ethno-centric. A more neutral question might have read as follows: "Do you think Russia and America will be able to cooperate after the war?" Given the in-nocent, often admirable idealism that permeated American culture in the 1940s, however, the question fit its time perfectly. Respondents could an-swer "yes," "no," or "no opinion."

From 1942 through 1944, there was typically a strong plurality of "yes" responses, and the overall trend of positive responses was upward. Although there were fluctuations between 36 and 50 percent, in 1942 the average per-centage of "yes" responses was 42.3 percent. It rose to 44.7 percent in 1943 and inched up to 45.3 percent in 1944. Despite the administration's and the news media's generally favorable portrayals of the U.S.S.R., roughly one-third of respondents consistently expressed distrust of Russia.

During 1944, virtually all Americans were pleased about continued Al-lied cooperation and progress in the war against Germany, and most people who followed the news were pleased as well that Soviet officials participated in the U.S.–sponsored conferences in the summer of 1944 that laid the groundwork for the United Nations and other international institutions. With regard to U.S.–Soviet relations, to FDR's relations with Polish Amer-icans and other Catholics, and to his party's ties to domestic groups with communist members, however, 1944 was not as good a year as 1943 had been.

Roosevelt's two main goals for 1944 were to continue working with the Allies for victory over Germany and Japan and a lasting peace, and to be elected for a fourth term in November. Viewing these goals as intercon-nected, FDR sought to play down growing differences with Stalin on sev-eral issues, notably Poland.

As German and Russian troops were conquering Poland in 1939, many prominent Poles fled to London, where they set up a government-in-exile. During the winter of 1943–1944, Churchill and Roosevelt tried to improve relations between this government, which deeply disliked and distrusted the U.S.S.R., and Stalin, who felt the same way about the London Poles. In essence, the Western leaders wanted the Poles to become conciliatory toward Stalin and, specifically, to accept Russia's insistence on regaining much of the territory in eastern Poland that it had lost in World War I and then regained at the start of World War II.

Western leaders also were prepared to ask Stanislaw Mikolajczyk, a leader in the government-in-exile, to remove its most strongly anti-Soviet officials. In return, Churchill and Roosevelt hoped, Stalin would agree to re-store the diplomatic relations with the London Poles that he had severed in the spring of 1943, negotiate with Mikolajczyk about the numerous unresolved issues relating to Poland's future that had become more urgent after Russian troops entered Polish territory in early 1944, and thus largely accept the political independence of this populous, predominantly Catholic nation.

Despite repeated pleas from Churchill and Roosevelt, Stalin held firm to his position that the London Poles, dominated by "pro-fascist imperialist elements," were "incorrigible" and "incapable of establishing friendly relations with the Soviet Union." Refusing to take "no" for an answer, Western leaders kept working to improve Russo–Polish relations. An apparent breakthrough occurred in midsummer, when Stalin agreed to hold a series of meetings with Mikolajczyk in Moscow in early August.

On August 1, two days before the first meeting took place, Polish underground fighters with ties to the government-in-exile began an uprising in Warsaw against German forces. Soviet policies toward the uprising raised more doubts in the West about postwar cooperation with Russia than any other wartime development. Because the Poles were assisting in the war against Hitler and because Russian radio broadcasts in Polish had encouraged an uprising as Soviet forces approached Warsaw, Western leaders and ordinary citizens alike assumed that Russia would aid the insurgents. In their final meeting on August 9, Stalin promised Mikolajczyk that he would do so.

To the surprise and anger of most Poles and their Western supporters, Stalin gave no aid to the insurgents for more than a month, by which time they had sustained more than 200,000 casualties and were largely defeated. Equally appalling to Western leaders, Stalin strongly discouraged British and U.S. efforts to aid the insurgents. He refused, for example, to permit U.S. planes to land on Soviet airfields after dropping supplies over Warsaw.

In a message to Western leaders on August 22, Stalin denounced the Polish underground army as·"a group of criminals" who began the uprising in order to seize power. This message appeared to explain his callousness: He wanted the Germans to defeat the insurgents in order to make it easier to establish Soviet control of Poland under the auspices of the highly unpopular group of Polish communists that he had assembled in Lublin.

The numerous U.S. officials angered by Soviet behavior during the Warsaw uprising included Averell Harriman, the level-headed ambassador to Russia whom FDR liked and respected. In a message on September 10, Harriman, who had gone to Moscow a year earlier with high hopes for U.S.–Soviet cooperation, deplored the Soviet leaders' "indifference to world opinion regarding their unbending policy toward Poland" and their tendency to "become a world bully wherever their interests are involved." Following the advice of aide Kennan, a longtime expert on the Soviet Union, Harriman urged "a firm but friendly *quid pro quo* attitude" in dealing with Stalin.

Still doubting the productiveness of a firmer approach and emphasizing Big Three cooperation during his campaign for reelection, FDR did not change U.S. policy. But at a conference in Quebec in September, he reinforced America's special relationship with Britain—and not with Russia—by agreeing with Churchill on joint U.S.–British control of atomic energy after the war. He also talked with Churchill and other leaders about whether it would be possible to have Western armies reach parts of central and eastern Europe before Soviet forces arrived.

On the home front, FDR spent considerable time and energy in 1944 trying to keep the votes of Polish Americans, many of whom feared that he and Churchill were not doing enough to prevent Poland from coming under Soviet control. Despite growing anger and well-organized protests against U.S. policy among Polish Americans throughout the year, the master politician succeeded remarkably well. He helped himself by deceptively telling Mikolajczyk during a meeting in June that he had not agreed at Teheran to give much of eastern Poland to Russia. Polish American leaders helped him during the campaign by accepting and publicizing vague promises, including Roosevelt's claim that he would ensure at the peace conference that Poland remained a "great nation."

The Republican candidate for president, Thomas A. Dewey, and his chief foreign policy adviser, John Foster Dulles, also helped FDR by agreeing in August to a State Department proposal to exclude foreign policy issues from the campaign. Most recent European immigrants, including Polish Americans, supported the president's liberal domestic policies (which Dewey attacked) and were not yet very afraid of domestic communists (whom Dewey also criticized). Agreeing to exclude an issue that many Americans *were* concerned about—the danger Soviet expansion posed to European peoples and to American ideals—was a big gift to FDR.

Browder's endorsement of Roosevelt gave Dewey an opening that he repeatedly tried to exploit. "In Russia, a Communist is a man who supports his government," Dewey commented. "In America, a Communist is a man who supports the fourth term so our form of government may more easily be changed."

The communist issue probably had the greatest resonance among voters—especially among Catholics and rural or small-town Protestants—of all the issues Republican candidates and their supporters raised in 1944. "The greatest potential menace to permanent peace is Soviet Russia," the editors of *Catholic World* wrote in October 1944. "Fascism is not and never was as dangerous as Communism." That same month, the editors of *Farm Journal and Farmer's Wife* put the communist danger exactly where Dewey was putting it, in America: "The coalition of the machine bosses with the spokesmen of radicalism and Communism is ominous for freedom, and a challenge to all American ideas of liberty and democracy."

Partly because of the communist/labor issue and partly because the public as a whole had become less liberal, the election results were surprisingly close—the closest, in fact, since 1916. Roosevelt had much going for him—a wealth of experience and political skills, the widespread popularity of both the New Deal and his internationalist foreign policy, the desire of many Americans for continuity of leadership in wartime, organized labor's skill in identifying Democratic supporters and getting them to vote, and Dewey's stiff personality and inexperience in national and world affairs. Yet FDR received only 53.4 percent of the vote, hardly a ringing endorsement of his leadership, and Republicans gained seats in the Senate.

On the defensive on the communist issue during the election, thereafter Roosevelt largely remained on the defensive in regard to U.S.–Soviet relations. He was caught politically between repeated promises to deliver a Wilsonian peace and Russian actions, especially in Poland, that threatened those promises. Happily playing offense in November, the conservative *Saturday Evening Post* urged Russia to ease Allied fears "with a broad and generous policy toward her neighbors and more assurances that she has no plans for a new hegemony over the European 'heartland.'" In December, William Green, the head of the AFL, warned the rival CIO that its representatives should not attend an international gathering of trade unions that would include delegates from the U.S.S.R. because the Russians "do not have free trade unions" and because U.S. and Russian workers' "fundamental philosophies and objectives are diametrically opposed."

Unhappily playing defense, Roosevelt met in the White House on December 23 with several internationalist senators and successfully urged them not to open a debate on foreign policy that could harm U.S. relations with Russia and Britain.

Roosevelt was less successful in dealing with Stalin. Fearing both domestic and international repercussions if the Soviet dictator decided to recognize the Lublin committee as Poland's government, FDR pleaded with him in mid-December not to do so before the next Big Three meeting occurred. When Stalin replied that he was going ahead, the president responded that he was "disturbed and deeply disappointed." Recognition followed in early January 1945.

Most Americans continued to hope, with Roosevelt, that the United States and the U.S.S.R. would find a way to cooperate in the postwar world. But America intended to remain heavily involved in international affairs, with or without Russian cooperation. Espousing a much broader conception of national security than before Pearl Harbor, and wishing to maintain what historian Melvyn P. Leffler has called "a preponderance of power" over all potential enemies, U.S. officials—with strong public support—were planning throughout the war to organize as much of the postwar world as possible along Wilsonian and geostrategic lines. Several agencies—notably the State Department and the War Department—did detailed planning for the peace in 1943 and 1944 based on the twin assumptions of the universal applicability of America's ideals and the continuing superiority of U.S. military power.

In short, by the winter of 1944–1945 America's leaders intended to run the postwar world economically, politically, and militarily, even as they hoped to do so in cooperation with Britons and Russians. As FDR stated in a radio message on January 6, 1945, "We can fulfill our responsibilities for maintaining the security of our country only by exercising our power and our influence to achieve the principles in which we believe and for which we have fought."

President Wilson, a deft wordsmith, had made many memorable speeches with virtually identical themes between 1917 and 1920. But it is doubtful that even he could have offered a clearer and more insightful summary of America's internationalist foreign policy.

FROM WARTIME ALLIES TO COLD WAR RIVALS: 1945–1946

There is a story, dating from the late 1960s or early 1970s when the American academic debate over the Cold War's origins was most heated, about a graduate student who had written his doctoral dissertation on the subject. Three professors would decide whether he passed: one thought that U.S. and British leaders' assertive actions and anti-Russian attitudes were responsible for the Cold War; another blamed Russia's expansionism and Stalin's uncooperative approach; and the third thought that the unstable, uncertain political and economic conditions in many nations at the end of World War II and the almost inevitable jockeying for power in these countries among the three main victors triggered the conflict.

Because of their contrasting, strongly held opinions, the three professors were barely on speaking terms with each other. One of them asked the first question: "How do *you* explain the coming of the Cold War?" After a long silence in which the tension in the room rose even higher, the flustered graduate student finally said in a low voice, "The answer is—uh, uh—in part."

Although the professors were disappointed, in fact the answer reflected the profound truth that all short answers to the question—or, indeed, lengthy ones like those that have appeared in hundreds of books on the subject—are likely to be partial and incomplete. One reason is that available Soviet sources have been much scarcer than Western ones. More important, the complexity and interrelatedness of all the factors involved, combined with scholars' diverse predispositions and values, have made it hard thus far to agree on any one set of relevant facts, much less on one interpretation. In reaching their own conclusions, readers thus are encouraged not only to weigh the perspectives offered in this book, but also to undertake further study of this fascinating subject.

Our short answer to the question begins by acknowledging the considerable truth reflected in each professor's viewpoint. We agree that Western leaders often were assertive and anti-Russian, that Stalin's government typically was expansionist and uncooperative, and that jockeying for power was almost inevitable, especially in the huge power vacuums in Europe and Asia left by Germany's and Japan's defeat.

Writing with a U.S.–centered focus, we would add that the overwhelming majority of both the public and officials in Washington believed in 1945–1946 and thereafter that a lasting peace would have to be based largely on Wilsonian—by then, bipartisan American—principles. They also believed that communism was an inherently evil system of government and that Soviet expansionism—like German and Japanese expansionism in the 1930s—threatened peace, freedom, and prosperity. Strongly nationalistic and proud, Americans thought that they lived in the world's most powerful, most virtuous, and most freedom-loving nation. Partly because they wanted above all to enjoy liberty and prosperity at home, they wanted a peaceful, cooperative world order. Because "isolationism" failed to ensure peace after World War I, Americans were determined not to repeat that perceived mistake.

Given beliefs like these, and given the fact that Britons and other Europeans generally shared Americans' love of freedom and distaste for expansionist dictatorships, it is hard to imagine that a Cold War with Russia could have been avoided unless Stalin had been willing to cooperate with Western governments and peoples largely on their own terms. Especially after the end of the war with Japan in August 1945, the strongest message that most Americans and Europeans thought they were getting from Stalin was his unwillingness to do so. "If we cannot have a world community with the Russians as a constructive member," a disappointed British Foreign Office official noted in early 1946 in words that easily could have been written in Washington, "it seems clear that the next best hope for peace and stability is that the rest of the world, including the vital North American arsenal, should be united in defense of whatever degree of stability we can attain."

Perhaps the biggest interpretive error that students of the early Cold War sometimes make is to assume practical and moral equivalence between U.S. and Soviet behavior. Both America and Russia were powerful militarily and expansionist for security and ideological reasons, and each stood firm for its vision of the postwar world. But there the similarities largely ended. Throughout eastern Europe and in their occupation zone in Germany, Russians and their local communist allies in the middle and late 1940s repeatedly deprived large numbers of people of every individual right valued in the West, including freedom of speech and religion, the right to own property, the right to choose one's place of residence, the right to a fair trial, and the right to choose political leaders through free and fair elections. Indeed, about the only positive the Russians had going for them in some of the countries they occupied was the fact that they were not the hated Germans. And even that did not help them in Germany and Austria, where Soviet soldiers and officials raped many thousands of women and carted off large quantities of property.

Some individual Western occupiers acted improperly, but in the main west Europeans, from Norway to Italy, welcomed the U.S. and British presence on the continent as a counterweight to Soviet influence. Local populations also generally understood that America and Britain sought to restore individual rights, prosperity, and democratic governments.

Another common interpretive error is to argue that America's "real motive" in leading an anti-Soviet coalition after World War II was economic. To be sure, most Americans valued money and, with the Depression a fresh memory, concern about postwar prosperity was widespread. The economic interpretation's great flaw, however, is that it is far too narrow and monocausal. Most Americans wanted friendly, democratic nations overseas not only for economic reasons, but also for political and strategic ones. As true Wilsonians, they wanted the horrors of war to be redeemed in the building of a freer, more democratic, prosperous, and peaceful world. Although most Americans disliked Stalin's communist system and did not want it to spread, his disregard for other people's basic human rights also helped to turn tens of millions of Americans against the U.S.S.R. in the early postwar years.

GROWING DIFFERENCES DURING ROOSEVELT'S FINAL MONTHS

On January 10, 1945, Arthur Vandenberg of Michigan, the leading Republican on the Senate Foreign Relations Committee, delivered a major address. Speaking on the Senate floor, Vandenberg called on the administration to "reassert, in high places, our American faith in . . . the Atlantic Charter." The former noninterventionist criticized "Russia's unilateral plan" that appeared "to contemplate the engulfment . . . of a surrounding circle of buffer States, contrary to our conception of what we thought we were fighting for in respect to the rights of small nations and a just peace." Instead of acting unilaterally, Vandenberg argued, Russia should work with its allies to establish "collective security" to prevent future German aggression. Although he did not mention Poland by name, he strongly implied that Soviet domination of that country and its neighbors would betray "our aspirations, our sacrifices and our dreams."

Vandenberg's speech was significant for two reasons. First, he was expressing the Wilsonian sentiments not only of most Republicans, including Luce, the highly influential publisher of *Time, Life,* and *Fortune,* but also of many Democrats, including the six million overwhelmingly Democratic Polish Americans and the roughly fifteen million other largely Democratic Catholics in the Northeast and Midwest, as well as most of the generally conservative Protestant Democrats in the South. Second, by making this well-publicized speech at a time when FDR had requested congressional silence on Big Three relations until after his upcoming meeting with Stalin and Churchill, Vandenberg was serving notice that, as in 1919–1920, Republican leaders intended to play a large role in shaping postwar U.S. foreign policy.

A second major development in Big Three relations during early 1945 was the Big Three meeting held at Russia's Black Sea resort of Yalta from February 4 to 11. As at Teheran, FDR's main goals at Yalta were to strengthen Allied cooperation and to fashion a communiqué that would convince the American people and Congress that the Big Three were working together effectively in waging the war and planning the postwar world. The physically ailing president achieved mixed results in both areas.

On issues other than the future of eastern Europe, FDR got most of what he wanted: agreement on several matters involved in setting up the United Nations Organization that spring; the division of Germany—and Berlin—into four sectors, with overall direction lodged in an Allied Control Council; and the renewed assurance that Russia, in exchange for territorial concessions in East Asia, would enter the war against Japan not more than three months after the end of the war against Germany.

Some key issues relating to Germany, including Stalin's insistence that Germany pay $10 billion in reparations to Russia, were not resolved. The same was true for Poland. The Big Three agreed on that nation's eastern border with Russia, but they did not agree where Poland's western border— the one with Germany—would be. Nor, more importantly, did they reach agreement on Poland's future government. Stalin wanted the group he dominated, the Lublin committee, to rule. He thought that Churchill and FDR should defer to him on this issue, just as he was deferring to them on the composition of the French government. In contrast, Western leaders wanted the Lublin committee to have not more than one-third of the power in Poland. Then the Poles would have a realistic chance to govern themselves and, equally significant, the large number of Americans and Britons who desired a self-governing future for Poland—including Roosevelt and Churchill themselves—could be satisfied.

Because Soviet troops and officials controlled Poland at the time, and because Western leaders had no thought of going to war with Russia to gain Poland's freedom, compromises on this issue favored Russia. The conference communiqué stated vaguely that the current Lublin government should be "reorganized on a broader democratic basis with the inclusion of democratic leaders from Poland itself and from Poles abroad," and that there should be "free and unfettered elections." The all-important details were to be resolved later. Details also were absent in the communiqué's Declaration on Liberated Europe, which promised that governments in all of the nations liberated from Germany would be based on free elections and other ideals mentioned in the Atlantic Charter.

After looking over the final report on Poland, Admiral William Leahy, the president's top military aide, told Roosevelt that "this is so elastic that the Russians can stretch it all the way from Yalta to Washington without ever technically breaking it." "I know, Bill," FDR replied. "I know it. But it's the best I can do for Poland at this time."

Partly because presidential assistant James Byrnes told journalists in Washington on February 12 that the Big Three leaders were united and supported U.S. ideals, the initial reaction to Yalta was highly positive. Largely favorable newspaper, magazine, and radio stories strengthened the public's hopes for a just and lasting peace. In a Gallup poll in late February, 55 percent—the highest percentage ever—responded that Russia could be trusted to cooperate after the war.

Not everyone was positive. "American idealism has been defeated as conspicuously at [Yalta] as it was at Paris 26 years ago," conservative columnist David Lawrence argued, complaining that "a Polish puppet state under

Russian domination has been set up and now its title and authority are confirmed." Following the lead of the London Poles, numerous Polish Americans denounced the Yalta agreements. The editor of the *Detroit Polish News*, Frank Januszewski, asserted in a long memorandum to Vandenberg that FDR's effort "to camouflage the violence done Poland ... will not succeed" (see document 2). Vandenberg commented publicly on March 8 that decisions made in regard to Poland and other nations "under the duress of war" should be reconsidered after Germany was defeated.

Angered by heavy-handed Soviet behavior in Romania and Poland after the conference, Churchill twice suggested to Roosevelt that they appeal jointly to Stalin to live up to the letter and spirit of Yalta. FDR refused, but he did cable Stalin on March 31 that the American people would view the Yalta agreements as a failure if the Big Three did not work out something more than "a thinly disguised continuation of the present Warsaw regime." "I wish I could convey to you," he added, "how important it is for the successful development of our program of international collaboration that this Polish question be settled fairly and speedily."

Two weeks later, on April 12, 1945, Roosevelt suffered a massive stroke and died, thus leaving the many difficult problems in U.S.–Soviet relations to his successor, Harry S. Truman.

UNDERSTANDING HARRY TRUMAN

Whereas Wilson is best characterized as a visionary intellectual and FDR as a charismatic, skillful politician who juggled conflicting ideas and pressures, Truman is best viewed, biographer Alonzo L. Hamby has observed, as a "man of the people." This familiar phrase has positive and negative connotations, both of which fit Truman. Positively, Truman was a modest, optimistic, religious, and honest American who believed that the country—and especially the Democratic party—stood for ideals and policies that would benefit average citizens both at home and abroad. Seeing America as a great nation, this man with middle-class, Baptist roots in Missouri strove to do his best in the office he had neither sought nor wanted. His modesty, faith, and desire to succeed came through in a comment to congressional friends the day after he became president: "Boys, if you ever pray, pray for me now."

Truman's view of himself as a man who kept his word had major implications for U.S.–Soviet relations. "When I say I'm going to do something, I do it," he wrote, "or [I] bust my insides trying to do it." Believing that the America he led kept its commitments, he judged the U.S.S.R. by the same standard and concluded with disappointment and growing anger that it was not living up to its agreements. The more relativistic Roosevelt was slower to take offense at Stalin's cavalier attitude toward his promises.

More negatively for one who had become president of the world's most powerful nation, Truman, like most Americans then and now, lacked the public speaking skills and the personal charisma that had helped FDR become a great leader. He also lacked the social and intellectual confidence and economic advantages that education beyond the high school level might have given him.

Aware of his limitations, Truman was unsure of his ability to succeed as president. He also lacked detailed knowledge and practical experience in world affairs at this pivotal moment in world history. Although Truman soon learned much about foreign relations, historians Randall B. Woods and Howard Jones rightly have noted that he "was never able to rid himself of a deep-seated inferiority complex." This sense of inferiority may well have contributed to his tendency to lash out, largely in private, at "professional liberals," "prima donnas," and others at home and abroad who opposed his policies or criticized him or members of his family.

As a senator, Truman had been mainly interested in domestic affairs and had supported FDR's New Deal programs. He considered himself a practical Wilsonian in foreign policy, strongly supporting overall U.S. leadership in world affairs, a new world organization, and freer trade. In a widely quoted comment that summed up what many American were thinking when Hitler attacked Russia in June 1941, Truman suggested that the United States should weaken both nations by aiding whichever one was losing, thus implying that both governments were equally bad. Like most Americans, Truman became at least superficially pro-Russian after Pearl Harbor. Also like most of his compatriots, he believed that true peace could be achieved only if Russia largely cooperated on U.S. terms.

During most of 1945, Truman thought, as had FDR, that this kind of peace might well be achieved. "I'm not afraid of Russia," he wrote in his diary on June 7. "They've always been our friends and I can't see any reason why they shouldn't always be." But he was more skeptical of Stalin's government than FDR had been, as comments in a memorandum to himself the previous month suggest: "I've no faith in any totalitarian state, be it Russian, German, Spanish, . . . or Japanese. They all start with the wrong premise—that lies are justified and that . . . the end justifies the means. . . . Honest Communism, as set out in the 'Acts of the Apostles,' would work. But Russian Godless Pervert Systems won't work."

One last point about Truman deserves emphasis. Especially in U.S.–Soviet relations, Truman set his compass on the political center and largely let it chart his course. Knowing that most Americans—and most members of Congress—wanted to try to work out a postwar accommodation with Russia, he made sincere, substantial efforts during his first nine months in office to do so. But when public and congressional opinion began to turn against the U.S.S.R. in late 1945 and early 1946, Truman moved with majority opinion toward a firm policy of opposition to further Russian expansion.

Truman did not make a single anti-Russian speech—or even a negative public comment—before his famous "Truman Doctrine" address of March 1947, even though a similar speech six months earlier almost certainly would have helped his party in the 1946 election. The president increasingly permitted administration officials to criticize Soviet actions, both in speeches and in conversations with journalists, but he himself remained remarkably cautious as a leader of public and congressional opinion on this issue.

The U.S. political system generally pushes presidents—even strong, charismatic presidents like FDR and Ronald Reagan—toward the political center. Nevertheless, the contrast between Roosevelt and Truman is clear: Whereas FDR had been a leader of public, congressional, and administration thinking on U.S.–Soviet relations, Truman was largely a follower in all three areas.

U.S.–SOVIET RELATIONS UNTIL WAR'S END

Like FDR earlier, Truman sought from April through August 1945 to continue to build a framework for postwar Great Power cooperation. In doing so, Truman permitted much more discussion and debate within the administration—and listened carefully to more opinions—than FDR had done. In particular, he listened in mid-April to the view, expounded by Ambassador Harriman and others, that the best way to gain Stalin's respect and cooperation was to replace U.S. generosity with reciprocity in the relationship and insist that the Soviets carry out their commitments in eastern Europe. A few advisers, including Secretary of War Henry Stimson, argued that America should remain magnanimous and that the United States should not press Stalin in a region of vital interest to him. This diversity of opinions, combined with Truman's lack of experience and initial lack of knowledge, led to a raggedness in policy from April through June that may well have damaged U.S.–Soviet relations. Three developments illustrate this raggedness.

The first was a meeting between Truman and Foreign Minister Molotov in the White House on April 23. With several U.S. and Soviet aides present, Truman bluntly told Molotov that Russia had not been carrying out the Yalta agreements on Poland. When Molotov disagreed, Truman cut him off and told him that the United States wanted to cooperate with Russia, but not as a one-way street. At one point, Molotov commented, "I have never been talked to like that in my life." According to Truman's later account of the meeting, he replied: "Carry out your agreements, and you won't get talked to like that."

U.S. officials disagreed about whether Truman had been wise to address Molotov so undiplomatically in his first substantive meeting with a Soviet official. Although some were pleased that Truman, in his words, had given Molotov a "straight one-two to the jaw," Harriman noted later that Truman's "behavior gave Molotov an excuse to tell Stalin that Roosevelt's policy was being abandoned. I regretted that Truman gave him that opportunity."

Whether or not Truman's blunt words to Molotov were a mistake, virtually everyone involved in U.S.–Soviet relations agreed that it was unfortunate that most Lend–Lease shipments to Russia were ended abruptly a couple days after the war in Europe ended on May 9. Under orders from Foreign Economic Administrator Leo Crowley based on a directive that Truman had signed casually, ships carrying Lend–Lease material not intended for the war against Japan were told to turn around and return to port.

Wrongly but understandably thinking that Truman was trying to use blatant economic pressure to gain political concessions, Stalin and other Soviet officials were furious. In fact, Truman never intended to cut off supplies already en route to the U.S.S.R., and he quickly countermanded the turnaround order. But the damage to U.S.–Soviet relations had been done: the apparent insult found a home in Stalin's proud, suspicious mind.

Having contributed to the downturn in U.S.–Soviet relations that was evident at the conference in San Francisco to establish the United Nations, and desiring "peace for the world for at least 90 years," Truman decided in mid-May to send FDR's close associate Harry Hopkins to Moscow in the hope that "Harry would be able to straighten things out with Stalin." As a longtime supporter of U.S.–Soviet cooperation who had Stalin's trust, Hopkins was a good choice for a mission with this goal. Yet the choice of Hopkins reflected a continuing unevenness in policymaking because it might well have suggested to Stalin that Truman did not mean what he had said to Molotov a month earlier.

At their first meeting on May 26, Hopkins worked hard to explain to Stalin why many Americans—including liberal supporters of "Roosevelt's policy of cooperation with the Soviet Union"—were deeply concerned about Soviet actions in Poland. Americans, Hopkins pointed out, believed that only a peace based on such universal principles as self-determination could last. Many Americans thus were upset about the unilateral, antidemocratic actions of the Russians and the Lublin Poles in Poland. "Without the support of public opinion and particularly of the supporters of President Roosevelt it would be very difficult for President Truman to carry forward President Roosevelt's policy," Hopkins presciently told Stalin.

Stalin admitted taking unilateral actions in Poland, but claimed he had done so only for military reasons. He offered a solution that fleshed out what had been agreed to at Yalta: The Lublin Poles would form the basis for a reorganized government, but representatives from other Polish groups would have four or five of the new government's eighteen or twenty ministries.

Wanting an agreement and recognizing his limited power, Truman accepted the offer that Hopkins passed along to him. To the dismay of many Polish Americans, other Catholics, and conservatives, Truman recognized the Polish government on the condition that free and fair elections would be held—even though he knew that they probably would not be. Basically, he accepted the argument that Poland and the rest of eastern Europe had to be abandoned for the sake of better relations with the U.S.S.R., including Russia's help in the war against Japan. Not surprisingly given Stalin's and other communists' contempt for democracy, the Soviet-controlled government did not permit elections until January 1947, and these were neither free nor fair.

With media coverage in June focused on the war against Japan, the typical American did not pay much attention to Hopkins's trip to Russia or to developments in Poland. Except for U.S. communists and the readers of a few liberal magazines, the public generally was not aware of an article written in Moscow in 1944 and published in April 1945 in a French communist journal under the name of a French communist, Jacques Duclos. The article sharply criticized Browder's support for class collaboration (i.e., the Popular Front). Instead, the article contended, the worldwide class struggle would resume after the war.

Reacting like the puppets that they were, party members quickly took away Browder's executive powers and then, early in 1946, expelled him from the party. Commenting in 1960, Browder called the rigidly ideological article "the first *public* declaration of the Cold War."

In America, the first noteworthy declaration may well have occurred the same month that the Duclos article appeared. In a speech in Cleveland, a city known for its large number of Catholics, many of whom were recent immigrants from eastern Europe, Father Edmund Walsh of Georgetown University predicted that a race for domination between communism and democracy would be the "next chapter in the history of civilization." Walsh's speech was well publicized in Catholic and immigrant media.

In addition to America's conditional recognition of the Polish government, the two main developments affecting U.S.–Soviet relations in the summer of 1945 were the Big Three meeting in Potsdam (just outside Berlin) from July 17 through August 2 and the dropping of atomic bombs on the Japanese cities of Hiroshima on August 6 and Nagasaki on August 9. Above all, the Potsdam Conference helped to shape policy toward postwar Germany, and the use of the atomic bombs increased U.S. leaders' confidence in foreign policy and heightened Soviet leaders' feelings of insecurity and fear.

The major issue at Potsdam was Germany's future. Before the conference, Russian leaders were upset that U.S. officials refused to agree to a dollar figure for reparations to be sent from Germany to Russia, and British and U.S. officials were upset that Russia had unilaterally given a large slice of eastern Germany to Poland. At Potsdam, Stalin and Molotov pressed for a major commitment to reparations, especially reparations from the more industrialized western zones. But Truman and Secretary of State Byrnes refused because they did not want Americans to end up subsidizing large-scale reparations from Germany, as had happened after World War I.

When Stalin and Molotov finally realized that U.S. leaders were not going to budge, they accepted a proposal from Byrnes that allowed each nation to take reparations from its zone and offered hope that Russia might get reparations from the western zones in the future. In return, Byrnes agreed to recognize the Soviet-imposed border between Poland and Germany that already had resulted in the forced westward displacement of millions of Germans. The Big Three hoped that the Allied Control Council would be able to make decisions on "matters affecting Germany as a whole." The Big Three also set up a Council of Foreign Ministers in which the German question and other unresolved issues could be discussed in future meetings.

The portentous issue that U.S. leaders never really discussed with Stalin and Molotov at Potsdam was how, if at all, the Big Three might be able to cooperate on atomic energy after the war. Through their large spy network in the West, Soviet leaders not only had known throughout the war about the U.S.–British project to build atomic weapons, but they also had obtained detailed instructions about how to construct them. Neither they nor their U.S. counterparts had exchanged even a word about the subject prior to Potsdam.

After a session on July 24, more than a week after the first successful test in New Mexico, Truman casually walked over to where Stalin and his interpreter were standing and told them that America now had an unusually destructive new weapon. With equal casualness, Truman recalled, Stalin said he was pleased and urged that it be used against Japan. To Byrnes's surprise, neither Stalin nor Molotov mentioned the subject again, and neither did U.S. officials.

America's use of atomic weapons in early August contributed greatly to Japanese leaders' decision to end the war a few days afterward. Despite the link between the use of the bombs and Japan's surrender, scholars long have argued about why the United States used the bombs when it did. Among the explanations has been historian Gar Alperowitz's well-publicized but unfounded contention that U.S. leaders, supposedly knowing that Japan was about to surrender anyway, used the devastating weapons—and thus needlessly killed and wounded hundreds of thousands of people—primarily to intimidate Russia, not to defeat Japan.

Although Truman and Byrnes did think that using atomic weapons against Japan might have the added value of inducing Soviet leaders to be more cooperative, "the fundamental reason for using the bomb," historian Daniel Yergin rightly has observed, was "to end the war in the Pacific as quickly as possible, and so save American lives." America dropped the bombs, historian John Lewis Gaddis has noted with equal succinctness, primarily "to achieve victory as quickly, as decisively, and as economically as possible."

Truman's first impression of Stalin at Potsdam was positive: "I can deal with Stalin. He is honest—but smart as hell." But before long he was writing his family that "you never saw such pig-headed people as are the Russians." On his voyage back to America, he commented that Stalin was "an S.O.B.," but then continued evenhandedly: "I guess he thinks I'm one too." Admiral Leahy, Truman's military aide, was less charitable: He considered Stalin "a liar and a crook." Overall, the conference produced few lasting agreements and little if any goodwill; and America's possession of atomic weapons was a source of anxiety and tension in postwar U.S.–Soviet relations.

THE COLD WAR BEGINS: SEPTEMBER 1945–MARCH 1946

From the U.S. perspective, the Cold War began during the seven months from September 1945 through March 1946. During these months, the major thrust of U.S. policy shifted from the long-standing effort to reach agreements to a determination to limit Russia's expansion. Such old issues as Soviet unilateralism in eastern Europe continued to strain relations. New issues, notably Russian pressure on Iran, tipped the balance in U.S. policy in the winter of 1945–1946 from grudging accommodation to open confrontation.

Except for Polish Americans and others who had ethnic or religious reasons for abhorring Soviet power in eastern Europe, most Americans still hoped for a cooperative peace and thus regretted that U.S.–Soviet relations were becoming tense. Most people wanted to "bring the boys home" from overseas military duty and turn to peacetime pursuits. From late 1945 through 1946, they also found much to worry about at home, including high inflation, shortages of housing and other products, and a wave of strikes that fueled inflation and shortages as well as antiunion sentiment. The president's typically low-key, ineffective efforts to deal with domestic problems prompted a joke popular in 1946: "What do you think Truman would do if he were alive?"

Intractable domestic problems like inflation and labor-management relations became even more frustrating to Truman when combined with equally difficult foreign policy issues, including whether to seek international control of atomic weapons or to try to maintain a U.S. monopoly. After much debate, Truman decided to seek international control with safeguards to protect U.S. interests. Without international control, Truman and many other Americans reasoned, there almost certainly would be a dangerous and destabilizing arms race in nuclear weapons that could contribute to distrust in other areas of East–West relations. Determined to build and control their own atomic weapons and totally opposed to international inspections of facilities in the U.S.S.R., Soviet leaders refused to negotiate seriously on this issue either before or after U.S. officials presented a plan for international control at the United Nations in July 1946.

From the U.S. perspective, Molotov refused to negotiate seriously on *any* issue at the first meeting of the Council of Foreign Ministers, held in London in September and early October of 1945. The most acrimonious exchanges occurred on the issue of peace treaties for Bulgaria and Romania. Byrnes and his Republican adviser, John Foster Dulles, did not want the United States to recognize Soviet puppet regimes in these countries as it had in Poland. They thus insisted that the treaties' preambles should state that the major powers would recognize only "broadly representative" governments that were committed to holding free elections. Seeking to maintain Soviet control of these countries, Molotov refused to accept any such wording. The three-week conference ended without any agreements.

The London Conference marked the first time that U.S. officials and journalists depicted a high-level meeting between Western and Soviet officials as, in *Newsweek's* words, a "dismal failure." Because most officials and journalists supported the Western outlook, the overall message that the news media conveyed was that the U.S.S.R. was not cooperating in establishing a just peace. This message, in turn, was reflected in the declining trust of Russia that pollsters soon discovered.

The failure of the London Conference left Truman and Byrnes uncertain about the direction of U.S. policy. In theory, both men wanted to continue to seek agreements with Russia. But whereas Byrnes considered making compromises in U.S. positions that in his view would be required to reach agreements, Truman, encouraged by Admiral Leahy and others, increasingly believed that compromises with untrustworthy Soviet leaders effectively resulted in losses for America.

By December 1945, several developments bolstered Leahy's viewpoint. These included: (1) Russian demands on Turkey and actions in Iran that suggested the need to take forceful action to limit Soviet expansionism; (2) strong support for Leahy's perspective among leading members of Congress of both parties; (3) concern among some officials and members of Congress that Byrnes might be overly willing to share control of atomic energy with Russia; and (4) Byrnes's tendency to make foreign policy on his own, which many people in Washington now saw as arrogant, disrespectful of Truman's authority, and damaging to U.S. interests. Angry that he "had to read the newspapers to get the U.S. foreign policy," Truman privately called Byrnes a "conniver" in early December.

At a meeting later that month in Moscow with Soviet leaders and British foreign minister Ernest Bevin, Byrnes obtained agreements on several issues that, in his view, restored the spirit of Big Three cooperation that had been absent since Potsdam. He was especially pleased that Stalin had agreed to a slight broadening of the Romanian and Bulgarian governments, to the main points in the U.S. plan for a UN Atomic Energy Commission, and to a peace conference in Paris in 1946. He returned to Washington "far happier" than he had been when he had come back from the London Conference three months before.

Byrnes's euphoria did not last long. Exhausted from the long trip home, he was summoned to the presidential yacht and then needled at dinner by Leahy in Truman's presence about whether he had defended Western interests at the meeting. A week later, on January 5, 1946, Truman called Byrnes to the White House and told him to conduct a much firmer policy toward the U.S.S.R. In a long memorandum that he wrote for the meeting but did not read to Byrnes, Truman said that recent Soviet actions in Iran "were an outrage if I ever saw one." One passage in the memo summed up Truman's thinking at the time: "Unless Russia is faced with an iron fist and strong language another war is in the making. Only one language do they understand—'how many divisions have you?' . . . I'm tired of babying the Soviets." Anti-Russian editorials, columns, and letters to the editor that appeared frequently in newspapers across the nation in the winter of 1945–1946 showed that many Americans shared Truman's privately expressed anger toward Russia and concern about World War III.

To Truman and other U.S. officials, Soviet behavior in Iran in late 1945 and early 1946 was a major cause of East–West tensions. Russia and Britain had moved troops into Iran in 1941 to keep that large, oil-rich country out of Axis hands; they had agreed in a 1942 treaty to respect Iran's independence and territorial integrity and to withdraw their troops not later than six months after the war's end. In late 1945 and early 1946, however, the Russians installed puppet rulers in the Iranian province adjacent to the U.S.S.R. and pressured Iran's government in Teheran to follow pro-Russian policies. Moreover, Soviet leaders indicated that they no longer intended to honor repeated pledges to remove their troops by March 2, six months after the formal end of the war against Japan.

Iran's government focused international attention on the issue when it lodged a complaint against Soviet behavior in the UN Security Council on January 19, 1946. Initially, Byrnes hoped that the dispute could be resolved largely through Russo–Iranian negotiations. But after Senator Vandenberg and others pressured him to become firmer, Byrnes decided in February to make Iran a test of U.S. resolve. In a major address on February 28, Byrnes said that America intended to act as a great power "not only to ensure our own security but in order to preserve the peace of the world." Clearly condemning Soviet behavior in places like Iran, Byrnes insisted that Americans "cannot allow aggression to be accomplished by coercion or pressure."

When Russia failed to meet the March 2 deadline for withdrawal, Byrnes sent a virtual ultimatum to Moscow demanding the removal of the troops, informed the media of his demand before receiving a reply, and encouraged Iran to raise the issue again in the UN Security Council. Continuing U.S., British, and Iranian pressure led Russia to announce that it was removing all its troops from Iran. U.S. leaders drew two conclusions: a firm approach had been required to halt Soviet expansionism in Iran, and a similar approach might be equally effective in dealing with Stalin in the future.

In addition to the Iran crisis, five other developments in early 1946 helped to precipitate the Cold War. The first was Russia's decision not to participate in the two U.S.–led institutions—the World Bank and the International Monetary Fund—that had developed from the 1944 Bretton Woods conference in New Hampshire. Stalin thus had decided that there would not be one cooperative world economy, as U.S. officials and many opinion leaders had hoped, but rather two competing ones.

In a major speech on February 9, Stalin seemed to confirm Russia's separation from the West. He used Marxist–Leninist theory to explain to the Russian people that the "contradictions" of international capitalism meant that more conflicts like the two world wars would occur among the capitalist nations. Warning that Russia might well be drawn into these wars, as had happened in 1941, he asserted that the nation needed to concentrate on heavy industry and military production instead of the consumer goods that the Russian people so greatly desired.

Presenting a middle-of-the-road reaction to the speech, the editors of the *New York Times* found it "disappointing to many of those who felt that the close wartime partnership of Russia and the western democracies" had offered hope for continuing cooperation. To many conservatives and even to some liberals, the speech suggested that U.S.–Soviet cooperation was now impossible. As historian Eduard Mark has observed, Stalin "could not reassert Marxist–Leninist fundamentalism at home without alarming the West."

News of a Soviet spy ring in Canada broke a week later. A Soviet defector having supplied detailed information, the Canadian government announced that it had arrested twenty-two persons on charges of trying to steal atomic secrets for Russia. A few days later, FBI director J. Edgar Hoover said that Russia had obtained secret data about the atomic bomb through its espionage operation in Canada.

Because Canadian communists were involved in the spy ring, some U.S. officials, journalists, and especially conservative members of Congress argued that it was now time to crack down on U.S. communists and communist-front organizations. In fact, the FBI had been working with vigor and considerable success to neutralize communist influence in the federal government since the previous November, when former spy Elizabeth Bentley provided the FBI with the names of well-placed communist spies whom she knew. Ironically, the communist threat in the federal government was declining at the very time that many officials and members of Congress were gearing up to attack that threat.

The fourth development was Kennan's "long telegram," sent by the highest-ranking official then in the U.S. embassy in Moscow to the State Department on February 23 (see document 3). Eight thousand words long,

Kennan's dispatch examined the "Soviet outlook" and, in particular, why Russian leaders were not cooperating with their wartime allies. Kennan blamed Russia's troubled history and the ruling party's communist ideology and tenuous hold on power. Because of the Kremlin's "traditional and instinctive Russian sense of insecurity" and because of the "importance of dogma in Soviet affairs," Kennan wrote, the "basic Soviet instinct" was "that there can be no compromise with rival power and the constructive work can start only when Communist power is dominant."

Just as "neurotic" Soviet leaders had ruthlessly destroyed all real and imagined opposition to their rule within Russia, so they felt compelled to act in a similar fashion toward perceived enemies abroad. Soviet foreign policy thus derived from "inner-Russian necessities" and not from an "objective analysis of [the] situation beyond Russia's borders"—or from U.S. and British policy. Western leaders thus should not blame themselves for the downturn in relations or believe that they could alter Stalin's basic approach, Kennan argued. Instead, they should offer "strong resistance" to further Russian expansion and patiently await internal changes in Russia.

The "long telegram" was the most influential U.S. diplomatic dispatch ever written. Copies spread like wildfire throughout Washington and U.S. embassies overseas. Truman and other top officials read it; Byrnes summed up the official reaction when he called it a "splendid analysis." Copies were made available to influential publications, including *Time* and *Life*, which used it as the basis for commentaries on Russia. A powerfully written analysis of the wellsprings of Soviet foreign policy, the "long telegram" bolstered a new firmness, coherence, and confidence in U.S. policy.

Also contributing to the onset of the Cold War in America was the "iron curtain speech" that former prime minister Churchill delivered at Westminster College in Fulton, Missouri, on March 5. Officially, Churchill spoke as a private citizen. Yet both the U.S. and British governments basically agreed with what he said and encouraged his U.S. speaking tour. Although Americans at the time were not aware that Truman and other U.S. officials had read and informally approved the speech, they knew that Truman accompanied him to Fulton and warmly introduced him. An eloquent speaker whom most Americans greatly admired, Churchill could help to solidify anti-Russian sentiment more effectively than any other living person.

Churchill made two main points: Soviet expansionism threatened world peace and a militarily strong "fraternal association of the English-speaking peoples" was needed to counter it. Agreeing with Kennan that Soviet leaders did not want war, Churchill argued that they sought "the fruits of war and the indefinite expansion of their power and doctrines." He urged

Americans to recognize the danger and work with Britain once again to halt the advance of an expanding dictatorship.

The immediate reaction to Churchill's speech was diverse: Most conservatives and many liberals agreed with his criticisms of Soviet behavior but many liberals opposed a British–American alliance, partly because it might undermine the United Nations. Skeptical African American leaders noted that Britain still colonized black people and that Westminster College did not admit black students.

A Gallup poll just after the speech found that twice as many respondents opposed U.S.–British military cooperation against Russia as supported it. Yet a poll taken three weeks later showed that 66 percent shared Churchill's belief that the United States should not appease Russia. By May, 83 percent favored a U.S.–British military alliance. Thus, in the aftermath of Churchill's speech and in the context of the Iran crisis and other difficulties in U.S.–Soviet relations, the longer-term trends in public attitudes toward Russia clearly were moving in the direction Churchill desired—namely, toward the generally firm public and governmental stance that characterized the Cold War.

THE NEW COURSE IS CONFIRMED: APRIL–DECEMBER 1946

During the last nine months of 1946, the U.S. government's relations with the U.S.S.R. continued to deteriorate, settling into a Cold War pattern in which the many negative developments greatly outweighed the few positive ones. The public, which generally shared officials' disappointment and anger that Stalin was opposing America's vision of the postwar world, also moved toward a solidly anti-Soviet stance. Rightly using "we" to refer to government and public alike in a speech in Boston on June 4, Undersecretary of State Dean Acheson summed up a widely held view of America's postwar struggle against international communism: "We are in for it and the only real question is whether we shall know it soon enough."

During this period, the administration called its policy toward Russia and its allies "patience with firmness." Truman and Byrnes, with strong bipartisan congressional support, vowed not to make concessions in pursuit of an illusory peace with an implacable adversary. From Germany on the west of the Soviet empire to Turkey on the south and Japan on the east, the United States took stands that limited Soviet influence. Only in China, which administration officials considered a secondary interest, did America not pursue a firmly anticommunist policy.

In Germany, U.S. officials reluctantly moved away from the Potsdam vision of four-power cooperation to working with Britain—and eventually France as well—against Russia. There were four main reasons for the administration's reluctance. First, because most Germans wanted to remain united, the nation or nations that Germans viewed as responsible for dividing their country might well become unpopular. Second, because the more agricultural east would no longer complement the more industrial west, division could damage Germany's—and hence Europe's—economy. Third, because Russia almost certainly would install a communist government in its zone in the eastern third of the country if Germany were divided, splitting Germany would hasten Europe's division into Western and communist blocs. And fourth, U.S. officials and ordinary citizens alike still hoped in 1946 that America and Russia could resolve enough of their disagreements—including disagreements over Germany—to avoid falling into a truly frigid cold war that might well lead to a hot one.

So why, despite this reluctance, did U.S. leaders move toward a policy that, by ignoring Soviet desires regarding western Germany, increased U.S.–Soviet tensions? There were five main reasons: (1) the realization that the U.S.S.R. was repressing people and property in its zone; (2) the fear that Russia would dominate any all-German government that it would agree to support, as was occurring in eastern Europe; (3) the importance of Germany's coal for western Europe's economic recovery; (4) the Soviet tendency to undermine efforts to resolve Germany's pressing economic and political problems; and (5) the resulting belief that, in the zones they controlled, the United States and Britain should wait no longer to stimulate prosperity, democracy, and especially hope.

At lengthy, often tedious meetings of the Council of Foreign Ministers in April–May and again in June–July, Byrnes was frustrated by Molotov's rejection of U.S. proposals regarding Germany and other issues. Byrnes also bristled at a July 9 speech in which Molotov sharply criticized U.S. and British policies in Germany and portrayed the U.S.S.R. as supporting the "rightful aspirations" of the German people.

Byrnes responded with a well-publicized speech in Stuttgart on September 6 in which he made it clear that Germans in the western zones could count on U.S. support in restoring self-government and prosperity (see document 4). Byrnes promised that U.S. forces would remain "as long as there is an occupation army in Germany" to ensure that Germany did not "become the satellite of any power" (i.e., Russia). Byrnes also repeated an offer made in July to merge the U.S. zone economically with any other zone—a British-inspired proposal that resulted in the creation of a combined U.S. and

British zone (Bizonia) on January 1, 1947. Unless Russia changed course and decided to cooperate largely on Western terms, the division of Germany was now almost certain.

The stiffening of U.S. policy in the summer and fall also resulted from Soviet pressure against Turkey. The pressure had been building since June 1945, when Molotov had demanded cession of two of Turkey's eastern provinces to the U.S.S.R.; joint defense of the Bosporus and the Dardanelles, the narrow straits through Turkey that link the Mediterranean and Black seas; and a major revision of the Montreux Convention that governed navigation through the straits.

After the war, the Soviet regime criticized the Turkish government repeatedly and concentrated armed forces to Turkey's east in Soviet territory and to its west in Bulgaria and Romania. On August 7, 1946, Russia sent a note to Turkey requesting joint Turkish–Soviet defense of the straits—that is, Soviet bases on Turkish territory that might well result in a Soviet takeover of the country.

In meetings in mid-August, the Truman administration decided to offer strong support to Turkey. On August 14, high-level officials agreed to recommend to Truman that America should be "prepared, if necessary, to meet [Soviet] aggression with force of arms." In a meeting at the White House the next day, Truman said that he would support the officials' recommendations "to the end," noting that "we might as well find out whether the Russians were bent on world conquest now as in five or ten years."

To carry out this policy, the administration sent a strong warning to Russia, dispatched a large naval force to the eastern Mediterranean, and secretly stepped up joint British–American planning for a possible war with Russia. Donald Maclean, a Soviet spy who held a high-level position in the British embassy in Washington, also secretly reported to Moscow that America was serious about fighting to protect Turkey. On September 24, Russia sent a much more conciliatory note to Turkey, effectively ending the crisis. As in Iran in the spring, U.S. firmness appeared to be both justified and effective.

In 1946, U.S. officials also worked to limit communist influence in South Korea. Near the end of the war with Japan, Russia agreed to a U.S. proposal to divide Korea temporarily at the thirty-eighth parallel, with Soviet troops supervising the Japanese surrender north of this line and U.S. troops assuming that responsibility south of it. Negotiations in early 1946 to form a provisional government for the entire country ended in stalemate: The U.S.S.R. and its Korean allies would accept only a communist-dominated regime like the one that Russia was installing in the north, whereas

America and its local allies would accept only a noncommunist government like the one it was favoring in the south.

Despite most Koreans' desire that their peninsula be unified under an independent government, Korea thus quickly slipped into an unfortunate division in which one government depended on Moscow and the other relied on Washington. This division led to repeated skirmishes between pro- and anticommunist Koreans in the late 1940s and, ultimately, to the devastating Korean War of 1950–1953.

Meanwhile, U.S. leaders were experiencing success in the Asian nation that they considered most strategically important, Japan, and finding frustration in nearby China. In Japan, U.S. officials obtained, in diplomat John Paton Davies's words, just what they wanted: A "stable Japan, integrated into the Pacific, friendly to the U.S., and, in case of need, a ready and dependable ally." Determined to exclude the U.S.S.R. and other nations from meaningful participation in decisions about Japan's future, U.S. officials—led by the commander of the occupying forces, General Douglas MacArthur—called the shots. They consulted with noncommunist Japanese and then insisted that the nation implement a new democratic constitution that included land reform, tax reform, educational reform, and other programs that reflected liberal U.S. ideals. As in Europe and the Middle East, America also provided food and other economic aid for the war-ravaged country.

To put it mildly, America did not control developments in postwar China. As in Japan, U.S. leaders wanted China to be democratic, capitalist, and pro-Western. More specifically, U.S. officials wanted China's pro-Western Nationalist party leader, Chiang Kai-shek, to accept their strong request that, in return for continuing U.S. aid, he become more democratic, less corrupt, and more willing to negotiate seriously with his communist opponents. They also hoped that Chiang's long-time communist challenger, Mao Zedong, would accept the idea of democratic change and reach a compromise with Chiang that would prevent a bitter and destructive civil war. Finally, they hoped that Russia would support their vision for China by urging compromise and not providing military aid to Mao.

Although there were occasional signs from early 1945 through late 1946 that at least some of America's hopes might be realized, in fact all the hopes were illusory and faced disappointment long before the final communist victory in the Chinese civil war in October 1949. To their credit, U.S. officials saw clearly by late 1946 and early 1947 that their hopes had been dashed. This was true of General Marshall, who had spent nearly all of 1946 in China in a futile attempt to work out a compromise peace between the nationalists and the communists. By year's end, he had concluded that additional U.S. aid to the undemocratic Chiang would be "useless." Acheson similarly became "convinced" by late 1946 that "the Chinese factions had no intention or desire to get together." A couple months later, Truman told his cabinet that the communists would win because they were "fanatical."

By early 1947, no high official believed that, under the circumstances, preserving a noncommunist China was a vital U.S. interest. Yet officials offered lukewarm support to the nationalists in order not to undermine Chiang's shaky position and, more importantly, not to lose Republican votes for aid programs to Europe and the Middle East.

Some vocal Republicans in Congress and elsewhere—notably publisher Henry Luce—viewed China as a vital interest in the struggle against communism and fervently believed that Chiang, with sufficient U.S. aid, could win the civil war. No one—not even the revered Marshall—could change their minds. To the administration's regret, the bipartisan foreign policy that was being applied elsewhere in the world thus did not extend to China. America's frustrations and bitter public debates regarding policy toward postwar China foreshadowed similar frustrations and bitter debates two decades later when America sent aid—and this time troops as well—to help anticommunists fight communists in an ongoing civil war in China's southern neighbor, Vietnam.

As U.S. officials pursued a strongly anticommunist policy in most parts of the world, they did so with overwhelming public support. Despite the administration's emphasis on firmness, large majorities in polls in 1946 and 1947 repeatedly characterized U.S. policy toward Russia as "too soft" and favored a more "firm" approach to prevent further Soviet expansion. In polls about domestic communists in summer 1946, more than 75 percent of those with opinions supported strong measures (including imprisonment and killing) to limit communist activities in America. An even higher percentage said that communists should not be permitted to hold government jobs.

By mid-1946, overall public opinion toward the U.S.S.R. and domestic communists thus had become as negative as it had been in 1939–1941 after the Nazi–Soviet pact and Russia's invasion of Finland. As in 1939–1941, dislike of Soviet expansion and hostility toward U.S. communists were rising together.

Because the anticommunist consensus that characterized the Cold War was developing so rapidly, 1946 generally was a good year for anticommunists in politics, in labor unions, in churches, in the news media, and in other major American institutions. It was a bad year for communists, for fellow travelers, and for Democratic politicians who had received support from communists and their sympathizers during the heyday of the Popular Front in the late 1930s or during its wartime revival. Emphasizing ideological roots of the conflict, the anticommunist editors of the *Charlotte Observer* noted on July 14 that the United States and the U.S.S.R. "are as far apart as the [North and South] poles on such vital and controlling questions as the nature of God, as the character of man, as the role of religion, as the function of the state, as the purpose of life. . . . Russia and America have nothing in common that is of social, ethical and religious value."

Catholics (typically Democrats and labor-union members) and Republicans led the verbal and institutional assault on international and domestic communists. Joining them—but often with less strident language—were large numbers of white Protestants (including many business leaders and journalists), anticommunist blacks and Jews, and non-Catholic, anticommunist liberals including historian Arthur Schlesinger Jr., theologian Reinhold Niebuhr, and the nation's most prominent woman, Eleanor Roosevelt. Postwar anticommunism, historian Philip Jenkins rightly noted, "arose from a genuinely comprehensive social movement."

From their viewpoint, Catholics, who made up roughly one-third of the population (and voters) in the Northeast and Midwest, had numerous reasons to fight communism vigorously in the early postwar years. Communists opposed all religions, including theirs. The Soviet government had persecuted Catholics while virtually stamping out religion in the U.S.S.R. during the 1920s. Making matters worse, the Russians and their allies in eastern Europe were vigorously repressing the church and killing Catholics there as well. Moreover, Catholics were aware that, if communists triumphed in Italy and elsewhere, believers would be repressed and killed, and the Church itself could be devastated. The evidence is overwhelming that most Catholics agreed with Philadelphia priest Vito Mazzone's depiction of communism as "red tyranny" and "the greatest enemy ever faced by religion in the history of mankind."

During 1946, large numbers of Catholics fought this "enemy" by words and deeds. In April, a priest wrote in *Catholic World* that America should remove the Russians from Poland, the Balkans, and the Baltic states not "with notes of protest . . . but with arms and men, with blood and death, with possibly a million casualties." More typically, Catholic writers couched the struggle against Russia in general terms. "We shall not win unless we can match and overmatch the tireless zeal of the enemy," a writer for a Catholic newspaper in Youngstown, Ohio, noted.

In contrast, Catholics typically used concrete language to denounce U.S. communists. Louis Budenz, a former communist who had returned to

Catholicism, warned that every communist was "a potential spy against the United States." An editorial in a Catholic newspaper put it simply: "There is no good Communist."

By voting Republican or by staying home and thus limiting the Democratic vote, Catholics contributed greatly to the Republicans' landslide victory in the 1946 election. Equally important, they played a vital role in setting in motion the process by which communists were removed from positions of leadership in CIO unions over the next several years. A revitalized Association of Catholic Trade Unionists fought against the communist presence, as did priests and lay people who insisted that the heavily Catholic unions should not tolerate as leaders people whose first loyalty was to the U.S.S.R. and hence to the destruction of religious and other freedoms.

In particular, Catholics worked throughout 1946 to convince the CIO's leader, the devout Catholic Philip Murray, to oppose communist involvement in the organization. Their efforts paid off: In September, in an obvious reference to communists and fellow travelers, Murray criticized American apologists for Soviet foreign policy. At the CIO convention in November, Murray worked to ensure passage of a resolution stating that the delegates "resent and reject efforts of the Communist Party . . . to interfere in the affairs of the CIO."

Like most Catholics, virtually all Republicans wanted to halt Soviet expansion and end domestic communists' influence in American institutions. But Republicans also used anticommunism for partisan purposes. A strong desire to gain control of Congress for the first time since 1930 contributed to their frequent criticisms of foreign policy "failures" in eastern Europe under FDR and Truman.

Political calculations also contributed to Republicans' tendency to link prolabor Democrats to communist influence in labor unions, a linkage to which many Democratic politicians were vulnerable because of their acceptance—in 1944 if not necessarily in 1946—of CIO funds and support through the organization's political action committee, CIO–PAC. Wishing to curb labor unions' economic and political power, Republicans naturally sought a vulnerable point to mount their attack. In his successful campaign for the Senate, for example, Governor Edward Martin of Pennsylvania vowed to help anticommunists in the CIO "in purging and removing the PAC element which is trying to overthrow our country."

A speech by FBI director Hoover to the strongly anticommunist American Legion on September 30 aided the Republican cause (see document 5). "During the past five years," Hoover observed, "American communists have made their deepest inroads into our national life. . . . Their propaganda, skillfully designed and adroitly executed, has been projected into practically every phase of our national life. . . . We are rapidly reaching the time when loyal Americans must be willing to stand up and be counted." Through speeches, magazine articles, interviews, and testimony before Congress in the postwar years, the widely admired, publicly nonpartisan Hoover epitomized the nation's commitment to anticommunism at home and abroad.

There were other important issues in the 1946 campaign—for example, inflation, large numbers of strikes by labor unions, and shortages of meat and other products. But the domestic/international communist issue clearly was a central one as well. In five populous northern states with large numbers of Catholics (including many immigrants from eastern Europe)—New York, Pennsylvania, Ohio, Michigan, and Illinois—Republicans increased their seats in the House of Representatives from 82 to 109, while Democrats dropped from 62 to 35. Aided by the large shift in these and other states, Republicans easily gained the majority in both houses of Congress.

On September 20, Truman demonstrated that he was part of the emerging Cold War consensus by firing Secretary of Commerce Henry Wallace, a New Deal liberal and longtime supporter of Russia. Wallace had become a fellow traveler by the time he secretly met with a Soviet official in Washington in the fall of 1945 and offered to share information about the U.S. atomic weapons program. The president and the American public were not aware of this meeting; if they had known, Wallace almost certainly would have been fired then. But Truman did know that he had embarrassed himself by approving a moderately pro-Russian speech that Wallace gave to a large audience composed mostly of communists and fellow travelers in New York on September 12 (see document 6). "'Getting tough' never bought anything real and lasting—whether for schoolyard bullies or businessmen or world powers," Wallace insisted. "The tougher we get, the tougher the Russians will get."

Because Wallace's views on U.S.–Soviet relations had been outside the mainstream during the previous six months and because Truman's approval of the speech appeared to undercut Byrnes's ability to negotiate with the Russians in Paris, the president was in the hot seat. Efforts to slither off by claiming first that Wallace's and Byrnes's views were "exactly in line" and then that he had approved Wallace's right to make the speech but not the contents failed to stem an avalanche of criticism that soon was directed as much at him as at Wallace. An angry Byrnes told Truman that he would resign immediately unless Wallace promised not to speak out on foreign policy. When Wallace refused Truman's request for silence, the president asked him to resign.

On the day before he fired Wallace, Truman privately affirmed that he agreed with Byrnes's views of U.S.–Soviet relations and disagreed with Wallace's. Writing in his diary, Truman lambasted the "Reds, phonies and . . . parlor pinks [who] can see no wrong in Russia's four and one half million armed forces, in Russia's loot of Poland, Austria, Hungary, Rumania, Manchuria. . . . But when we help our friends in China who fought on our side it is terrible."

Wallace's firing and Hoover's anticommunist speech ten days later made it clear that the administration's views of Soviet expansion and of U.S. communists and their sympathizers were broadly similar to the views of most Catholics, Republicans, and other anticommunists. With the numbers of communists and fellow travelers already declining in the federal government, in labor unions, and elsewhere, and with the public, the political parties, the news media, the administration, and most religious and civic groups overwhelmingly opposed to Russia's postwar foreign policy, Americans by late 1946 were more united on the broad principles of the communist issue than on any other major issue they faced. But they would spend the next few years—indeed, the entire Cold War era—arguing about the details.

THE COLD WAR INTENSIFIES: 1947–1950

In an analysis written in December 1946 and published as an article in the influential magazine *Foreign Affairs* seven months later, George F. Kennan argued that, in view of the persistent "Soviet pressure against the free institutions of the western world, . . . the main element of any United States policy toward the Soviet Union must be that of a long-term, patient but firm and vigilant containment of Russian expansive tendencies." America now had a word—"containment"—to name the fundamental policy that the nation and its allies would pursue toward the U.S.S.R. and its allies for more than four decades, including the last three years of the 1940s.

Containment's immediate goal was to inhibit the further spread of Soviet power, hopefully without war with Russia. Its ultimate objective, Kennan contended, was "to promote tendencies which must eventually find their outlet in either the break-up or the gradual mellowing of Soviet power." If America and its allies implemented containment wisely, Kennan was confident about the Cold War's outcome.

Although Kennan's article did not mention domestic communists, governmental and nongovernmental institutions were adopting an equally tough-minded approach to dealing with them. Detesting communism and fearing that domestic communists and their allies would aid Russia if a U.S.–Soviet war broke out, the overwhelming majority of Americans supported efforts during the late 1940s and early 1950s to ensure that the influence of domestic communists was first contained and then, if possible, eliminated. The nation thus pursued a two-pronged policy of containment—containing communists abroad and at home. To most Americans, this two-pronged policy seemed both logical and necessary for the country's safety.

Because so many questions that Americans had about U.S.–Soviet relations in the postwar world had remained unanswered during 1945 and well into 1946, an intriguing tension between hope and frustration marked that period's thinking regarding relations with their former ally, a tension that is largely missing for the years that followed. In 1945–1946, the key question for most Americans had been whether the United States could pursue its major goals for the postwar world while avoiding a serious conflict with Russia. That question having been answered by late 1946 with a strong "no," the central question shifted to how America could best contain Russia's influence—including the influence it exercised through the United States and other communist parties—outside the Soviet bloc. Because the latter question relates at least as much to the Cold War's evolution as to its origins, this subsection can be briefer and more selective than the preceding one.

Four major foreign-policy developments between early 1947 and early 1950 illustrate the implementation of containment and the intensification of the Cold War: the issue of aid to anticommunists in Greece and Turkey; the Marshall Plan to provide aid to cooperative nations in Europe; the Berlin blockade and its consequences; and America's most important Cold War planning document, National Security Council Study No. 68 (NSC-68). In the domestic Cold War, three developments in the first half of 1947 highlight the declining influence of communists and fellow travelers in the nation's public life. Although these seven developments were highly significant, a dozen or more additional examples easily could be discussed. To put it mildly, Americans at the time were waging the Cold War on many fronts.

INITIATIVES/RESPONSES ABROAD

During the late 1940s, U.S. leaders largely saw themselves as being on the defensive, reacting to Soviet advances (e.g., in eastern Europe) or trying to prevent potential communist gains (e.g., in Greece and Germany). In noncommunist nations in western Europe (e.g., France and Italy), in Latin

America (e.g., Costa Rica and Chile), and in Asia (e.g., Vietnam and China), U.S. officials feared that local communists would gain power. Because both U.S. and Soviet leaders saw their own and their allies' actions as defensive and their opponents' actions as offensive, in retrospect most distinctions between "defensive" responses and "offensive" initiatives in East–West relations in the late 1940s are blurred.

In U.S. relations with its European allies, the distinction between initiator and responder also was fuzzy because U.S. and west European officials often saw themselves as working together toward common goals. What was important was not where the idea originated but whether it could help strengthen noncommunist nations and thus aid the Western cause. Moreover, as ideas like the Marshall Plan and the North Atlantic Treaty Organization (NATO) developed over many months from concept to fruition, there were numerous initiatives and responses on both sides of the Atlantic, thus combining the threads of initiative and response into a single cloth.

The issue of aid to Greece and Turkey in early 1947 is a perfect example of the combination of initiative and response in the making of U.S. policy. The spark for this highly publicized U.S. venture came from the British government, which on February 24 informed the State Department of its decision to stop providing aid to Greece and Turkey and urged America to assume this burden. Because of financial constraints exacerbated by the worst winter weather in modern history, Britain could afford neither to help Turkey nor to continue the substantial assistance to the virtually insolvent Greek government that was fighting a civil war against communist-led insurgents aided by communist nations to the north with close ties to Moscow. Western leaders feared a falling-domino effect in the Mediterranean and Middle East if either Greece or Turkey became communist.

Led by Undersecretary of State Acheson, the administration quickly decided to ask Congress to appropriate $400 million in aid for Greece and Turkey. The problem was how to persuade the Republican-controlled Congress, many of whose members wanted cuts in expenditures and taxes and doubted whether the large amounts of aid already given to Europe had accomplished much.

Fortunately for the administration, the overwhelming majority of congressional Republicans (and Democrats) were strongly anticommunist and anti-Soviet. As Acheson, Truman, and leading Republicans recognized, most members of both parties were almost certain to approve a request that emphasized freedom's struggle against tyranny. Although political considerations contributed to what Acheson later called the speech's "clearer than truth" language, Truman believed what he said. "I wanted no hedge in this speech," he recalled. "This was America's answer to the surge of communist tyranny."

Truman's address to a joint session of Congress on March 12, 1947, was one of the most important presidential pronouncements of the twentieth century (see document 7). Although the request to aid the Greek and Turkish governments in containing communism was important, even more significant for the future was the sentence that quickly became known as the Truman Doctrine: "I believe it must be the policy of the United States to support free peoples who are resisting attempted subjugation by armed minorities or by outside pressures."

Under this precept, aid would be given mainly to governments in western Europe and East Asia in the late 1940s, and extended in subsequent decades to governments threatened by communist movements throughout the world. Moreover, hundreds of billions of dollars in aid would be provided not only for strategic and economic reasons, but also because U.S. leaders from Truman through Reagan believed that clear moral issues relating to basic human freedoms were at stake in the struggle against communism. As it did during the two world wars, U.S. foreign policy combined realism and idealism during the Cold War.

This speech went a long way toward establishing Truman as the strong, decisive leader that millions of Americans had longed for since Roosevelt's death almost two years before. The speech especially raised Truman's standing with ethnic Americans from eastern Europe and with Catholics and evangelical Protestants from other backgrounds who had doubted his conviction and effectiveness as an opponent of communism. Normally Democratic voters in these groups had been decisive in the Republican victory in 1946, but would undergird the Democratic triumph in 1948.

The address's strongly anticommunist theme, combined with Vandenberg's advice to Truman beforehand that, to ensure Congress's approval, he should "scare the hell out of the American people," created the inaccurate impression that the speech turned the public against communism and thus "manufactured consent" for anticommunist policies. As we have seen, most Americans were strongly anticommunist and anti-Russian by mid-1946. Thus Truman, like most presidents, was actually following public opinion at the time of the speech much more than he was leading it. When an aide urged him to stay in Washington afterward to lobby for the bill's passage, Truman replied that he was taking his vacation as planned because he believed that the public and Congress already supported him. Public opinion polls soon showed that he was right, as did the large majorities in Congress who voted for the aid package later that spring.

Even before Congress approved military and economic aid to Greece and Turkey on May 22, 1947, U.S. officials were contemplating a much larger economic aid package for Europe. This time the initiative came largely from officials in Washington, though European officials, U.S. diplomats abroad, and journalists on both sides of the Atlantic helped to alert U.S. leaders to the fact that the economies of most European nations had declined sharply since war's end and were in danger of falling even further if America did not provide large-scale, well-planned assistance. If the downward spiral continued, despair among the unemployed and the hungry might turn to desperation and communists might win elections or stage coups in France and Italy, which had large, Soviet-funded communist parties.

In a memorandum to Acheson and Secretary of State Marshall, Will Clayton, the undersecretary of state for economic affairs, summed up the situation in the spring of 1947 as the administration saw it: "Without further prompt and substantial aid from the U.S.A., economic, social and political disintegration will overwhelm Europe." Clayton, a successful Texas cotton broker, was blunt about America's economic interest in a prosperous Europe: "We need markets—big markets, in which to buy and sell." Only growing international trade, U.S. leaders believed, could prevent another Depression and foster democratic institutions.

Marshall, who had replaced Byrnes as secretary of state in January, made his most significant speech at Harvard University's commencement exercises on June 5. After describing the grave economic conditions in much of Europe, Marshall called on America to help "in breaking the vicious circle and restoring the confidence of the European people in the economic future of their own countries and of Europe as a whole" in order to "permit the emergence of political and social conditions in which free institutions can exist."

Three additional points stood out in the speech. First, Marshall insisted that the "initiative" for working out a specific proposal for U.S. aid "must come from Europe." Second, Marshall implied that America no longer wanted to aid individual nations, but instead sought to contribute to the continent's economic and political integration through "friendly aid in the drafting of a European program." And third, by stating that U.S. policy was "directed not against any country or doctrine but against hunger, poverty, desperation and chaos," Marshall was inviting Russia and east European nations to participate in developing a proposal for aid.

Although U.S. officials doubted that Stalin would choose to participate in a program premised on open, cooperative economies throughout Europe, they wanted Russia, not America, to bear the onus for the lasting division of the continent into communist and noncommunist blocs that might well result from Soviet refusal to participate in the Marshall Plan or to permit its client states to do so. Understandably reluctant to be the bad guys, Soviet leaders blamed the Marshall Plan's "imperialism" for dividing Europe when they withdrew from negotiations on the plan in early July and then ordered east European officials not to participate in the program.

With the Eastern bloc out of the picture, U.S. officials still had to reach understandings with the representatives of the sixteen west European nations who requested $22 billion in aid over four years. In discussions with the Europeans, U.S. officials emphasized that they wanted to support projects that grew out of careful planning both within and between countries, that resulted in reduced barriers to trade and investment, and that increased productivity in both industry and agriculture—in other words, to support projects that were likely to contribute to lasting economic growth and political stability in western Europe as a whole.

In these discussions, and in the subsequent implementation of the Marshall Plan (officially called the European Recovery Program [ERP]), U.S. officials achieved many of their goals, but usually with the tacit understanding that the recipients had at least as much influence as the donors in working out the program's many details. As historian Michael J. Hogan has noted, Europeans exercised "a considerable degree of autonomy within the framework of the ERP." Assuming, as U.S. officials did, that Europeans should be treated as equals, this sharing of power seemed both natural and praiseworthy.

The administration's biggest challenge was to get the Republican Congress to appropriate the large sums needed for the program. By December 1947, U.S. officials had cut $5 billion from the Europeans' request. Although Congress approved $522 million in short-term aid to Italy, France, and Austria on December 15, it was in no hurry to approve the larger program. The most influential critic was Senator Robert Taft of Ohio, a fiscally conservative, highly partisan Republican who derisively called the plan an "international New Deal."

Fortunately for western Europe and for U.S. relations with the region, the widely admired, nonpartisan Marshall was a masterful spokesman for the plan on Capitol Hill during the winter of 1948. A communist coup in Czechoslovakia in late February that shocked and angered many Americans also contributed to the bill's passage, as did Senator Vandenberg's effective support. With an initial appropriation of $5.3 billion for one year and with a Republican businessman, Paul Hoffman, slated to head the program, the ERP passed both houses in March 1948 by margins of more than four to one. By late 1951, when the program ended, America had contributed more than $13 billion, the equivalent of more than $80 billion in year 2002 dollars.

The Marshall Plan was America's most successful aid program ever. It reinforced the widely held belief that Americans were generous as well as self-interested. It helped to spur rapid economic growth in most of western Europe. It lifted the spirits of most Europeans and helped to diminish communist influence. It contributed to economic, political, and military integration in the region. It helped to demonstrate, through comparison between western and eastern Europe, that democratic capitalism was superior to communism in meeting most human needs and aspirations. And it helped to link the people and governments of America and western Europe in many ways, including the "big markets" on both sides of the Atlantic that Clayton had envisioned. In short, this cooperative, far-sighted program provided a huge boost for Western nations and values in the Cold War.

Whereas U.S. aid to Greece and Turkey and the Marshall Plan primarily involved U.S. relations with other Western governments, the Soviet blockade of the road, rail, and water routes that linked the three western zones in Germany to Berlin from June 24, 1948, through May 12, 1949, directly affected Soviet relations with America, Britain, and France. From Russia's perspective, the blockade was a legitimate response to the West's unilateral decision to unify the three western occupation zones and to move toward establishing a West German government, including the decision in the spring of 1948 to institute a new currency in the western zones and in the three western sectors in Berlin.

Detesting the Soviet government, most Americans by 1948 did not seek to understand its viewpoint, much less to find merit in it. Having read and heard many news stories about Soviet "aggression," they generally saw the blockade as an effort to gain control of Berlin's western sectors and absorb them into Russian-controlled East Germany—which it partly was, as recently released documents show.

The issue facing Western leaders in late June was how to respond. On June 25, the day after the blockade went into effect, British and U.S. military leaders in Germany, acting separately, began airlifts to supply West Berlin. Although Truman and his top advisers did not approve the U.S. airlift in advance, they agreed that "determined steps must be taken by the U.S. to stay in Berlin." Many officials doubted that an airlift would be able to deliver the minimum of 4,000 tons of supplies per day needed for the roughly 2.5 million people who lived in Berlin's western sectors.

In subsequent meetings, the administration authorized the airlift but rejected General Lucius Clay's proposal that U.S. troops use force if necessary to try to open one of the roads from West Germany to Berlin. Truman was determined to stay in Berlin, but he also wanted to avoid a military confrontation with Russia that might well escalate into full-scale war. Once again, Truman's approach mirrored the thinking of most Americans: Remain in Berlin even at the risk of war with Russia, 80 percent responded in a Gallup poll in July, but also try to avoid war.

Meetings with Stalin and other Soviet officials in July and August made it clear that Russia was willing to end the blockade only if the West agreed to abandon its plans to develop a West German government. Having decided well before the blockade that an independent, prosperous West Germany was their only realistic choice, Western leaders rejected Stalin's terms. The only question that remained by late summer was which policy would be more successful: the Soviet blockade or the West's airlift coupled with a counterblockade on deliveries of goods from West Germany to East Germany.

Like the Marshall Plan that was being implemented at the same time, the airlift quickly proved successful. The roughly 1,000 tons of supplies per day that U.S. and British planes averaged in the airlift's early weeks grew by autumn to the required 4,000 tons per day and then to 4,500 by December. As the weather improved with the coming of spring, the average daily shipment of food, fuel, medicine, and other supplies increased to 8,000 tons, as much as had been carried by road and rail before the blockade.

Ordinary Germans, Britons, and Americans—including the tens of thousands of industrial workers, coal miners, military personnel, and laborers who loaded and unloaded the planes—deserve much of the credit for the airlift's success. Stalin also showed restraint by not ordering Soviet forces to shoot down the planes while they were flying over the Russian zone. Like Truman and British prime minister Clement Atlee, Stalin deserves credit for not starting a war in this highly charged situation.

The airlift provided a huge victory for the West in the battle for German public opinion. Whereas Russia appeared to be trying to starve, freeze, and force communism on the West Berliners, America and Britain were seen as trying to help them survive and remain free. Most Germans also appreciated the sacrifices—both in money and in the lives of the forty-eight airmen who died in crashes that usually occurred in bad weather—that America and Britain made for freedom in West Berlin.

Contrary to Stalin's hopes, the blockade increased support among Germans for the speedy development of a separate West German government. It also increased support on both sides of the Atlantic for NATO, a military alliance that the United States, Canada, and ten European nations established in Washington in April 1949. As observers long have noted, NATO's three most important goals were to keep America in western Europe, to keep the U.S.S.R. out, and to ensure that a revived West Germany did not threaten its neighbors. Together with the Marshall Plan and other initiatives, NATO helped to integrate the nations of western Europe and forge lasting partnerships with Americans and Canadians.

By the winter of 1948–1949, Stalin realized that the airlift was helping the West more than the blockade was hurting it. Moreover, the Western counterblockade was damaging East Germany's already depressed economy. On January 30, Stalin told a U.S. journalist that fruitful negotiations to end the stalemate were possible. Secret U.S.–Soviet discussions took place at the United Nations in subsequent months, leading to an announcement on May 5 that the blockade and counterblockade would be lifted on May 12 and that a Council of Foreign Ministers meeting to focus on German issues would convene in Paris two weeks later. The Berlin crisis of 1948–1949, which had raised Americans' fear of war to high levels and their hatred of Russia and domestic communists even higher, was finally over.

Despite occasional bursts of overblown rhetoric, during the Cold War's first three years—from early 1946 through early 1949—U.S. leaders generally had pursued a balanced, well-calculated policy in which they treated the U.S.S.R. as an adversary to be contained, not an enemy to be demonized. They also had made distinctions among the threats to Western interests posed by particular communist leaders. After Stalin broke with Yugoslavia's Josef Tito in June 1948, for example, U.S. leaders cautiously aided Tito. But the Berlin blockade and other developments in 1948 and early 1949 undermined this relatively balanced approach, leading to increasingly self-righteous attitudes among U.S. officials and the public.

Two developments in the fall of 1949—the announcement of Russia's testing of an atomic bomb and the victory of Mao's communist forces in the Chinese civil war—triggered an even greater hardening in U.S. attitudes and policies toward the U.S.S.R. and communism at home and abroad. Mao's victory increased U.S. leaders' fears of communist expansion in the politically weak, economically underdeveloped nations of Southeast Asia. Russia's possession of nuclear weapons made it possible that Soviet leaders might use them to try to intimidate noncommunist nations and thus gain an advantage in the Cold War.

These and other fears and concerns were reflected in NSC-68, which epitomized hard-line thinking among U.S. officials during a time of high

Cold War tensions. Presented to Truman in April 1950, the top-secret report was written largely by Paul Nitze, who had replaced the more moderate Kennan as head of the State Department's Policy Planning Staff. Nitze was especially concerned about Soviet superiority in conventional forces in Europe at a time when Russia was also developing nuclear capabilities.

NSC-68's basic premises were (1) the U.S.S.R., "animated by a new fanatic faith [communism]," was "developing the military capacity to support its design for world domination"; (2) "the cold war is in fact a real war in which the survival of the free world is at stake"; (3) U.S. military strength was "becoming dangerously inadequate"; and (4) it would be "unacceptable, if not disastrous" to try to negotiate with the Kremlin at a time when the West was relatively weak. Not surprisingly, the report's major conclusion was that America and its allies should undertake a "rapid and concerted build-up" of their military forces in order to prevent any further Soviet/communist expansion.

NSC-68 did not consider the possibility that America's substantial lead in nuclear weapons and aircraft, coupled with Truman's decision in January 1950 to attempt to build hydrogen bombs, might give the West adequate deterrent power for the foreseeable future. Scientists at the time calculated that hydrogen bombs would be able to release hundreds or even thousands of times as much destructive power as the bombs dropped on Hiroshima and Nagasaki, thus making war between powers equipped with these weapons virtually unthinkable except as exercises in mutual suicide.

Because NSC-68 also called for efforts to weaken communist power inside the U.S.S.R. and other communist nations, it blurred the distinction between containing communism and seeking to win the Cold War. And because the emphasis on "international communism" failed to acknowledge differences and disagreements among the national communist parties, NSC-68 ignored the possibility that nations like U.S.S.R. and China might eventually become enemies and thus in effect contain each other, as Russia and Yugoslavia were doing on a small scale in Europe.

NSC-68 argued that "a defeat of free [i.e., noncommunist] institutions anywhere is a defeat everywhere." Based partly on the logic of this sweeping generalization, U.S. leaders in May 1950 agreed to supply military aid to the French colonialists (who also were key U.S. allies in Europe) who were fighting the communist-led nationalists in Vietnam. The next month, U.S. officials—with more justification—sent troops to repel an attack by Soviet-supplied North Korean troops against South Korea. The international Cold War was entering a new, even more dangerous phase.

ACTING TO REDUCE COMMUNIST INFLUENCE AT HOME

In 1946, the domestic Cold War had taken the form of increasingly harsh criticisms, by liberals and especially by conservatives, of U.S. communists and fellow travelers. In the first six months of 1947, anticommunists continued to criticize, but they also acted to curb communist influence. Three actions in these months illustrate the ending of the Popular Front, the often uneasy communist–liberal collaboration that had marked the Roosevelt years. These actions, together with many others that governmental bodies and private groups at all levels undertook in 1947 and in subsequent years, virtually ended communist influence in government, in the labor movement, in education, in the arts, and in other areas of American life.

The first development that isolated communists and fellow travelers was the founding of Americans for Democratic Action (ADA) at a meeting of four hundred anticommunist liberals—mostly Democrats—in Washington in January 1947. Prominent members included Eleanor Roosevelt, a well-known liberal and former first lady; New Deal official Leon Henderson; labor leaders Walter Reuther and David Dubinsky; the head of the National Association for the Advancement of Colored People, Walter White; the Democratic mayor of Minneapolis, Hubert Humphrey; historian Arthur Schlesinger Jr.; and theologian Reinhold Niebuhr. Another founding member was actor Ronald Reagan, then a liberal Democrat who opposed communist influence in the movie industry's labor unions.

Concerned about the Republican victory in the 1946 election and about Truman's half-hearted support for liberal causes, ADA called for an expansion of New Deal programs and sought civil rights for "all Americans regardless of race, color, creed, or sex." Most important for the domestic Cold War, ADA renounced "any association with Communists or sympathizers with Communists in the United States as completely as we reject any association with Fascists or their sympathizers. Both are hostile to the principles of freedom and democracy on which this republic has grown great." Energetic in fighting for liberal causes and in opposing communists, fellow travelers, and Henry Wallace's communist-directed Progressive party campaign for president in 1948, ADA was an important influence in the domestic Cold War.

The second action that demonstrated that the Popular Front was out of fashion was Truman's Executive Order No. 9835 issued on March 22, 1947, ten days after the president's Truman Doctrine speech. The order set up "loyalty boards" within each federal agency that were instructed to recommend the firing of "subversives" and prevent the hiring of "security risks." This action resulted from the growing awareness after World War II that U.S. citizens who spied for Russia had infiltrated the federal government and had gained access to highly classified information. Pressure to ensure the loyalty of federal employees came mostly from Republicans, who had raised concerns about the issue during the 1946 election. Now that they controlled Congress and had solid public support for removing communists from government, Republicans were ready to pass strong legislation and maintain a popular issue for the 1948 election if the president failed to act.

Although Truman promised that there would be no "witch-hunt," in fact the program that resulted from his order failed to protect accused employees' civil liberties. Because the names of accusers generally were kept secret, the accused often did not have a fair chance to defend themselves. Moreover, government agencies were permitted to fire employees—793 in the first year alone—without due process of law. Finally, the loyalty program may well have been unnecessary because, as we have seen, in 1945–1946 the FBI had collected large amounts of information about Americans who were spying for Russia and had taken effective steps to deal with the problem.

The third action—the one that almost certainly diminished the influence of communists and fellow travelers the most—was Congress's inclusion in the June 1947 Taft-Hartley Act of a provision that, if labor unions wished to have access to the services of the National Labor Relations Board in their disputes with management, their leaders would have to sign affidavits certifying that they were neither communists nor communist sympathizers. As long as they appeared to be sincere in doing so, leaders could resign from the Communist party, sign the oath, and keep their offices—as happened in several cases. The provision—section 9(h)—was popular not only in Washington but among the American people: a Gallup poll found that 78 percent of respondents who expressed an opinion supported it.

Section 9(h) boosted anticommunists in such major unions as the United Auto Workers in their ongoing struggle against communists and fellow travelers. It also strengthened unions that complied with section 9(h) at the expense of the communist-led unions that defied it. Together with other developments in the late 1940s, including most workers' hatred of communism and a bitter split in the CIO over whether to support Truman or Wallace for president in 1948, section 9(h) contributed to the decisive victory of anticommunist union leaders within the CIO and to the marked decline of most communist-led unions. In retrospect, the majorities who supported section 9(h) in Congress and in public opinion polls appear justified: by the late 1940s communist labor leaders clearly could not be trusted to advance America's democratic ideals.

CONCLUSION: EVALUATING AMERICA'S APPROACH TO U.S.–SOVIET RELATIONS

Historians and social scientists are rightly reluctant to use the word "in-evitable" because it suggests that historical developments are predetermined and hence are beyond people's capacity to influence decisively. In retrospect, however, the rapidly rising tensions in U.S.–Soviet relations beginning in 1945 appear all but inevitable given the fact that the overwhelming major-ity of America's leaders and the public were determined to pursue a peace based on the nation's perceived interests and ideals.

The economic isolationism that the Depression had discredited and the political and military isolationism that the Japanese attack on Pearl Harbor had destroyed were to be replaced, in most Americans' eyes, with economic, political, and military internationalism based on Wilsonian principles backed by the nation's superior industrial capacity and military power. In retrospect, it is clear that, if Soviet leaders did not accept America's internationalism and instead pursued their own goals, a wide-ranging, multifaceted conflict would ensue. In a speech in Paris on October 3, 1946, Secretary of State Byrnes highlighted the ideological antagonism that underlay the conflict: "In our view human freedom and human progress are inseparable."

We believe that U.S. leaders generally pursued wise policies toward the U.S.S.R. and toward communist parties in other nations during World War II and the early postwar years. We believe that Roosevelt was right to give pri-ority during the war to defeating Germany and Japan and to trying to estab-lish a foundation for constructive postwar U.S.–Soviet relations. Pursuing these goals, FDR sent large quantities of Lend–Lease aid to Russia and sought to establish cooperative relations with Stalin. We think that Truman was wise largely to continue Roosevelt's approach until the war's end, and then to shift to an approach that put more emphasis on America's ideals and on a tangible Soviet concession for every U.S. concession. The varied but generally firm ap-proach to containment that U.S. leaders implemented in Europe, the Middle East, and East Asia between 1946 and 1949 seems equally sensible. America's cooperative, generous policies toward noncommunist European nations are especially praiseworthy.

Beyond specific policies, U.S. leaders and the public deserve credit for grasping the central truth about the contest with the U.S.S.R. and its sup-porters in other nations. Historian Frank Ninkovich's 1999 depiction of the Cold War's essence echoes the Truman Doctrine speech of 1947: "The cold war was a historical struggle over which ideology or way of life would be able to form the basis of a global civilization." As we have seen repeatedly, most Americans supported their nation's determined involvement in that struggle.

By 1949–1950, however, U.S. officials, members of Congress, non-governmental opinion-molders, and ordinary citizens increasingly were exhibiting a self-righteous confidence in the complete validity of America's anticommunist policies—and of the total "evil" of "international communism"—that made clear thinking and wise diplomacy difficult. This dualistic, oversimplified approach to world affairs now characterized not only the main author of NSC-68, Paul Nitze, but also most other officials, including President Truman.

The virtue of U.S. leaders' anti-Soviet views of 1946–1947 was becoming the vice of undiscriminating global anticommunism (often called globalism) in 1949–1950, the vice that contributed even then to an unwise policy toward Vietnam. As William Shakespeare wrote in *Romeo and Juliet*, "virtue itself turns vice, being misapplied."

Shakespeare's insight also fits America's domestic Cold War. In the late 1940s, communists who could aid Russia from well-placed jobs in the federal government, in labor unions, and in defense industries clearly should have been required—and often were required—to find other employment. Indeed, given the Communist party's blatant disloyalty, FDR and Congress should have acted decisively in these areas between August 1939 and June 1941, when the totalitarian Soviet and German governments worked together in the war against democratic, U.S.–supported Britain and France. But communists who posed no direct threat to national security—teachers and social workers, for example—generally should have been permitted to keep their jobs. In employment and on other fronts, the domestic Cold War often resulted in unnecessary violations of civil liberties.

Although anticommunist measures often went too far, it is important to acknowledge, as historian John E. Haynes has argued, that it was "potentially dangerous and intolerable" to permit the U.S. Communist party to continue to operate "with the institutional power it possessed in the late 1940s." Haynes thus argues, we believe convincingly, that America's "cold war mobilization required an anti-Communist consensus" that limited the political and economic power of those in a position to serve the Soviet cause. The fact that other democratic nations limited communists' influence at the time lends support to this view, as does the fact that U.S. officials had established a popular precedent by cracking down on Nazi sympathizers during the war.

By 1947, the vast majority of Americans thought that fellow citizens who were self-proclaimed communists or who openly sympathized with communism and the U.S.S.R. should no longer have significant influence in society and government. Students of modern U.S. history are free to praise, criticize, or offer (as we do) a mixed assessment of this conviction and the ways it was translated into action. Before making a final evaluation, however, all of us first should try to understand the difficult challenges of these fateful years.

During the early 1940s, Americans made many sacrifices to defend their country and its allies against the aggression of fascist dictatorships in Europe and of militarists in Japan. Then starting in 1945 they provided much of the wherewithal needed to counter the expansionism of the communist-ruled Soviet Union. In thus stepping in to fill the vacuum created by World War II's weakening of central and western Europe and East Asia, the United States helped fulfill Alexis de Tocqueville's famous prediction, made more than a hundred years before the Cold War began, that one day America and Russia would each hold in its hands the destiny of half the world.

Although the Cold War did not require wartime levels of mobilization and sacrifice, it was by no means a peacetime era comparable to the years between the two world wars. Even before the Korean War of 1950–1953, a "peacetime" military draft, substantial inflation, and a high federal income tax rate—all linked to America's decision to aid allies and to limit Soviet/communist expansion—exemplified the nation's sacrifices in a crucial struggle destined to stretch over four decades. Americans should feel great satisfaction that their perseverance not only protected their fundamental interests, but also ultimately made the world safer for democracy than it had been in a long time, perhaps than it had ever been.

Documents

1

THE ATLANTIC CHARTER, AUGUST 14, 1941

Joint declaration of the President of the United States of America [Franklin Roosevelt] and the Prime Minister, Mr. Churchill, representing His Majesty's Government in the United Kingdom, being met together, deem it right to make known certain common principles in the national policies of their respective countries on which they base their hopes for a better future for the world.

First, their countries seek no aggrandizement, territorial or other;

Second, they desire to see no territorial changes that do not accord with the freely expressed wishes of the peoples concerned;

Third, they respect the right of all peoples to choose the form of government under which they will live; and they wish to see sovereign rights and self-government restored to those who have been forcibly deprived of them;

Fourth, they will endeavor, with due respect for their existing obligations, to further the enjoyment by all States, great or small, victor or vanquished, of access, on equal terms, to the trade and to the raw materials of the world which are needed for their economic prosperity;

Fifth, they desire to bring about the fullest collaboration between all nations in the economic field with the object of securing, for all, improved labor standards, economic advancement, and social security;

Sixth, after the final destruction of the Nazi tyranny, they hope to see established a peace which will afford to all nations the means of dwelling in safety within their own boundaries, and which will afford assurance that all the men in all the lands may live out their lives in freedom from fear and want;

Seventh, such a peace should enable all men to traverse the high seas and oceans without hindrance;

Eighth, they believe that all of the nations of the world, for realistic as well as spiritual reasons must come to the abandonment of the use of force. Since no future peace can be maintained if land, sea, or air armaments continue to be employed by nations which threaten, or may threaten, aggression outside of their frontiers, they believe pending the establishment of a wider and permanent system of general security, that the disarmament of such nations is essential. They will likewise aid and encourage all other practicable measures which will lighten for peace-loving peoples the crushing burden of armaments.

2

"COMMENT ON THE RESULTS OF THE DECISIONS MADE AT THE YALTA CONFERENCE"

By Frank Januszewski, editor of the
Detroit Polish News, typewritten manuscript sent
to Senator Arthur Vandenberg (Rep., Mich.) in
late February or early March 1945

At Yalta a new system of handling international affairs was established and President Roosevelt's signature on the report compels the United States to recognize that system. This system agreed upon by Stalin, Roosevelt and Churchill destroys a civilization that humanity has been centuries in building. This system means:

1. Morally—recognition of the priority of might before right,
2. Juridically—legalization of aggression,
3. Politically—abolition of democratic principles in international relations,
4. Strategically—end of the balance of power and the recognition of Soviet hegemony,
5. Economically—restriction if not abolition of free trade and consequently of free enterprise. . . .

Anxious to achieve the appearance of personal success, Roosevelt, playing against the hard and inflexible Stalin, lost in every negotiation, whether political or military. At Moscow, Teheran, and Dumbarton Oaks he pursued this policy until it became nothing more than the dictation of Moscow in matters concerning both the conduct of the war and the organization of the peace. . . .

From the standpoint of morals . . . the question of Poland at the Yalta Conference was a test case. Once President Roosevelt referred to Poland as "the inspiration of the world." Yalta has made Poland an eternal reproach for every decent man or woman. . . .

The Polish cause has become the morality test of the governments of the United States, Great Britain and Russia—a test they must pass in the court of world opinion—for Roosevelt and Churchill did not succeed in camouflaging the partitioning of Poland and depriving it of its independence. . . . In the hour when that violence and crime can no longer be covered, the treatment of Poland will be the yardstick of *our* political morality. . . .

Twice in twenty years a wave of barbarism has swept over the world. The first was the Bolsevist [*sic*] wave of 1918. The second was the fascist in its Italian and later its German manifestation. The third is that of Soviet imperialism. One common characteristic of these waves in their use of all possible technical and scientific methods and processes, a second is their absolute rejection of all ethical principles, whether in relation to domestic or international affairs. . . . It seems now as if the defeat of the Germans will not mean victory of the principles of our civilization but on the contrary, the subjection of this civilization to Soviet barbarism. So it comes to this: either we save our civilization and preserve our way of life or, gradually capitulating, we shall be responsible for the destruction of Western culture. Such is the task facing us.

The Democratic Party has shown that it not only cannot save, it cannot even defend our civilization. If the Republican Party does not feel that the preservation or the loss of the achievements of ages of civilized life and of Christianity is its affair and if it makes no effort to save America and with it the world, we shall not only lose the war but shall be in part responsible for the fall of the civilized world.

3

GEORGE F. KENNAN'S "LONG TELEGRAM," FEBRUARY 1946

At bottom of Kremlin's neurotic view of world affairs is *the* traditional and instinctive Russian sense of insecurity. Originally, this was *the* insecurity of a peaceful agricultural people trying to live on *a* vast exposed plain in *the* neighborhood of fierce nomadic peoples. To this was added, as Russia came into contact with *the* economically advanced West, fear of more competent, more powerful, more highly organized societies in that area. But this latter type of insecurity was one which afflicted rather Russian rulers than Russian people; for Russian rulers have invariably sensed that their rule was relatively archaic in form, fragile and artificial in its psychological foundation, unable to stand comparison or contact with *the* political systems of Western countries. For this reason they have always feared foreign penetration, feared direct contact between Western world and their own, feared what would happen if Russians learned *the* truth about *the* world without or if foreigners learned *the* truth about *the* world within. And they have learned to seek security only in *a* patient but deadly struggle for total destruction of rival power, never in compacts and compromises with it.

It was no coincidence that Marxism, which had smouldered ineffectively for half a century in Western Europe, caught hold and blazed for *the* first time in Russia. Only in this land which had never known a friendly neighbor or indeed any tolerant equilibrium of separate powers, either internal or international, could a doctrine thrive which viewed *the* economic conflicts of society as insoluble by peaceful means. After *the* establishment of *the* Bolshevist regime, Marxist dogma, rendered even more truculent and intolerant by Lenin's interpretation, became a perfect vehicle *the* for sense of insecurity with which Bolsheviks, even more than previous Russian rulers, were afflicted. In this dogma, with its basic altruism of purpose, they found justification for their instinctive fear of outside world, for the dictatorship without which they did not know how to rule, for cruelties they did not dare not to inflict, for sacrifices they felt bound to demand. In the name of Marxism they sacrificed every single ethical value in their methods and tactics. Today they cannot dispense with it. It is *the* fig leaf of their moral and intellectual respectability. Without it they would stand before history, at best, as only the last of that long succession of cruel and wasteful Russian rulers who have relentlessly forced *the* country on to ever new heights of military power in order to guarantee *the* external security of their internally weak regimes. This is why Soviet purposes must always be solemnly clothed in trappings of Marxism, and why no one should underrate *the* importance of dogma in Soviet affairs. Thus Soviet leaders are driven [by] necessities of their own past and present position to put forward a dogma which [depicts the] outside world as evil, hostile and menacing, but as bearing within itself germs of *a* creeping disease and destined to be wracked with growing internal convulsions until it is given *a* final coup de grace by *the* rising power of socialism and yields *a* to new and better world. This thesis provides justification for that increase of military and police power of *the* Russian state, for that isolation of *the* Russian population from *the* outside world, and for that fluid and constant pressure to extend *the* limits of Russian police power which are together the natural and instinctive urges of Russian rulers. Basically this is only the steady advance of uneasy Russian nationalism, a centuries old movement in which conceptions of offense and defense are inextricably confused. But in *the* new guise of international Marxism, with its honeyed promises to a desperate and war torn outside world, it is more dangerous and insidious than ever before.

It should not be thought from [the] above that Soviet party line is necessarily disingenuous and insincere on *the* part of all those who put it forward. Many of them are too ignorant of *the* outside world and mentally too dependent to question [their] self-hypnotism, and [many] have no difficulty making themselves believe what they find it comforting and convenient to believe. Finally we have the unsolved mystery as to who, if anyone, in this great land actually receives accurate and unbiased information about *the* outside world. In *the* atmosphere of oriental secretiveness and conspiracy which pervades this Government, *the* possibilities for distorting or poisoning sources and currents of information are infinite. The very disrespect of Russians for objective truth—indeed, their disbelief in its existence—leads them to view all stated facts as instruments for furtherance of one ulterior purpose or another. There is good reason to suspect that this Government is actually a conspiracy within a conspiracy; and I for one am reluctant to believe that Stalin himself receives anything like an objective picture of *the* outside world. Here there is ample scope for the type of subtle intrigue at which Russians are past masters. . . .

In summary, we have here a political force committed fanatically to the belief that with *the* US there can be no permanent modus vivendi, that it is desirable and necessary that the internal harmony of our society be disrupted, our traditional way of life be destroyed, the international authority of our state be broken, if Soviet power is to be secure. This political force has complete power of disposition over *the* energies of one of *the* world's greatest peoples and *the* resources of *the* world's richest national territory, and is borne along by deep and powerful currents of Russian nationalism. In addition, it has an elaborate and far flung apparatus for exertion of its influence in other countries, an apparatus of amazing flexibility and versatility, managed by people whose experience and skill in underground methods are presumably without parallel in history. Finally, it is seemingly inaccessible to considerations of reality in its basic reactions. For it, the vast fund of objective fact about human society is not, as with us, the measure against which *an* outlook is constantly being tested and re-formed, but a grab bag from which individual items are selected arbitrarily and tendenciously [*sic*] to bolster an outlook already preconceived. This is admittedly not a pleasant picture. Problem of how to cope with this force [is] undoubtedly *the* greatest task our diplomacy has ever faced and probably *the* greatest it will ever have to face. It should be *the* point of departure from which our political general staff work at *the* present juncture should proceed. It should be approached with *the* same thoroughness and care as *the* solution of major strategic problem in war, and if necessary, with no smaller outlay in planning effort. I cannot attempt to suggest all answers here. But I would like to record my conviction that *the* problem is within our power to solve—and that without recourse to any general military conflict. And in support of this conviction there are certain observations of a more encouraging nature I should like to make:

1. Soviet power, unlike that of Hitlerite Germany, is neither schematic nor adventuristic. It does not work by fixed plans. It does not take unnecessary risks. Impervious to *the* logic of reason, and it is highly sensitive to *the* logic of force. For this reason it can easily withdraw—and usually does—when strong resistance is encountered at any point. Thus, if the adversary has sufficient force and makes clear his readiness to use it, he rarely has to do so. If situations are properly handled there need be no prestige-engaging showdowns.

2. Gauged against *the* Western World as a whole, *the* Soviets are still by far the weaker force. Thus, their success will really depend on *the* degree of cohesion, firmness and vigor which *the* Western World can muster. And this is *a* factor which it is within our power to influence.

3. *The* success of *the* Soviet system, as *a* form of internal power, is not yet finally proven. It has yet to be demonstrated that it can survive *the* supreme test of successive transfer of power from one individual or group to another. Lenin's death was *the* first such transfer, and its effects wracked *the* Soviet state for 15 years. After Stalin's death or retirement will be *the* second. But even this will not be *the* final test. *The* Soviet internal system will now be subjected, by virtue of recent territorial expansions, to *a* series of additional strains which once proved *a* severe tax on Tsardom. We here are convinced that never since *the* termination of *the* civil war have *the* mass of Russian people been emotionally farther removed from doctrines of Communist Party than they are today. In Russia, *the* party has now become a great and—for the moment—highly successful apparatus of dictatorial administration, but it has ceased to be a source of emotional inspiration. Thus, *the* internal soundness and permanence of *the* movement need not yet be regarded as assured.

4. All Soviet propaganda beyond *the* Soviet security sphere is basically negative and destructive. It should therefore be relatively easy to combat it by any intelligent and really constructive program.

For these reasons I think we may approach calmly and with good heart *the* problem of how to deal with Russia. As to how this approach should be made, I only wish to advance, by way of conclusion, *the* following comments:

1. Our first step must be to apprehend, and recognize for what it is, the nature of the movement with which we are dealing. We must study it with *the* same courage, detachment, objectivity, and *the* same determination not to be emotionally provoked or unseated by it, with which *a* doctor studies *an* unruly and unreasonable individual.

2. We must see that our public is educated to *the* realities of *the* Russian situation. I cannot over-emphasize *the* importance of this. *The* press cannot do this alone. It must be done mainly by *the* Government, which is necessarily more experienced and better informed

on *the* practical problems involved. In this we need not be deterred by [ugliness?] of *the* picture. I am convinced that there would be far less hysterical anti-Sovietism in our country today if *the* realities of this situation were better understood by our people. There is nothing as dangerous or as terrifying as the unknown. It may also be argued that to reveal more information on our difficulties with Russia would reflect unfavorably on Russian–American relations. I feel that if there is any real risk here involved, it is one which we should have *the* courage to face, and *the* sooner the better. But I cannot see what we would be risking. Our stake in this country, even coming on *the* heels of tremendous demonstrations of our friendship for *the* Russian people, is remarkably small. We have here no investments to guard, no actual trade to lose, virtually no citizens to protect, few cultural contacts to preserve. Our only stake lies in what we hope rather than what we have; and I am convinced we have *a* better chance of realizing those hopes if our public is enlightened and if our dealings with Russians are placed entirely on *a* realistic and matter-of-fact basis.

3. Much depends on *the* health and vigor of our own society. World communism is like *a* malignant parasite which feeds only on diseased tissue. This is *the* point at which domestic and foreign policies meet. Every courageous and incisive measure to solve *the* internal problems of our own society, to improve *the* self-confidence, discipline, morale and community spirit of our own people, is a diplomatic victory over Moscow worth a thousand diplomatic notes and joint communiques. . . .

4. We must formulate and put forward for other nations a much more positive and constructive picture of *the* sort of world we would like to see than we have put forward in *the* past. It is not enough to urge people to develop political processes similar to our own. Many foreign peoples, in Europe at least, are tired and frightened by *the* experiences of *the* past, and are less interested in abstract freedom than in security. They are seeking guidance rather than responsibilities. We should be better able than Russians to give them this. And unless we do, *the* Russians certainly will.

5. Finally we must have *the* courage and self-confidence to cling to our own methods and conceptions of human society. After all, the greatest danger that can befall us in coping with this problem of Soviet communism, is that we shall allow ourselves to become like those with whom we are coping.

4

SECRETARY OF STATE JAMES BYRNES'S SPEECH IN STUTTGART ON GERMANY'S FUTURE, SEPTEMBER 6, 1946

I have come to Germany to learn at first hand the problems involved in the reconstruction of Germany and to discuss with our representatives the views of the United States government as to some of the problems confronting us.

We in the United States have given considerable time and attention to these problems because upon their proper solution will depend not only the future well-being of Germany, but the future well-being of Europe.

We have learned . . . that we live in one world, from which we cannot isolate ourselves. We have learned that peace and well-being are indivisible and that our peace and well-being cannot be purchased at the price of peace or the well-being of any other country.

I hope that the German people will never again make the mistake of believing that, because the American people are peace-loving, they will sit back hoping for peace if any nation uses force or the threat of force to acquire dominion over other people and other governments.

In 1917 the United States was forced into the first world war. After that war we refused to join the League of Nations. We thought we could stay out of Europe's wars and we lost interest in the affairs of Europe. That did not keep us from being forced into a second world war.

We will not again make that mistake. We intend to continue our interest in the affairs of Europe and of the world. . . .

The American people want peace. They have long since ceased talk of a hard or a soft peace for Germany. This never has been the real issue. What we want is a lasting peace. We will oppose soft measures which invite breaking the peace. . . .

It is the view of the American government that the German people throughout Germany, under proper safeguards, should now be given the primary responsibility for the running of their own affairs. . . .

Security forces will probably have to remain in Germany for a long period. . . . We are not withdrawing. As long as an occupation force is required in Germany, the Army of the United States will be a part of that occupation force.

The United States favors the early establishment of a provisional German government for Germany. Progress has been made in the American zone in developing local and state self-government in Germany, and the American government believes similar progress is possible for all zones. . . .

While we shall insist that Germany observe the principles of peace, good neighborliness and humanity, we do not want Germany to become the satellite of any power or to live under a dictatorship, foreign or domestic. . . .

The American people want to return the government of Germany to the German people. The American people want to help the German people to win their way back to an honorable place among the free and peace-loving nations of the world.

5

SPEECH BY J. EDGAR HOOVER, DIRECTOR, FEDERAL BUREAU OF INVESTIGATION, AT THE ANNUAL CONVENTION OF THE AMERICAN LEGION IN SAN FRANCISCO, SEPTEMBER 30, 1946

During the past five years, American Communists have made their deepest inroads upon our national life. In our vaunted tolerance for all peoples the Communist has found our "Achilles' heel". . . .

The fact that the Communist Party in the United States claims some 100,000 members has lulled many Americans into feeling[s] of false complacency. I would not be concerned if we were dealing with only 100,000 Communists. The Communists themselves boast that for every Party member there are ten others ready to do the Party's work. These include their satellites, their fellow-travelers and their so-called progressive and phony liberal allies. They have maneuvered themselves into positions where a few Communists control the destinies of hundreds who are either willing to be led or have been duped into obeying the dictates of others.

The average American working man is loyal, patriotic and law-abiding. He wants security for his family and himself. But in some unions the rank and file find themselves between a Communist pincers, manipulated by a few leaders who have hoodwinked and browbeaten them into a state of submission. . . .

The Communist influence has projected itself into some newspapers, magazines, books, radio and the screen. Some churches, schools, colleges and even fraternal orders have been penetrated, not with the approval of the rank and file but in spite of them. . . .

We are rapidly reaching the time when loyal Americans must be willing to stand up and be counted. The American Communist Party, despite its claims, is not truly a political party. The Communist Party in this country is not working for the general welfare of all our people—it is working against our people. It is not interested in providing for the common defense. It has for its purpose the shackling of America and its conversion to the Godless, Communist way of life.

. . . Its unprincipled converts would sell America short if it would help their cause of furthering an alien way of life . . . whose ultimate aim is the destruction of our cherished freedom. Let us no longer be misled by their sly propaganda and false preachments on civil liberty. They want civil license to do as they please and, if they get control, liberty for Americans will be but a haunted memory. For those who seek to provoke prejudice and stir up the public mind to angry resentment against our form of government are a menace to the very powers of law and order which guarantee and safeguard popular rights.

We, of this generation, have faced two great menaces in America—Fascism and Communism. Both are materialistic; both are totalitarian; both are anti-religious; both are degrading and inhuman. In fact, they differ little except in name. Communism has bred Fascism and Fascism spawns Communism. Both are the antithesis of [the] American belief in liberty and freedom. If the peoples of other countries want Communism, let them have it, but it has no place in America.

6

HENRY A. WALLACE'S SPEECH IN NEW YORK CITY, SEPTEMBER 12, 1946

Tonight I want to talk about peace—and how to get peace. Never have the common people of all lands so longed for peace. Yet, never in a time of comparative peace have they feared war so much. . . .

During the past year or so, the significance of peace has been increased immeasurably by the atom bomb, guided missiles and airplanes which soon will travel as fast as sound. Make no mistake about it—another war would hurt the United States many times as much as the last war. We cannot rest in the assurance that we invented the atom bomb—and therefore that this agent of destruction will work best for us. He who trusts in the atom bomb will sooner or later perish by the atom bomb—or something worse. . . .

To achieve lasting peace, we must study in detail just how the Russian character was formed—by invasions of Tartars, Mongols, Germans, Poles, Swedes, and French; by the czarist rule based on ignorance, fear and force; by the intervention of the British, French and Americans in Russian affairs from 1919 to 1921; by the geography of the huge Russian land mass situated strategically between Europe and Asia; and by the vitality derived from the rich Russian soil and the strenuous Russian climate. Add to all this the tremendous emotional powers which Marxism and Leninism give to the Russian leaders—and then we can realize that we are reckoning with a force which cannot be handled by a "Get tough with Russia" policy. "Getting tough" never bought anything real and lasting—whether for schoolyard bullies or businessmen or world powers. The tougher we get, the tougher the Russians will get. . . .

We must not let our Russian policy be guided or influenced by those inside or outside the United States who want war with Russia. This does not mean appeasement.

We must earnestly want peace with Russia—but we want to be met half way. We want cooperation. And I believe that we can get cooperation once Russia understands that our primary objective is neither saving the British Empire nor purchasing oil in the Near East with the lives of American soldiers. . . .

For her part, Russia can retain our respect by cooperating with the United Nations in a spirit of openminded and flexible give-and-take.

The real peace treaty we now need is between the United States and Russia. On our part, we should recognize that we have no more business in the *political* affairs of Eastern Europe than Russia has in the *political* affairs of Latin America, Western Europe and the United States. We may not like what Russia does in Eastern Europe. Her type of land reform, industrial expropriation, and suppression of basic liberties offends the great majority of the people of the United States. But whether we like it or not the Russians will try to socialize their sphere of influence just as we try to democratize our sphere of influence. . . .

The Russians have no more business in stirring up native communists to political activity in Western Europe, Latin America and the United States than we have in interfering in the politics of Eastern Europe and Russia. . . .

Under friendly peaceful competition the Russian world and the American world will gradually become more alike. The Russians will be forced to grant more and more of the personal freedoms; and we shall become more and more absorbed with the problems of social–economic justice.

Russia must be convinced that we are not planning for war against her and we must be certain that Russia is not carrying on territorial expansion or world domination through native communists faithfully following every twist and turn in the Moscow party line. . . . There will always be an ideological conflict—but that is no reason why diplomats cannot work out a basis for both systems to live safely in the world side by side. . . .

In the United States an informed public opinion will be all-powerful. Our people are peace-minded. But they often express themselves too late—for events today move much faster than public opinion. The people here, as everywhere in the world, must be convinced that another war is not inevitable. And through mass meetings such as this, and through persistent pamphleteering, the people can be organized for peace—even though a large segment of our press is propagandizing our people for war in the hope of scaring Russia. And we who look on this war-with-Russia talk as criminal foolishness must carry our message direct to the people—even though we may be called communists because we dare to speak out.

I believe that peace—the kind of peace I have outlined tonight—is the basic issue, both in the Congressional campaign this fall and right on through the Presidential election in 1948. How we meet this issue will determine whether we live not in "one world" or "two worlds"—but whether we live at all.

7

PRESIDENT HARRY S. TRUMAN'S SPEECH TO CONGRESS, MARCH 12, 1947

The gravity of the situation which confronts the world today necessitates my appearance before a joint session of the Congress. The foreign policy and the national security of this country are involved.

One aspect of the present situation, which I present to you at this time for your consideration and decision, concerns Greece and Turkey. . . .

The very existence of the Greek state is today threatened by the terrorist activities of several thousand armed men, led by Communists, who defy the Government's authority at a number of points, particularly along the northern boundaries. . . .

Meanwhile, the Greek Government is unable to cope with the situation. The Greek Army is small and poorly equipped. It needs supplies and equipment if it is to restore authority to the Government throughout Greek territory.

Greece must have assistance if it is to become a self-supporting and self-respecting democracy. . . .

Greece's neighbor, Turkey, also deserves our attention. . . . Since the war Turkey has sought additional financial assistance from Great Britain and the United States for the purpose of effecting that modernization necessary for the maintenance of its national integrity. That integrity is essential to the preservation of order in the Middle East. . . .

As in the case of Greece, if Turkey is to have the assistance it needs, the United States must supply it. We are the only country able to provide that help. . . .

One of the primary objectives of the foreign policy of the United States is the creation of conditions in which we and other nations will be able to work out a way of life free from coercion. This was a fundamental issue in the war with Germany and Japan. Our victory was won over countries which sought to impose their will, and their way of life, upon other nations.

To ensure the peaceful development of nations, free from coercion, the United States has taken a leading part in establishing the United Nations. The United Nations is designed to make possible lasting freedom and independence for its members. We shall not realize our objectives, however, unless we are willing to help free peoples to maintain their free institutions and their national integrity against aggressive movements that seek to impose upon them totalitarian regimes. . . .

The peoples of a number of countries of the world have recently had totalitarian regimes forced upon them against their will. The Government of the United States has made frequent protests against coercion and intimidation, in violation of the Yalta agreement, in Poland, Rumania, and Bulgaria. I must also state that in a number of other countries there have been similar developments.

At the present moment in world history nearly every nation must choose between alternative ways of life. The choice is too often not a free one. One way of life is based upon the will of the majority, and is distinguished by free institutions, representative government, free elections, guarantees of individual liberty, freedom of speech and religion, and freedom from political oppression.

The second way of life is based upon the will of a minority forcibly imposed upon the majority. It relies upon terror and oppression, a controlled press and radio, fixed elections, and the suppression of personal freedoms.

I believe that it must be the policy of the United States to support free peoples who are resisting attempted subjugation by armed minorities or by outside pressures.

I believe that we must assist free peoples to work out their own destinies in their own way.

I believe that our help should be primarily through economic and financial aid which is essential to economic stability and orderly political processes.

The world is not static, and the status quo is not sacred. But we cannot allow changes in the status quo in violation of the Charter of the United Nations by such methods as coercion, or by such subterfuges as political infiltration. . . .

It is necessary only to glance at a map to realize that the survival and integrity of the Greek nation are of grave importance in a much wider situation. If Greece should fall under the control of an armed minority, the effect upon its neighbor, Turkey, would be immediate and serious. Confusion and disorder might well spread throughout the entire Middle East. . . .

I therefore ask the Congress to provide authority for assistance to Greece and Turkey in the amount of $400,000,000 for the period ending June 30, 1948. . . .

In addition to funds, I ask the Congress to authorize the detail of American civilian and military personnel to Greece and Turkey, at the request of those countries, to assist in the tasks of reconstruction, and for the purpose of supervising the use of such financial and material assistance as may be furnished. I recommend that authority also be provided for the instruction and training of selected Greek and Turkish personnel. . . .

If further funds, or further authority, should be needed for purposes indicated in this message, I shall not hesitate to bring the situation before the Congress. On this subject the executive and legislative branches of the Government must work together.

This is a serious course upon which we embark.

I would not recommend it except that the alternative is much more serious. The United States contributed $341,000,000,000 toward winning World War II. This is an investment in world freedom and world peace.

The assistance that I am recommending for Greece and Turkey amounts to little more than 1/10 of 1 percent of this investment. It is only common sense that we should safeguard this investment and make sure that it was not in vain. . . .

The free peoples of the world look to us for support in maintaining their freedoms.

If we falter in our leadership, we may endanger the peace of the world—and we shall surely endanger the welfare of this Nation.

THE RUSSIAN PERSPECTIVE

Vladimir O. Pechatnov and C. Earl Edmondson

THE SOVIET ROAD TO THE COLD WAR

To people in the Soviet Union, the coming and the nature of the Cold War looked greatly—indeed, almost diametrically—different from the way most Americans saw things. Officials in the Kremlin were confident that they were pursuing legitimate security interests of the Union of Soviet Socialist Republics (commonly abbreviated to U.S.S.R., and also known as the Soviet Union) against aggressive machinations of the "imperialist" powers. "We do not conduct any cold war," Josef Stalin wrote in a rare note to himself in May 1948. "The cold war is being waged by the U.S.A. and its allies."

Although this view, almost a mirror-image of the one held in the West, became the standard one in the Soviet Union, it evolved only gradually following the surrender of Nazi Germany in May 1945. Soviet officials' perception of their place in the world then was much different from that three years later. In order fully to understand the coming of the Cold War, one must have an awareness of the evolution of the Soviet leaders' perceptions of their country's vital interests and of ways to defend them. Fortunately, the recent opening of important Russian archives has made available documents that permit a reasonably thorough examination of the motives and decision making of Soviet leaders during the years in which the Cold War began.

This section examines interwoven threads of perceptions, concerns, hopes, and decisions that contributed to and helped shape developments leading to what became known as the Cold War. Recurring in the tapestry are threads colored by Russia's imperial and revolutionary past, by the devastating impact of World War II, by Stalin's personality, by differing and often inconsistent perceptions among Soviet officials, and by hopes and plans for the postwar world.

85

GENERAL CONDITIONS AND ASSUMPTIONS

World War II took an enormous toll on the Soviet Union. In contrast to the United States, the country emerged from World War II with its human resources depleted and much of its infrastructure destroyed. At least 27 million people died during the war, and according to estimates made by the Soviet reparations commission, the country lost about 25 percent of all its reproducible wealth. In the western part of the country, over 1,700 cities and towns and thousands of villages were destroyed, most of the livestock stolen or slaughtered, and more than 31,000 industrial enterprises demolished. In sum, the German invasion left in ruins the most populous and developed part of the country—an area comparable, in the words of President John F. Kennedy, to "one-third of the continental United States east of Chicago."

Having gone through horrendous sufferings, the Soviet people longed for peace and security. The country was still on a strict rationing system (including bread), and people were weary of semistarvation. According to confidential surveys by the Communist party and the secret police, the public mood was a mixture of exhaustion, yearnings for relaxation of state controls, and hopes for a better life. Members of the intelligentsia, heartened by the country's cooperation with its allies, looked forward to greater intellectual freedom and widening contacts with the West. In a sampling of the public's mood reported to the Kremlin late in 1943, a university professor in recently liberated Kharkov asserted, "The ongoing changes will have to go further toward a greater democratization of the country's life." Peasants, still reeling from the upheavals of the 1930s, whispered hopefully about dissolution of collective farms (kolkhozes), which was rumored to be part of a deal between Stalin and the Western allies. Industrial workers, still laboring seven days a week, expected lower quotas and shorter hours. "The war is over now. Why should we work as hard as before?" asked a worker at a clothing factory in Siberia. And an ordinary worker in Moscow told a party official, "During the war we sacrificed everything for the sake of victory; now we want to be taken better care of"—simple words that expressed a widespread mood. Millions of Red Army soldiers, having seen the outside world, were becoming more critical of things back home.

Such reports do not tell the whole story, however. Many communist "true believers" and party officials felt troubled by the same changes that gave hope to much of the public. They wondered whether the price of cooperation with the Western allies might be too high. In particular, the dissolution in 1943 of the Communist International (Comintern), nominally the headquarters of international communism, disturbed many of them. Communist functionaries complained that although the dissolution might "help us now," it might "turn us backwards" in the long run. One person asked, "Who will now lead the world revolution? Will other communist parties continue to consult with comrade Stalin?"

A summary of such views sent to Moscow by the party boss in Sverdlovsk, a city in the Ural Mountains, stated that "there are people who interpret this step as a clear capitulation before the capitalist countries." He also reported the circulation of disturbing rumors about the introduction of private trade and of competing political parties. Some rumors held "that soon there will be a new tsar and that after the war the world would be governed by America and England."

Whether hopeful or worried, most Russians shared a new sense of pride and self-confidence when contemplating total victory over a lethal enemy. After the initial shock of invasion, the Stalinist system withstood the test of the titanic war (much to the surprise and relief of its chief guardian) and proved its ability to concentrate resources, maintain internal discipline, and act decisively under life-or-death circumstances. The emerging image of Russia as savior of Europe was a welcome and natural change after years of inferiority and isolation. Official propaganda identified the war with Russia's heroic past and glorified Soviet achievement. In many respects, the Great Patriotic War, which came to be known among the people as a "sacred war," endowed the regime with broader legitimacy than sterile Marxist ideology alone was ever able to provide and brought Stalin to the height of his popularity. Victory, in its turn, enabled Stalin to boast, as he did at a meeting of the Central Committee of the Communist Party of the Soviet Union (CPSU) in March 1946: "The war has shown that our social order is very firmly established."

The question remained, however, whether the regime could survive peace as well as war, especially in view of the changes that had occurred during the war. Because it was a war for national survival and not a communist crusade, Marxist ideology was overshadowed by Russian nationalism and Soviet patriotism, a shift symbolized by the fact that the formerly suppressed Russian Orthodox Church received official recognition while the Comintern was being disbanded. Moreover, conditions of war gave greater autonomy to military commanders, industrial managers, and local authorities. The Communist party itself, greatly expanded by the wartime inflow of military personnel, had been transformed from a small elite group into a much broader and more representative organization. So the key question was whether these trends toward greater openness would continue after the war, or whether strict ideological controls and administrative centralization would be reimposed.

Externally, the Soviet position was also marked by contradictions. On the one hand, victory over Germany and Japan, two mortal enemies, brought the U.S.S.R. to new heights of strategic and political influence. With expanded borders and an array of neighbors under its control, the country established military hegemony over the Eurasian landmass for years to come; it also gained recognition as a major power and a key member of the victorious antifascist alliance. On the other hand, the war clearly exposed critical strategic vulnerabilities: easily penetrable borders, lack of ready access to key seaways, and absence of a strategic air force and an ocean-going navy, all of which greatly restricted the Soviet Union's global reach. The very fact that the country came so close to defeat at the hands of a much smaller but technologically more advanced country could not fail to make Soviet leaders realize how vulnerable and backward their regime really was.

In view of such perceived vulnerabilities, it should not be surprising that, despite the apparent gains made during the war, security concerns remained paramount in Soviet leaders' thinking about the postwar world. All countries worry about security, and after 1945 leaders in the United States and Great Britain were also preoccupied by such concerns (in part, it must be admitted, because they saw the Soviet Union's gains more readily than its vulnerabilities). But given Russian history, the huge war damages, and the country's perceived vulnerabilities, as well as the mentality of Stalin and his subordinates, concerns about security were especially pronounced in the Soviet Union.

As a Marxist-Leninist, Stalin was revolutionary in many respects, but he also had a keen interest in history and strategy and saw himself as heir to a long tradition of Russian imperial statecraft. Shaped by Russia's geography, history, and national culture, that tradition was a unique combination of expansion to counter insecurity, on the one hand, and of a sense of inferiority and hostility vis-à-vis the more advanced West, from which invasion through Russia's penetrable borders had occurred repeatedly over six centuries, on the other hand. Yet this sense of insecurity and inferiority was intermingled with a strong sense of Russia's spiritual superiority, of its global mission, and of the necessity of autocratic rule and self-reliance.

Leninist-Bolshevism, of which Stalin and his lieutenants were true disciples, intensified and aggravated these traditional characteristics. The Russian Revolution transformed the culture's traditional messianism into a much more aggressive and implacable secular faith that Russia's way would redeem, or at least remake, the world. Thus, even before World War II, vir-

Wartime closeness: General George C. Marshall talks with Ambassador Maxim Litvinov at Bolling Field, Washington, D.C., on June 4, 1942. (National Archives.)

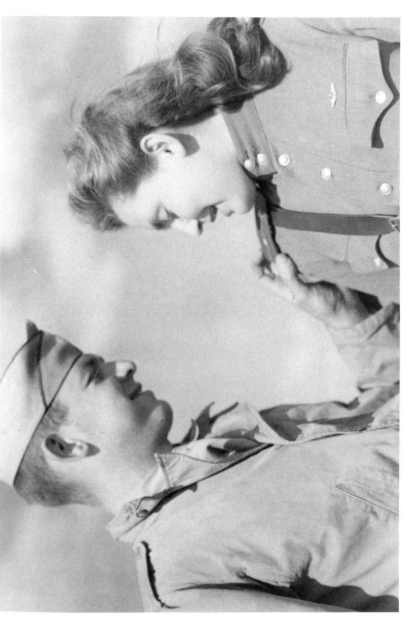

Allied soldiers: A Russian female officer and an American soldier socialize in the summer of 1944 when a detachment of U.S. forces was stationed in the Soviet Union to stage bombing attacks against Germany. (Library of Congress.)

Allied propaganda: A Russian poster (1945) depicts the bleeding Nazi wolf stabbed by the bayonets of the British, American, and Russian Allies. The poster reads: "So it will be with the Fascist beast!" (Library of Congress.)

Discussing diplomatic strategies: Soviet Premier Josef Stalin and
Foreign Minister Vyacheslav Molotov confer during the Yalta conference.
Andrei Vyshinsky is in the background. February 1945. (National
Archives.)

The Big Three: Churchill, Roosevelt, and Stalin meet at Yalta. February 1945. (National Archives.)

The occupation of Germany: A Russian convoy moves up a German highway to relieve U.S. troops in the zone of occupation near Leipzig. July 1945. (National Archives.)

Friend or foe? Stalin and President Harry S. Truman meet at Potsdam (near Berlin). At the extreme right is young Andrei Gromyko, Soviet ambassador to the United States. July 1945. (National Archives.)

Moscow foreign ministers conference: British Foreign Secretary Ernest Bevin, Soviet Foreign Minister Vyacheslav Molotov, and U.S. Secretary of State James Byrnes smile for the camera. December 1945. (National Archives.)

American policy advisor: George F. Kennan, chargé d'affaires in Moscow, wrote the "long telegram" in February 1946. (National Archives.)

Future enemies in the Far East: Mao Zedong, chairman of the Chinese Communist Party, and Patrick J. Hurley, U.S. ambassador to China, seem hopeful about a unified China in 1946. But civil war ensued. (National Archives.)

Berlin airlift: Airplanes from the United States and other Western allies bring food and supplies to Berlin during the blockade imposed by the Russians. 1948. (National Archives.)

Food for body and soul: Thanks to the Cooperative for American Relief Everywhere (CARE), German children receive nutritious aid from their former enemies in the United States. (National Archives.)

ulent anticapitalist ideology widened Russia's separateness from the West and intensified its isolation and sense of insecurity. As seen from Moscow, events between the world wars lent substance to this sense: military intervention by Western powers in Russia's civil war of 1918–1920; nonrecognition of Vladimir Lenin's government for many years; the creation of a barrier of anti-Russian countries, a "cordon sanitaire," along Russia's borders; and apparent efforts, as at Munich in 1938, to nudge Adolf Hitler's aggression eastwards.

In addition, factors as broad as the nature of the Bolshevik experience before 1917 and as narrow as Stalin's personality greatly affected Soviet policies in the international arena. Life in the revolutionary underground, which provided formative experiences for Bolsheviks, was a brutal school of survival that taught them conspiracy, self-righteousness, cruelty, single-mindedness, and contempt for written rules and compromises. It also taught them how to repress opposition more efficiently than the tsarist system had managed to do. Superimposed on these historical layers was the personality of Stalin himself. Stalin surpassed his comrades not only in the ability to run the huge country almost single-handedly, but also in boundless suspiciousness, ruthlessness, and sheer Machiavellianism. Thus shaped, Stalin and his circle created dictatorial institutions that gave them far greater control over Russia's resources and people than the tsars had ever dreamed about.

Stalin was determined to exploit his power at home and the possibilities opened by the defeat of Germany. Now was the time to right history's wrongs and to provide his country with an extra margin of safety for the future. The U.S.S.R. could be made into an invincible fortress against foreign, especially capitalist, enemies. If in the process it became a major actor on the world stage, so much the better.

In the most immediate sense, Soviet policymakers acted on the basis of what may be called the "Barbarossa syndrome"—the fear of another invasion from the West, presumably by a revived Germany bent on revenge and perhaps backed by other capitalist powers. Given the number and scale of past invasions, Russia's Barbarossa syndrome was surely more deeply felt than the "Pearl Harbor syndrome" in the United States. To prevent invasion in the future, Stalin was determined to keep Germany enfeebled and to extend Soviet borders to the line of 1941 (i.e., to retain control over the Baltic states, the western part of Ukraine, and Bessarabia, all of which Russia had lost after World War I and repossessed in 1939–1941, as well as the northern Bukovina). Without those expanded borders, most initially gained through the infamous Molotov–Ribbentrop (Soviet–German) Pact of 1939, Russian forces most probably would have lost both Moscow and

Leningrad in 1941. To provide a still greater depth of defense, a buffer zone of "friendly states" along the Soviet Union's western borders—a sort of "cordon sanitaire" in reverse—was to be created in eastern Europe, the traditional base for military aggression against Russia.

The same line of thinking applied also in the Far East, where twice in the twentieth century Japan had posed a serious threat to Russia's security. On that front, Soviet leaders wanted at the least to regain territory lost to Japan in the Russo–Japanese War of 1904–1905, primarily Sakhalin Island, as well as to acquire the Kurile Islands chain, all strategically important.

Another lesson of World War II, which Stalin aptly called "a war of engines," was the critical importance of a country's military–industrial base. The industrial sector of the Soviet Union needed rebuilding both to cover war losses and to catch up with potential competitors, for "those who lag behind get beaten," as Stalin liked to say. Hardly had the war against Germany ended when, on May 14, 1945, the Central Committee of the CPSU instructed editors-in-chief of major newspapers to concentrate "on our people's tasks in further strengthening the military–economic might of our Motherland." In short, control of adjacent space and enhanced military–industrial capacity were key components of Soviet thinking about the postwar world.

EARLY PLANNING FOR THE POSTWAR ERA

Soviet officials started to prepare for peace when the war was still in its early stages. The initial impulse for these preparations came from Solomon Lozovsky, a deputy to Foreign Minister Vyacheslav Molotov. In a memorandum to Molotov and Stalin late in December 1941, after German forces had been pushed away from Moscow, Lozovsky warned that "after the war we will again face, on every important question, a united front of capitalist countries which would be mostly concerned with preserving a capitalist system (including in the defeated countries) and above all with containing the Soviet Union within the old pre-1939 borders." Foreshadowing subsequent themes, Lozovsky offered three main tasks for planning the postwar agenda: compensation to the U.S.S.R. for wartime losses, securing new borders, and rendering Germany and its allies harmless for the future. The following month, Stalin authorized the creation of a special commission to work on this agenda.

The planning process picked up speed after major turning points in the war occurred in 1943. Soon after the great battles of Stalingrad and Kursk, three new bodies were organized to deal with issues likely to be faced in reaching a peace settlement.

One interagency commission, headed by Marshal Kliment Voroshilov, worked out a basic pattern for armistices to be signed with Germany's satellites. These armistices would provide for a predominant Soviet role in occupation policies for Hungary, Romania, and Bulgaria. In the Soviet view, such a role was critical for insuring a pro-Soviet orientation in those countries in the future.

A Foreign Ministry commission on reparations, headed by Deputy Foreign Minister Ivan Maisky, prepared a reparations program intended to keep Germany weak by requiring that it contribute massively to Soviet reconstruction. According to this scheme, the Soviet Union would receive $20 billion worth of reparations, half of which would presumably be supplied by Germany. As Maisky wrote, Germany, "the main problem," was "to be rendered harmless" for the next thirty years through a combination of Allied occupation, disarmament, reparations, and "re-education."

Finally, a Foreign Ministry commission on peace treaties and the postwar order, chaired by former Foreign Minister Maxim Litvinov, now a deputy to Molotov, made a strong geopolitical case for creating a wide security zone in Europe and acquiring additional strategic strongholds. Litvinov's commission proposed getting some control over the Turkish straits; internationalizing the Kiel Canal; maintaining a Soviet presence in the northern part of Iran in order to protect the Caucasus border and to open lines of communication to the Persian Gulf; and securing trusteeships over the Dodecanese Islands, Tripolitania (Libya), Somalia, Eritrea, and even Palestine.

Although very ambitious, these strategic desiderata were not conceived in absolutist terms of global hegemony or world revolution. The main justification for the claims was "the experience of the war," which had demonstrated severe constraints on the country's communications by sea and on its ability to project power beyond its borders. Based on continuity with goals of the late tsarist period, these desiderata remained, in terms of Realpolitik, fairly limited—from Moscow's perspective, anyway. Characteristically, there were no blueprints for expanding Soviet influence in western Europe, Latin America, or China, which were obviously considered to be within the West's sphere of interest.

Many of these proposals were fleshed out during the war. Although the Western allies were reluctant to grant formal recognition of the 1941 borders, they did give promising hints about the matter, and Stalin came to rely on their de facto recognition after the war. "The problem of borders, or rather of security guarantees of our specific borders, will be decided by force," he told Molotov in 1942. Soviet ambassadors in Washington and

London predicted that despite pro forma objections, both Washington and London "will ultimately bow to the inevitable and recognize the boundaries adequate to our needs." Aside from the special case of Poland, Stalin expected little Western resistance to Soviet domination of eastern Europe. In this matter, he relied on the realities of power.

All in all, Soviet leaders considered their expectations to be modest and legitimate. In their view, such claims represented a "fair share" of the spoils of war won by great sacrifice, spoils that were, moreover, vital for the future security of their country. In Stalin's brutal logic, each victor's share should be proportionate to the number of soldiers "spent" (his favorite expression) and of enemy killed. On both of these accounts the Soviet contribution was overwhelming indeed: The Red Army suffered fifty-five times more casualties than did U.S. forces and inflicted 93 percent of German combat losses during the three-year period between Barbarossa (June 22, 1941) and D day (June 6, 1944). Even including naval and air operations in all the war's theaters, the Soviet share of the total Allied war effort was, according to Soviet estimates, no less than 75 percent.

Stalin might also have sincerely considered his requests modest especially in comparison with his partners' possessions and gains. "The U.K. has India and her possessions in the Indian ocean in her sphere of interest; the U.S. has China and Japan, but the Soviet Union has nothing," Stalin complained to British foreign secretary Ernest Bevin late in 1945 in making his case for Soviet trusteeship over Tripolitania (Libya). "Could not the interests of the Soviet government also be taken into account?"

Stalin may have seen his agenda as reasonable, and his Western partners may have seemed open to much of it, but he doubted that he would achieve all of his desiderata. Both Russian history and Bolshevik ideology conspired to make him apprehensive about the postwar settlement. In 1877, 1904, and 1914, Russia had been lured into war by the prospect or promise of major strategic gains either in southeastern Europe (control over the Balkans and the Straits) or in eastern Asia (control over Manchuria), only to be left empty-handed in the end.

Even more treachery could be expected from the West now that Russia had become its ideological and class enemy. In 1944, Stalin said to Yugoslav communist allies, pointing to the map of the Soviet Union, "They will never accept the idea that so great a space should be red, never, never!" And in March 1945 he told Czechoslovak communists that after the war "our allies will try to save the Germans and conspire with them [against us]," echoing suspicions he had uttered as early as 1942. Molotov, citing Stalin to the effect that tsarist Russia used "to win wars but was unable to enjoy the fruits of her victories," joined in the refrain: "Russians are re-markable warriors, but do not know how to make peace: they are deceived, underpaid."

Thus obsessed by the idea of "not being fooled" yet again, Stalin and Molotov were ready for tough bargaining with their allies. They were deter-mined to secure as many gains as possible—first of all in east-central Europe, preferably with their allies' consent, but unilaterally if necessary. Hoping for the best (i.e., formal recognition of their rights and claims), they were prepared for the worst. Although important, collaboration with the West was subordinate to the main task of building a buffer zone along the western border. At least some Western observers were aware of that order of Soviet priorities, as illus-trated by a report from the U.S. Office of Strategic Services (OSS) in March 1945: "[T]o the Soviet leadership, adherence to the pro-Soviet foreign policy on the part of the border countries is more important than the success or fail-ure of general international cooperation after the war."

The experience of interallied relationships during the war was another factor shaping Soviet postwar plans and expectations. Despite the unex-pectedly large-scale cooperation with "a class enemy," necessitated by a common threat, underlying ideological hostility and suspicions remained alive throughout the war, as fully confirmed by newly available Russian documentation. From the Soviet standpoint, certain Western policies were the chief culprits. Soviet leaders viewed the failure of the Western allies to open a second front in Europe early in the conflict as particularly serious and symptomatic. They saw it as a clear sign that Britain and the United States wanted Russian blood to win the war for them. In a dispatch from Washington in June 1943, even such a Western-oriented Soviet diplomat as Litvinov concluded "beyond doubt" that "military calculations of both gov-ernments [Britain and the United States] are [intended] to . . . wear down the Soviet Union's strength to the maximum extent possible in order to di-minish its role in the solution of postwar problems." Stalin and his diplomats placed most of the blame for such policies on Winston Churchill, however, for they sensed that he was "towing Roosevelt."

Soviet leaders also resented what they viewed, with good reason, as an Anglo–American plot to keep the development of atomic weapons a com-plete secret from them. Thanks to the Kremlin's extended spying network in both Britain and the United States, it knew about the secret project early on, however. Accordingly, Stalin showed no surprise when President Harry S. Truman referred obliquely to the atomic bomb at the Potsdam Confer-ence in July 1945. At the same time, Stalin told his diplomats, "Roosevelt clearly felt no need to put us in the picture. He could have done it at Yalta.

He could simply have told me that the atomic bomb was going through its experimental stages. We were supposed to be allies." On other matters, too, spies provided grounds for persistent Soviet suspicions about the intentions of the country's Western allies.

Finally, as the war neared its end, disagreements among the Allies about the future of eastern Europe became more pronounced, despite earlier efforts to paper them over. Poland in particular proved to be a major bone of contention, "an open wound in the relations between the Soviet Union and the Anglo–Saxon countries," as Churchill put it. Hostility between Poles and Russians went back several centuries, but Stalin saw Poland less as an old enemy than as a strategic "corridor for attack" against Russia, as he said at Yalta. Now he wanted its territory to be his own corridor of communication to the future Soviet occupation zone in Germany.

The U.S.S.R. and its Western allies disagreed about who should speak for Poland. For domestic political as well as strategic reasons, London and Washington supported the London-based government-in-exile and its underground military wing in Poland. In the Kremlin's eyes, however, the Poles in London were true heirs of Poland's Russophobic tradition and were only too willing to act, as U.S. intelligence acknowledged, as "a counterpoise" to the U.S.S.R. in eastern Europe. Openly anti-Soviet and irredentist, the "London Poles" were a major obstacle to Soviet plans for Poland, and Stalin was determined to deny them a political role in the country. In the summer of 1944, a rival pro-Soviet group, which came to be known as the Lublin government, was set up in Poland. At the same time, much to the indignation of his Western allies, Stalin refused actively to support the uprising in Warsaw by forces loyal to the London Poles. In a more muted way, the same contradiction between independence and friendliness toward the Soviet Union was present in Romania and Bulgaria, where the West also tacitly supported anti-Russian political forces.

Despite all these problems, the interallied relationship also had positive features from the Soviet standpoint. Procuring large-scale aid from the West for the deadly fight against fascism was considered by the Kremlin a major political feat. "Lenin could not even dream of such a correlation of forces as we achieved in this war," Stalin told Yugoslav communists early in 1945. Thanks to the mutual interest in defeating the common enemy and laying the bases for a postwar order, the underlying ideological hostility receded into the background for a while. New habits of cooperation developed within parts of the Soviet bureaucracy and eroded some of its orthodox anti-Western stereotypes and prejudices. Among the public at large a new image of friendly allies superseded the old one of class enemies. Several Soviet diplomats dealing with the West—notably Litvinov, Maisky, and Andrei Gromyko—came to base their planning for the postwar period on the presumption of continued cooperation among the Big Three. They viewed such cooperation as the best basis for a stable postwar order, one that would also be protective of their country's interests.

This presumption in turn required a fairly revisionist view of the capitalist West, which some people in the Kremlin came to appreciate as a staunch opponent of fascism and German–Japanese militarism. Fully aware of interallied differences, these Soviet diplomats still believed that the vital security interests of their country were largely compatible with those of the United States and Great Britain and even that cooperation with the Western allies was required in order to realize and safeguard those interests. The young Gromyko, a loyal protégé of Molotov, predicted in June 1944 that the United States would want to "preserve international peace" after the war in order to secure its "greatly enhanced world position."

Although Stalin, with his boundless suspicion of everything foreign, was hardly prone to such a benign view of the West, his cynical pragmatism prompted him to keep open the option of continued cooperation after the war. His future-oriented policies during the war spoke louder to this effect than his private words of distrust. Soviet diplomacy played an active role in laying the foundation for the Bretton–Woods international financial system and in creating the United Nations. For a while, Stalin was serious about the United Nations's peacekeeping potential, at least as long as the Allies policed the world (a scheme that corresponded to his own vision of dividing the world into spheres of influence). In May 1942, for example, he overruled Molotov's skeptical reaction to the "four-policemen" idea put forward by President Franklin Delano Roosevelt (FDR); this notion was "absolutely correct," he cabled to his deputy. "There is no doubt," he went on, "that without Great Britain, the U.S.A., and the U.S.S.R. creating a joint military force capable of preventing aggression, it would be impossible to secure peace in the future." (FDR also foresaw China as one of the "four policemen.") And in August 1944 Stalin assured pro-Soviet Polish leaders that prospective UN military forces would hold Germany in check.

Important psychological incentives also contributed to an inclination toward international cooperation. For the first time, the West accepted the Soviet Union as a legitimate great power thanks to its impressive military performance and the sacrifices it made during the war. In only a couple of years, the former international pariah state became a full partner in the councils of world powers, which seemed respectful of its power, interests, and newly gained status. Such respect was especially important for Stalin, who developed a reasonably close working relationship with his Western counterparts and clearly enjoyed his new status of being, in his view, first among equals, a view that spread throughout the Soviet leadership and was generally cultivated.

Of course, this new sense of recognition and legitimacy worked two ways. Although it provided incentive for international cooperation, it also enhanced the Soviet Union's appetite and created a sort of entitlement complex.

There were also vital practical reasons for continued Soviet cooperation with the West. Stalin and his team were fully aware of the awesome military–industrial potential and global strategic reach of the Anglo–American world. They did not want to make that world an enemy. At the least, they wanted to postpone doing so until a correlation of forces more favorable for the U.S.S.R. was achieved. ("A bad peace is better than a good quarrel," goes a Russian saying.) In general, Soviet leaders thought it best to have the Western allies as partners in preventing a resurgence of Germany and Japan, for those countries were deemed to be potentially more deadly enemies than the liberal democracies.

Besides, the West, especially the mighty and prosperous America, was seen as a potential source of desperately needed economic assistance for the postwar reconstruction of the Soviet economy. In December 1944, the State Defense Committee approved a request for a $6 billion loan from the United States, in addition to other plans to use Lend-Lease for getting industrial equipment for postwar use. In Soviet planning guidelines, Western assistance was listed, along with domestic sources and reparations, as one of the three main resources for reconstruction.

As for the nature of cooperation with the West, Soviet planners saw it largely in terms of a great-power concert based on some kind of a division of the world into spheres of influence. Litvinov recommended "an amicable separation of security spheres in Europe" (mainly between the U.S.S.R. and Britain) and saw "our maximum sphere of security" to be "Finland, Sweden, Poland, Hungary, Czechoslovakia, Romania, the Slavic countries of the Balkans, as well as Turkey." Maisky also argued for a British–Soviet condominium in Europe, one that would "strengthen friendly relations with the United States." Thus, the "three- [or four-] policemen" formula of cooperation was expected to provide for the major strategic imperatives of the U.S.S.R.: keeping it in the council of world powers, legitimizing its postwar borders and spheres of influence, and keeping Germany and Japan down. Stalin demonstrated his preference for arrangements based on spheres of influence when he accepted the "percentage deal" for southeastern Europe proposed by Churchill in Moscow in October 1944.

Again, the ultimate controlling factor was military presence on the ground. "Whoever occupies a territory also imposes in it his own social system," was Stalin's famous dictum recorded by Yugoslav communist leader Milovan Djilas in 1944. This line of thinking did not mean that the Kremlin had definite plans early on for sovietizing the whole of eastern Europe. With regard to Poland, for example, the battle order for the Red Army forbade "setting up Soviet-type regulations" and "interfering with local Catholic churches." Specific forms of Soviet control in different countries were to be worked out in accordance with evolving conditions. But in crude Bolshevik thinking, military presence was a critical variable for influencing an occupied country's sociopolitical development. Internal Soviet documents of 1945–1946 are full of references to the Red Army's key role in bringing "people's democracy" to east European countries, while a "totally different political process" was expected to develop in Western-occupied countries. Molotov's handwritten comments regarding the post-Yalta reorganization of the Lublin government provide a vivid illustration of the Soviet view: "Poland—big deal! But how governments are being organized in Belgium, France, Greece, etc., we do not know. We do not say that we like one or another of these governments. We have not interfered, because there it is the Anglo–American zone of military action."

Indeed, Stalin was very careful about interfering with the Western sphere. He demonstrated that early on, when the Kremlin grudgingly accepted a negligible role in the occupation of Italy in 1943. Not that Stalin gave up on spreading communism or Soviet influence there altogether, but he subordinated those interests to his larger strategic goals. Later, in 1944 and 1945, Stalin restrained French and Italian communists from attempts to take power in their countries and refused actively to support communist-led campaigns against the British-backed government of Greece and the American-backed government in China.

Stalin's strong support for a British–American invasion through northern France, instead of the Mediterranean strategy favored by Churchill, also indicated his priorities. He knew that the latter would tie Western forces down in Europe's southern periphery, thus allowing the Red Army to advance much further westward than it ultimately did. But a speedy defeat of the common enemy was more important to him than exporting revolution or extending Soviet military presence into western Europe.

He was, of course, fully aware of the geopolitical advantages of the other course. "Had Churchill delayed opening the second front in northern France by a year, the Red Army would have come to France," he told Maurice Thorez, the leader of France's communists, in 1947. He acknowledged having thought about "reaching Paris," as did Tsar Alexander I, who led Russian troops into the French capital in 1814. But Stalin resisted the temptation to emulate his illustrious predecessor (see document 7).

No wonder that analysts in Washington saw these priorities, along with the disbanding of the Comintern, as evidence of "increasingly cooperative policy on the part of the U.S.S.R.," to quote an OSS report of September 1943. The OSS was impressed by the fact that "despite the overwhelming success of its summer offensive, the Soviet Union continues to urge the Allies to invade Europe with a large military force, the presence of which could hardly be conducive to Soviet expansion in that area."

GAINS AT YALTA AND MISTAKEN ASSUMPTIONS

Many of the threads examined thus far came together at the Yalta Conference in the Crimea. There, the Allies reached broad consensus on many important issues. Compromises blunted the sharpening tensions over Poland. Faced with a "correlation of forces" favoring the Soviet Union, Roosevelt and Churchill agreed to move Poland's borders westward by about 200 miles. The shift allowed the U.S.S.R. to keep the territory in the eastern part of prewar Poland that it had gained through the Molotov–Ribbentrop Pact in 1939 (and giving it at least part of the Polish territory that the Romanov empire controlled before World War I). In return, Stalin agreed to allow free elections and a democratic reorganization of the pro-Soviet Lublin government—a formulation representing the maximum price Stalin was willing to pay for preserving "comity" with his Western allies. In addition, he mollified Roosevelt and Churchill by signing the Declaration on Liberated Europe, which formally emphasized democracy and self-determination. All the while, he reassured the worried Molotov: "Do not worry. We can implement it in our way later. The heart of the matter is in the correlation of forces."

Even with regard to more ambitious Soviet strategic aspirations, the initial Western response was apparently positive. The U.S. government agreed in principle to consider Soviet claims to former Italian colonies, while both FDR and Churchill informally supported a review of the Montreaux Convention of 1936, thus implicitly acknowledging the Soviet request for a greater role in controlling the Turkish straits. They also secretly assured Stalin that his country could regain former tsarist possessions in the Far East as a reward for entering the war against Japan within three months after the surrender of Germany. Another incentive to participate in the war in Asia was Stalin's aspiration to take part in the postwar occupation of Japan, thus to play a major role in that part of the world.

The Yalta Conference was regarded as a success by the Soviet side. "The general atmosphere at the conference was very friendly," Molotov reported to Soviet ambassadors abroad. "There was obviously a desire to come to agreement on issues in dispute. We consider the conference as a positive development on the whole and specifically on Poland, Yugoslavia, and reparations."

But a serious downturn in interallied relations soon followed the Yalta Conference. It was caused primarily by disputes over implementation of the decisions regarding the reorganization of the Polish government and by the so-called Bern incident. The latter grew out of the Soviet response to secret contacts between U.S. agents and Nazi emissaries in Bern, Switzerland, in March 1945. When denied participation in the talks, the Soviet side interpreted them as a sinister plot designed to bring about unilateral German capitulation on the western front. Although Roosevelt tried to play the matter down in his last message to Stalin, the incident left bad feelings on both sides.

One likely fallout from the incident was Stalin's abrupt decision to downgrade the Soviet representation at the upcoming conference to found the United Nations Organization. Instead of sending a large, top-level delegation headed by Molotov, as originally decreed by the Politburo, Stalin proposed at the end of March to send a much smaller group led by the young Andrei Gromyko, a proposal that annoyed Washington.

Even so, as the war in Europe neared its end, Stalin was less of an expansionist than some of his lieutenants. The mood of the Red Army's officer corps, as they advanced triumphantly through Europe, was euphoric, according to reports by various Russian witnesses and American intelligence operatives. Many officers seemed ready to go all the way to the English Channel, and the normally reasonable Litvinov proposed a much wider Soviet security zone than Stalin ever supported. Even among the Soviet public there were sentiments, according to party and secret-police reports, in favor of annexing much of eastern Europe and Germany to the U.S.S.R.

Although more modest than that, Stalin's own security agenda, as deduced from his actions rather than from his words, was overly ambitious and ultimately proved unacceptable to the West. As noted, his minimum goals were to keep Germany and Japan down while securing the Soviet sphere in eastern Europe. But he was also ready, as we will see, to knock on other doors looking for soft spots around the periphery of the U.S.S.R. and beyond—in Iran, Turkey, and even the Mediterranean. And all of these acquisitions were to be made while preserving the fruits, especially the economic fruits, of a stable relationship with the West. At that point, Stalin did not view the wartime alliance as an impediment to his plans for security through expansion. To the contrary, it was only within the framework of the Big Three that he could hope to achieve his main goals. Ultimately, this combination proved to be incompatible, for Soviet leaders had, in William Taubman's words, "not so much a plan, with all contingencies taken into account, as a hope."

The Kremlin's hope was propped up by several largely illusional assumptions. Despite occasional worries about a "united front of capitalist countries," in general Soviet leaders firmly believed, in line with a long-held Bolshevik view of the capitalist world, that the postwar British–American relationship would be marked by "contradictions" and competition. Maisky expected that in this relationship the United States would play an "offensive" role, the British a "defensive" one. Furthermore, Soviet thinking postulated not only that Americans and Britons would be locked in a deadly struggle for markets and colonies, but also that they both would be keenly interested in keeping the German and Japanese economies weak. Why, Gromyko asked, would the "industrial–financial bourgeoisie of the U.S.A." strengthen future competitors?

British–American discord and a weak Germany were the Kremlin's best hope for avoiding the emergence of a hostile Western coalition, the specter of which had haunted the Soviet leadership since the Entente's intervention in Russia's civil war and the diplomatic isolation of 1920s. A bedrock of Soviet policy was "to prevent formation of a bloc of Great Britain and the U.S.A. against us," as Lozovsky stated during a staff meeting of top Soviet diplomats in the spring of 1944.

Soviet leaders entertained another illusion of an ideological nature: a grossly exaggerated notion that it would be in the West's economic interest to assist postwar reconstruction in the Soviet Union. Like some Americans, they expected the U.S. economy to go into another big depression after the war. Understandably, then, Soviet leaders saw their request for American goods and credits almost as a favor, one that the U.S. government should be only too glad to accept.

A final Soviet miscalculation was more geopolitical than ideological. Soviet leaders counted on an eventual withdrawal of U.S. military forces from Europe, which would leave the U.S.S.R. and Britain as the only two great powers on the continent. They saw it "in our best interest," according to a report by Maisky that reflected a predominant Soviet view of an optimal European balance of power, "that postwar Europe have only one great land power—the U.S.S.R.—and only one great sea power—England." Such an arrangement would "prevent the formation in [west-central] Europe of any power or combination of powers with powerful armies." President Roosevelt's assurance to Stalin at Teheran late in 1943 that the U.S. military forces would be out of Europe two years after the war ended gave added plausibility to such projections. Both tradition and common wartime expectations, then, pointed to a limited American role in the postwar world, even though such thinking clearly overlooked the expansion of American security requirements during World War II, an expansion that soon made the United States far more assertive and globalist in a strategic sense, especially in Europe, than Soviet leaders (and perhaps most Americans) expected.

Such, in brief, were Soviet plans and expectations, hopes and fears for the future as the terrible war came to an end. But soon this fairly optimistic picture began to unravel under the pressure of new, often unforeseen developments.

THE FIRST FREEZE: FROM THE DEATH
OF FDR TO THE TRUMAN DOCTRINE

FDR's sudden death on April 12, 1945, was a serious blow to Soviet calculations. Stalin was obviously distressed by the news, as confirmed by Ambassador Averell Harriman, and personally saw to it that mourning ceremonies in the U.S.S.R. were at the highest national level. Despite Stalin's lingering mistrust of Roosevelt, the American president was his favorite and most reliable Western partner, as well as a personal guarantor of the continuation of what Moscow called the "Roosevelt trend" in U.S. foreign policy, a policy of cooperation with the Soviet Union based on recognition of and respect for Soviet security needs. Stalin knew from his diplomats and intelligence reports that this trend was under mounting pressure even when FDR was still alive; without him, Washington was likely to become more anti-Soviet. Characteristically, Stalin suspected some evil plot behind Roosevelt's death and suggested to the U.S. ambassador that the president's body should be examined for evidence of poison.

Soviet leaders had misgivings about Roosevelt's successor from the start. In Moscow, Truman was known mostly for his memorable statement, at the time of the German invasion of the Soviet Union, to the effect that the United States should help whichever side was losing "and that way let them kill as many [of each other] as possible." That phrase haunted Truman in all internal Soviet assessments, including the first profile of the new president sent to the

Kremlin by the Foreign Ministry on April 13. Nevertheless, accurately describing Truman as a moderate Democrat and "a loyal New Dealer," that report hopefully predicted that he would "generally continue Roosevelt's policy" in foreign affairs.

But Truman soon confirmed the worst Soviet apprehensions. His famous scolding of Molotov in the White House on April 23, during a discussion of the Polish problem, was perceived by the Soviet foreign minister as a deliberate demonstration of a new tougher line toward the U.S.S.R. Then three weeks later the Truman administration, without any warning, abruptly stopped Lend–Lease shipments to the U.S.S.R. and even called back several ships already headed for Soviet ports. Officially, the Soviet government responded to the shock by tersely taking note of Truman's action. But in his talks with Harry Hopkins in June, Stalin called it a "brutal" act and asserted that if it was "designed to put pressure on the Russians in order to soften them up, then it was a fundamental mistake."

Clearly, Stalin was reading the worst possible meaning into Washington's action. The Kremlin's internal reaction was even more somber and far-reaching. As recalled by some government officials, a special Kremlin advisory to top Soviet leaders and to missions abroad characterized termination of Lend-Lease as a sign of a new, more adversarial U.S. policy "now that the war is over." The intensity of the Kremlin's indignation, mixed with defiance, also shows in Molotov's order for the Soviet trade representative in New York "to stop popping up with his miserable protestations and begging American authorities for deliveries; if the Americans want to stop deliveries, so much the worse for them."

This new tension between the emerging superpowers was soon eased by steps taken in Washington. Perhaps realizing that he had acted precipitously, Truman decided to resume Lend–Lease deliveries for the Far East and to send Hopkins, a Roosevelt aide highly regarded by the Russians, on a troubleshooting mission to Moscow. Most notably, the Stalin–Hopkins talks resolved thorny disagreements about the reorganization of the new Polish government in a way satisfactory to the Kremlin and its Polish clients. The compromise called for several members of the old London-based government-in-exile to join the pro-Soviet Lublin government, but the latter group would still be dominant. The arrangement was hailed as a "clear victory" by the Lublin government's representative in Moscow, since his group would control seven key posts out of twelve, thus "having a decisive voice." The compromise opened the way for Britain and the United States to recognize the Soviet-backed Polish government. But other contentious problems remained to be handled at the Potsdam Conference in mid-July.

THE POTSDAM CONFERENCE

The Potsdam Conference, and preparations for it, gave Stalin his best chance to consolidate Soviet war gains and to squeeze additional concessions from his allies. In the weeks following the unconditional surrender of Germany on May 8, the Soviet Union stood at the peak of its military glory. The Red Army controlled all of Berlin, and the Western allies, particularly the United States, still desired Soviet help for a final offensive against Japan. In preparing for the conference, the Soviet side was determined not just to lock in deals about eastern Europe, Germany, and the Far East agreed to at Yalta, but also to seek extra gains in the Mediterranean and along the southern borders of the U.S.S.R.

From Turkey, the Soviet Union wanted control over the Bosporus and the Dardanelles. For decades, first tsars and then commissars had vainly sought to gain control of the great geostrategic narrows connecting the Black and the Mediterranean Seas, passages that in the past had been used to Russia's detriment. During the Crimean War (1853–1856), British and French fleets passed through the straits to lay siege to Sevastopol, and during the world wars they had been at the disposal of Germany. In 1916, the tsarist government negotiated a secret treaty, never fulfilled, with the Entente powers to get the straits, and in 1940 Stalin, too, secretly tried to make a deal about them, this time with Hitler. At the end of World War II, Soviet leaders saw a new opportunity to extract that "bone in Russia's throat," as Stalin put it in talks with FDR and Churchill.

Soviet planners produced a number of possible options to reach this goal, ranging from a moderate revision of the Montreux Convention to a much more radical plan for joint Soviet–Turkish defense of the straits. Stalin, encouraged by his successful test of the first option at Teheran and Yalta, as well as by Turkey's accommodating mood, decided to raise the stakes by presenting Ankara with an ultimatum on June 7, 1945. Moscow demanded not only military bases at the straits, but also territorial concessions in Trans-Caucasus areas south of the Caucasus Mountains where Soviet Armenia and Georgia had some historical claims—the latter demand meant as a bargaining chip. Stalin obviously counted on Turkey's weak nerves and the Allies' grudging acceptance. But as subsequent events would demonstrate, he miscalculated on both counts.

Stalin's second project, the penetration of Britain's strategic domain in the Mediterranean, was no less ambitious, and it, too, presumed acquiescence, even support, by the United States. The Litvinov commission did most of the preparatory work on the future of Italian colonies. Fully aware of "the great strategic importance" of those areas to Britain and anticipating its strong resistance, Litvinov banked on U.S. help: "To knock Britain down from her positions," he wrote to Stalin and Molotov, "we would undoubtedly need strong support from the USA." In such thinking, Soviet officials relied on the initially positive American response to Gromyko's low-key request, in a note to Edward Stettinius in May, for a share in any trusteeship established over former Italian colonies in Africa. The combination of control over the Turkish straits with strongholds in the Mediterranean would give the U.S.S.R. a powerful strategic presence throughout the whole area, a stark fact that could not fail to impress the British and their American cousins, and at Potsdam Soviet leaders encountered diminishing tolerance for their growing appetites. The Western allies essentially rebuffed all Soviet efforts to go beyond the European sphere, although they left the door open for further discussion about the Turkish straits and the Italian colonies.

On issues relating to Europe, however, the Soviet Union gained more than it lost at Potsdam. After intense struggle, the Soviet delegation got what it wanted with regard to Poland, recognition of its new government and its new western border along the Oder and western Neisse Rivers. The three allies also agreed on basic principles for dealing with Germany, although the Soviet Union did not win internationalization of the Ruhr valley's industrial area or the desired amount of reparations. In disposing of former German territory east of the new Oder–Neisse line, the U.S.S.R. established direct control over—in effect, it annexed—the northern part of old East Prussia, which gave it an ice-free port at Koenigsberg, soon to be renamed Kaliningrad.

At Potsdam, the Soviet Union also gained the upper hand in preparing peace treaties for former German satellites in southeastern Europe (excluding Italy). "It is especially satisfactory," Molotov stated in a report about the conference sent to Soviet ambassadors abroad, "since it unties our hands in [the matter of] diplomatic recognition of Romania, Bulgaria, Hungary, and Finland." In private conversation with Georgy Dimitrov, Molotov was even more candid: The decisions, he said, "in effect recognized [the Balkans] as a [Soviet] sphere of influence." In an unsuccessful attempt to have a say in establishing democratic governments in that sphere, the Western allies proposed monitoring forthcoming parliamentary elections in Romania, Bulgaria, and Hungary. "We rejected this proposal as incompatible with democratic principles," Molotov wrote in the circular. (He might have added, more tangibly, that the Soviet Union had had no say in the formation of the Italian government, so now it was simply returning the favor.)

Despite such tensions, the Soviet side managed to preserve a Big Three format for negotiations about peace treaties in Europe. The Allies agreed that all key decisions were to be made by the U.S.S.R., the United States, and Britain assembled in a Council of Foreign Ministers. Molotov wrote: "This decision, which confines the number of our partners to a sufficient minimum, is the most flexible and satisfying from our viewpoint. . . . The conference ended with quite satisfactory results for the Soviet Union."

At Potsdam, Truman "casually" and vaguely informed Stalin about the first successful test of a new weapon of mass destruction, although he did not call it an atomic bomb. Without showing any particular interest in public, Stalin knew immediately what Truman meant and soon instructed his subordinates "to speed up our work" in the same field. But it was not until Hiroshima that the real magnitude and implications of the new weapon became clear.

HIROSHIMA AND ITS FALLOUT

"Hiroshima has shaken the whole world. The balance has been broken. Build the Bomb—it will remove a great danger from us." Such was Stalin's appeal to the managers of the Soviet atomic project after the United States had used atomic bombs against Japan. Despite all the intelligence about the Manhattan Project, Stalin was clearly unprepared for the destructive power of the "absolute weapon." The "Fat Boy" that exploded over Hiroshima also shattered many of Stalin's previous assumptions and calculations.

The first victim was the Soviet perception of the United States as a remote and relatively harmless giant that would be unable to present a real threat to Soviet security and would moreover be likely to withdraw to its traditional sphere of influence after the war. Only two months earlier, Stalin was almost asking Hopkins for a greater U.S. role in the world, hoping to use it as a counterweight against British imperialism. Now, it did not really matter whether the United States returned to isolationism, for with its strategic aviation and atomic bombs it could easily threaten any country in the world. Defenseless against such an attack, the Soviet elite was shaken back into insecurity. "The whole Soviet government interpreted [Hiroshima] as atomic blackmail against the U.S.S.R., as a threat to unleash a new, even more terrible and devastating war," Yuli Khariton, a physicist working with the Soviet nuclear program, later recalled about the mood of the time.

Hiroshima also undermined Stalin's calculations regarding Japan. Like U.S. military leaders before the bomb, he was counting on an extended final stage of the war against Japan and planned to convert Red Army participation in it into a role in deciding Japan's postwar development comparable to that of the United States. Stalin's overriding strategic goal was to use Soviet participation in the Asian war to ensure a zone of security in Outer Mongolia, Manchuria, North Korea, and possibly northern Japan—where he planned to occupy the island of Hokkaido. Now, all those plans and perhaps even the Yalta agreements themselves were endangered by the rapidity with which the war in Asia came to an end. Stalin was greatly concerned. Years later, Nikita Khrushchev remembered his worrying, "What if Japan capitulates before we enter the war? The Americans might say, 'We don't owe you anything.'"

In fact, some of Stalin's fears were borne out. Although the Soviet Union entered the war as promised and forced the capitulation of the large Japanese army in Manchuria, the military collapse of Japan came too rapidly to allow the prominent Soviet role once envisioned. The United States immediately began to rule Japan single-handedly without any consultations with Moscow. Faced with the firm resolve of Truman, Stalin had to cancel the Red Army's landing on Hokkaido at the last moment, but he did not give up his ambition to get a foothold in Japan by other means.

The month of August brought some other unpleasant surprises for Stalin. On August 18, Stalin received a shocking message from Truman. In addition to flatly rejecting a Soviet occupation of Hokkaido, Truman demanded use of an airbase on the Soviet-occupied Kurile Islands. In a chilling response, Stalin dismissed Truman's request as appropriate only for "a defeated country" or a weak ally; the U.S.S.R. was neither. Then on August 20–21, the United States and Britain made it clear that they would not recognize Soviet-sponsored governments in Bulgaria and Romania unless they included pro-Western candidates from the opposition parties. Covertly, Washington and London stepped up their support of these parties to strengthen local noncommunist forces that were already resisting Soviet dominance. Soviet representatives in Romania and Bulgaria began reporting to Moscow about "a mounting Anglo–American offensive." Even in friendly Bulgaria, cabinet members spoke publicly about postponing elections until inspections by Western observers were in place.

The Kremlin began to perceive a new pattern in American behavior. As seen from Moscow, the Americans, obviously encouraged by the awesome new weapon in their hands, were encroaching on the vital Soviet spheres in the Balkans and the Far East in violation of previous agreements and understandings, and were moreover maintaining exclusive control of Japan. For Stalin and his circle, shaped as they were by Russian history and Bolshevik ideology, the Western concern with national self-determination in eastern Europe seemed to be a hypocritical and deliberate attempt to undermine Soviet security along its western borders by creating a new pro-Western "cordon sanitaire."

Stalin's multifaceted response to what he saw as the first postwar American offensive was logical and typical of him. On August 20, he moved to revamp the previously sluggish atomic program into a giant crash project, for it had become abundantly clear that to preserve its great-power status the Soviet Union had to possess atomic weapons. To the newly created Special Committee, the operational branch of which was named Chief Directorate N1 and headed by the feared security chief Lavrenti Beria, he gave extraordinary powers to use all human and material resources available, including espionage, for the purposes of building a workable bomb in the shortest time possible (see the long-secret part of Stalin's order in note appended to document 8).

To impose such a massive and immensely costly program on a starving, war-ruined country was a fateful decision, one that meant a radical shift in national priorities for years to come. And with regard to foreign policy, Stalin decided, in an effort to compensate for his weakness, to meet toughness with toughness, thus to devalue the Americans' atomic ace. As Gromyko recalled, Stalin was certain that the Americans would try to use their atomic monopoly "to force us to accept their plans on questions affecting Europe and the world. Well, that is not going to happen." Small wonder that the next round of allied diplomacy—the London session of the Council of Foreign Ministers in September—quickly headed toward the rocks.

Instructions for the Soviet delegation to the conference excluded any concessions to the Western allies with respect to southeastern Europe. They prescribed, if needed, a link between the fate of peace treaties for Romania and Bulgaria to the one for Italy on a tit-for-tat basis. In Stalin's logic, Western support of "anti-Soviet elements" in those countries was "incompatible with our allied relations." With regular and revealing cables, Stalin guided Molotov through the negotiations. Here, one sees Stalin communicating with his right-hand man with no diplomatic or propagandistic camouflage.

On September 12, Stalin instructed his foreign minister: "You must also stand firm and make no concessions to the allies on Romania. In case the allies remain implacable . . . , you should, perhaps, let [Secretary of State James] Byrnes and [Foreign Minister Ernest] Bevin know that the government of the U.S.S.R. would find it difficult to give its agreement to the conclusion of a peace treaty with Italy." The next day Stalin continued: "It might happen that the allies could sign a peace treaty with Italy without us. So what? Then we have a precedent. We would have a possibility in our turn to reach a peace treaty with our satellites without the allies. If such a development would mean that the current session of the Council of Ministers winds up without making decisions on major issues, we should not be afraid of such an outcome either." With both sides unwilling to compromise, discussions about southeastern Europe led nowhere.

Despite this impasse, Stalin made another attempt to get a foothold in Japan. He instructed Molotov to push for the creation of an Allied Control Council for that country similar to the one established in occupied Germany. But Byrnes and Bevin refused even to put this issue on the agenda, a rejection that brought a rare outburst of indignation from Stalin. He wrote Molotov that it was "the height of impudence that the British and the Americans, who call themselves our allies, did not even want to hear us on the Control Council in Japan. . . . This demonstrates that they lack a minimal sense of respect for their ally."

A similar fate befell the renewed Soviet request for a foothold in the Mediterranean. Molotov's instructions charged him with getting for the U.S.S.R. an individual trusteeship over Libya. Stalin ordered his deputy to "remind Americans about their promise" (i.e., the Gromyko–Stettinius correspondence in May) and to push at least for the right for the Soviet navy "to call at Tripolitanian ports." Molotov tried hard, but Bevin, strongly supported by Byrnes, would have none of such strategic intrusion into an area traditionally dominated by Britain.

For their part, the Americans had a surprising offer for the Russians to consider. Byrnes unexpectedly proposed a treaty calling for the demilitarization of Germany for the next twenty to twenty-five years. The proposal envisaged gradual dismantling of the allied military occupation in Germany and providing security guarantees by the great powers against a revival of German militarism. At first glance, the idea looked logical and tempting. A guarantee against a revived German threat, the primary security concern for the Soviet Union, would spare that country all the extraordinary security measures that the Soviet Union was taking in eastern Europe. Molotov liked the idea and recommended that Stalin pursue it.

Stalin saw the matter differently, however. His vigorous negative reaction was revealing of his own motives and calculations. Byrnes's initiative, he explained to Molotov by cable, was really about the following goals:

> First, to divert our attention from the Far East, where America assumes a role
> of tomorrow's friend of Japan, and to create thereby a perception that every-
> thing is fine there; second, to receive from the U.S.S.R. a formal sanction for
> the U.S. playing the same role in European affairs as the U.S.S.R., so that the
> U.S. may hereafter, in league with England, take the future of Europe into its

hands; third, to devalue the treaties of alliance that the U.S.S.R. has already reached with European states; fourth, to pull the rug out from under any future treaties of alliance between the U.S.S.R. and Romania, Finland, etc.

Several things become clear from this analysis by Stalin, a rare archival window into his thinking, and from records of a subsequent internal discussion of this issue that took place a few months later. First, he was already beginning to see the United States as a potential rival for hegemony over the European continent (especially if it were allied with Britain). Stalin had no intention of sharing that role with the United States or anybody else. Indeed, minimizing the American role in Europe became even more important in the light of U.S. domination of Japan. Accustomed to thinking in global terms, Stalin saw that a prominent American role in both Europe and Japan would mean a radical, unprecedented shift in the global balance of power.

Second, Stalin evidently did not plan to withdraw his troops from Germany in the near future, not even in exchange for a possible but still problematic treaty regarding German demilitarization. He and his lieutenants considered a Soviet military presence in the heart of Europe as indispensable leverage in the forthcoming struggle over Germany's future. Recently declassified documents make it clear that Stalin's optimal goal was for a reunified Germany to be pro-Soviet. He hoped to achieve that goal by keeping the Red Army in eastern Germany and by using German communists to penetrate the western zones politically. Toward the latter end, in April 1946 he instructed German communists to merge their party with the large old Social Democratic party to form a Socialist Unity party (a merger accomplished only in the Soviet zone of occupation, as things turned out). He intended thereby to create a pro-Moscow "national front" as a political basis for German reunification. "All of Germany must be ours, that is, Soviet, Communist," Stalin explained to Yugoslav visitors early in 1946.

Without the trump card of Soviet military presence in eastern Germany, the Soviet Union had little chance of winning the economic and political competition for German allegiance, as its leaders fully understood. Molotov's deputy Lozovsky wrote: "Our acceptance of Byrnes's proposal would have led to the liquidation of occupational zones, the withdrawal of our troops, the political reunification of Germany, and U.S. economic domination of that country." Political and economic unification of Germany under American leadership would also mean, Lozovsky feared, "the military revival of Germany and, in a few years, a German–British–American war against the U.S.S.R." Soviet leaders increasingly perceived a revived German threat as part of a wider-ranging U.S.–led combination against their country.

Besides, Soviet leaders did not want to lose a key rationale for stationing troops in Poland and other eastern European countries: the necessity of maintaining lines of communication with the Soviet zone in Germany. The Supreme Soviet Commander in Germany, Marshal Georgy Zhukov, who also took part in this discussion, fully understood the strategic implications of Byrnes's plan for the Soviet position in Europe. "The Americans," he wrote, "would like to end the occupation of Germany as soon as possible and to remove the armed forces of the U.S.S.R. from Germany, and then to demand a withdrawal of our troops from Poland, and ultimately from the Balkans." Finally, Stalin understood that the course proposed by Byrnes was likely to devalue the Soviet Union's bilateral treaties with several European countries, security guarantees that were cemented by the specter of German revanchism (see document 2).

The negative reaction to the proposed treaty does not mean, however, that Soviet leaders minimized a possible German threat and thus felt no need to neutralize it. Such fears and presumed needs were very much part of their mind-set. But they also had a larger goal in mind: to use Soviet military–political presence in Europe and the specter of a revived Germany to build up a buffer zone of client states and security guarantees that would protect the Soviet Union on the west against not just Germany, but all other eventualities, including the increasingly likely emergence of a U.S.–led "western bloc."

The London Conference ended on an angry note, one occasioned by sharp disagreement over a secondary issue. In London, the Western delegations asked that France and China be allowed to take part in discussions of peace treaties with former German satellites. Molotov's initial response to the Allies was positive, but Stalin quickly brought him to heel. Stalin saw the request as another assault on the Yalta–Potsdam framework calling for the Big Three to work out the postwar settlement. He angrily ordered his deputy to retract his concession, a step that torpedoed the whole conference. In his circular cable on the conference's results, Molotov summarized his new view of British–American policy while trying to claim a moral victory: "The first session of the Council of Ministers ended in the failure of an attempt by certain American and British quarters to launch for the first time since the war a diplomatic attack on the foreign policy gains that the Soviet Union made during the war."

Molotov was giving voice to a theme that Stalin was to emphasize. In short, Stalin saw this post-Hiroshima British–American offensive as an attempt to "rewrite" the results of World War II. In his view the Western allies, encouraged by the new card in their hands and liberated from their dependence on Soviet arms, were trying to renege on their wartime promises and obligations, hoping to cancel Soviet gains by means of "atomic diplomacy" and pressure. In this vein, Stalin told Polish communists in November 1945 that the Western allies were "trying to intimidate us and force us to yield on contentious issues concerning Japan, the Balkans, and reparations . . . to tear away our allies Poland, Romania, Yugoslavia, and Bulgaria."

In sum, the Kremlin saw the tougher line taken by the Truman administration as "new American arrogance" and a retreat from the "Roosevelt tendency" of accepting the U.S.S.R. as an equal great power. Both Stalin and Molotov approvingly underlined one passage in the memorandum that Maisky wrote after a conversation with Harriman in December 1945. According to the report, Maisky criticized the Americans for their "unconscious arrogance" and appealed for understanding "that we all live on the same small planet, which becomes smaller and smaller while different countries get closer to each other, and that the United States, if it wants to maintain world order, should pay more attention to the principle of equality in their relations with other countries."

Despite his deep suspicion of the Western allies, Stalin did not intend to disrupt relations with them. He viewed the London Conference as an exploratory operation, a kind of "combat reconnaissance," and wanted to continue bargaining, albeit in a firm, even harsh, manner and on terms as close as possible to Soviet ones. To signal his displeasure with his allies' behavior, he recalled the Soviet representative from Japan and canceled a scheduled visit by Marshal Zhukov to the United States. But he kept the door to negotiations open. Soviet propaganda presented the outcome of the London Conference as but a temporary setback. In a speech on the anniversary of the October Revolution, a speech edited by Stalin himself, Molotov said that "similar difficulties" within the anti-Hitler coalition had "occurred even during the war." About the same time, Stalin accepted Truman's proposal for the simultaneous withdrawal of Soviet and American troops from Czechoslovakia.

Although ready to rub at the edges of the declining British empire, Stalin took care not to provoke the more powerful United States. With regard to China, for example, he did not openly side with the communists in that country's civil war, and after efforts to squeeze additional concessions met with firm U.S. and nationalist resistance, he agreed to a Sino–Soviet Treaty of Friendship and Alliance with the nationalist government in August 1945, a pact that incorporated the territorial agreements made at Yalta. In general, Stalin appeared to play the role of broker between China's warring factions, even as the United States was increasing its assistance to the nationalist government.

Stalin's primary goal in the region was to turn Manchuria into part of the Soviet security belt. He was not yet ready to entrust that task to the Chinese communists, however. Accordingly, in November 1945 he ordered the Soviet military commander in the Far East strictly to observe the new Sino–Soviet treaty, "to maintain good relations" with nationalist forces in Manchuria, and "to hold so-called communist troops away" from the main cities of the area, "keeping in mind that they want to entangle us in a conflict with the U.S.A., which cannot be allowed to happen."

Deeds did not wholly match words, however. As in the case of Iran, Stalin delayed the withdrawal of Soviet troops from Manchuria beyond February 1, 1946, a date agreed on with the nationalist government. Moreover, Soviet authorities prevented nationalist troops from entering key port cities, and Soviet troops stripped Japanese-built factories of most of their machinery, thus leaving the nationalists a hollow victory. When they finally departed, Soviet forces allowed Japanese military equipment to fall into the hands of Chinese communist troops, who gained control of much of northern Manchuria. Nevertheless, the Soviet departure did leave some Chinese communist personnel susceptible to military setbacks and purges at the hands of pronationalist administrators. With regard to China, Stalin was clearly keeping his options open.

Late in October 1945, Stalin took the unprecedented step of interrupting his vacation to receive Ambassador Harriman at his dacha on the Black Sea. He and his colleagues were eager to see whether Harriman would bring any retreat from the tough positions the Americans had taken at the London Conference, for they assumed that the Americans would have reassessed the situation. Harriman did not offer any new concessions, but came prepared to continue bargaining about Japan and southeastern Europe. Soon after Harriman's departure, Stalin sharply criticized a draft document in which the party's Politburo accepted (or planned to accept) most of the U.S. positions with regard to postwar governance of Japan. He was still determined to keep up the pressure and wait for the Americans to take the first step toward cooperation.

This time his calculations proved to be astute. In mid-November, Secretary of State Byrnes, in an effort to untie the post-London knot, offered to hold another meeting of foreign ministers, this time in Moscow and in the framework of the Big Three. That Byrnes took this step without consulting the British made it even more pleasing to the Kremlin, for it seemed again to offer an opening for playing the two Western allies against each other. Stalin was also encouraged by recent victories of pro-Soviet parties in parliamentary elections in Bulgaria and Yugoslavia.

These events seemed to vindicate Stalin's strategy. With great satisfaction, he reviewed the results of his tough line in another message sent from his dacha on the Black Sea to the leading members of the Politburo: "Thanks to our tenacity, we won the struggle" over the composition of the Moscow Conference. The exclusion of China and France means "a retreat of the U.S.A. and England from their positions in London. . . . We won the struggle in Bulgaria and Yugoslavia [as seen in] the results of elections in those countries. If we had stumbled on the issues regarding those countries and had not held on, then we would have definitely lost there." Stalin concluded with a main lesson on dealing with the Western allies-turned-rivals: "It is obvious that in dealing with partners such as the U.S. and Britain, we cannot achieve anything serious if we begin to give in to intimidation or betray uncertainty. To get anything serious from partners of this kind, we must arm ourselves with a policy of tenacity and steadfastness." Stalin urged his lieutenants to let that policy guide them in preparing for the upcoming "conference of three ministers" (see document 1).

In general, the Kremlin was pleased with the outcome of the Moscow Conference of December 1945. If the main goal of Soviet diplomacy was, as Maisky put it in a preparatory memorandum, "to achieve a de-facto recognition" by the Americans and British that eastern Europe and the Balkans (except for Greece) formed a Soviet "security zone," then a big step toward that goal was made in Moscow. Stalin and Molotov obtained U.S. and British agreement to recognize pro-Soviet governments in Romania and Bulgaria in return for their including token members of the opposition and vague assurances to respect "political freedoms." As Molotov reported after the conference, "Decisions on Bulgaria and Romania strengthen the situation of their democratic governments friendly to the Soviet Union and at the same time, because of small concessions [on our part], they allow England and the U.S.A. to recognize the Romanian and Bulgarian governments in the near future."

To make sure these concessions remained small, Stalin immediately sent a cable ordering his allies in both countries to select suitable representatives from the opposition and give them "insignificant ministries." The Kremlin rightly believed that decisions made at the Moscow Conference would greatly curtail Western interference in southeastern Europe. "Of course, behind the scenes the British and Americans will continue their support of the opposition," Molotov told top Bulgarian communists, "but they would no longer be able to do it publicly."

In other areas, there was some give-and-take at the Moscow Conference. The Americans made a small concession by agreeing to establish a Far

Eastern Advisory Commission. Although falling short of Stalin's demands, such a forum could provide a promising opening for future encroachments. For its part, the Soviet side agreed to a broader composition of a future peace conference than it originally wanted and to the creation of a UN Commission on Atomic Energy. But the Kremlin saw the overall outcome of the conference as favorable. It almost seemed that interallied relationships were getting back on their wartime track, an encouraging conclusion asserted by Molotov in his internal assessment of the conference: "We managed to reach decisions on a number of important European and Far Eastern issues and to sustain development of the cooperation among the three countries that emerged during the war."

SPEECH WARFARE: STALIN AND CHURCHILL

This period of relaxation, which turned out to be short, did not alter Stalin's basic plans for postwar development at home. He disclosed them publicly in a major speech on February 9, 1946, on the eve of Soviet-style elections to the Supreme Soviet. He first described the sources of Soviet victory in World War II: a socialist system, a Soviet state, effective armed forces, and a strong "material base" (referring to the rapid industrialization of the 1930s). For the first time since the beginning of the war, he evoked an ideological image of world capitalism and imperialistic rivalry as the principal engine of war. Finally, he laid out a new five-year program of accelerated economic development with a special emphasis on heavy industry. In five years, the Soviet economy was to surpass the prewar level and in the longer run to produce annually, among other things, 60 million tons of steel and 500 million tons of coal. Stalin's basic message to the Soviet people was clear: A world inhabited by capitalist rivals was still a dangerous place, and the Soviet people must brace themselves for a new round of sacrifice and mobilization to ensure their hard-won security against all eventualities. To mobilize a war-ravaged and exhausted country for a huge new effort was a monumental task. But Stalin did not see any other choice.

The postwar economic reconstruction had to be combined with massive rearmament. In addition to the atomic project, Stalin was about to launch similar long-term programs in rocketry and air defense (both started during the summer of 1946). It had become clear that for its postwar reconstruction, the U.S.S.R. would have to rely on its own resources plus reparations and industrial dismantling in the occupied territories. The hoped-for reconstruction loan from America did not materialize; a renewed

Soviet request was at first ignored (the Kremlin surely could not believe the official explanation about its having been misplaced) and then became loaded with so many conditions that Stalin decided not to pursue it.

About that time the Kremlin also decided to withdraw from the Bretton–Woods international financial system it had helped create only a year and a half earlier. In vigorous debates within the Soviet bureaucracy, the isolationists prevailed over the "integrationists" by appealing to Stalin's reluctance both to make the Soviet economy more transparent and to deposit part of the Soviet gold reserve with the new International Monetary Fund. That decision deprived the U.S.S.R. of another possible source of outside credits. To finance enormous military–industrial efforts, civilian production and consumption had to be severely restricted, the forced labor system expanded, and taxes and prices increased. Food prices were to go up 100 percent to 150 percent in 1946; taxes on peasants were to be increased by 30 percent by 1948, and by 150 percent by 1950; and obligatory, confiscatory war bonds were replaced by new reconstruction bonds—all sacrifices on the part of the Soviet citizenry that they had to accept and that Stalin had to legitimize.

Stalin steeled himself for new campaigns to bring both his lieutenants and the general populace into line. He knew how desperate people were for a normal, relaxed life, but for him that was more of a danger to be averted than a legitimate aspiration to be realized. In his view, postwar relaxation would undermine the drive for economic mobilization and perhaps of the stability of the Stalinist system itself, built as it was on one-man rule, tight discipline, and pervasive control. He worried that even his own inner circle had begun to show autonomy that bordered on insubordination. He thought that Molotov in particular, even after his mistakes in London should have taught him better, continued to display lack of vigilance as acting head of the Soviet government during Stalin's long vacation in the Caucasus. Stalin was annoyed that Molotov, without even informing his boss, first authorized publication of a speech that Churchill gave in the House of Commons in November 1945 (the speech seemed very complimentary of Stalin) and then proceeded to relax censorship of the foreign press in Moscow.

Stalin decided to use the situation to teach Molotov and other Politburo members a lesson in class vigilance and at the same time to eradicate any lingering respect for the Western allies, respect that had developed during the war and that in Stalin's view was no longer needed. In a special cable to the Politburo, he called publication of Churchill's speech "a mistake," since the former prime minister was using his praise of Russia and Stalin only "to camouflage his hostile attitude toward the U.S.S.R." But Stalin's main message was a warning to the top Soviet leadership: "There are now many in the seats of authority who hurl themselves into infantile ecstasy when hearing praises from the Churchills, the Trumans, the Byrneses, and conversely, who lose heart after unfavorable references from these misters. In my view these are dangerous attitudes, since they spawn in our ranks servility before foreign figures. Against this servility before foreigners we must fight tooth and nail."

Stalin's response to Molotov's decision about censorship was much harsher. He orchestrated a humiliating harassment of Molotov before the Politburo "troika" of Georgy Malenkov, Beria, and Anastas Mikoyan, during which he accused him of "placating" Western circles. Though Molotov was ultimately pardoned, he and his colleagues must have learned the lesson well: From now on, the premium was on anti-Western toughness. This small episode is a vivid illustration of how Stalin's personal urge to tighten control over his immediate circle dovetailed with his larger strategy concerning the country's economic mobilization.

Curiously, this dressing-down also mirrored Truman's famous reprimand of Byrnes after the latter's return from Moscow. "I am tired of babying the Soviets," Truman recalled telling Byrnes. However different in style and character, the two leaders had essentially the same aim: to shake their subordinates into a tougher line toward the former ally now becoming an enemy. For Stalin, the scolding of Molotov was a sort of dress rehearsal for his imminent public anti-Western campaign, a campaign for which another speech by Churchill provided a convenient target.

Churchill's famous "iron curtain" speech at Fulton, Missouri, on March 5, 1946, long considered in the Soviet Union to be a formal declaration of the Cold War, became both a challenge and an opportunity for Stalin. It not only confirmed his view of Churchill as the main instigator of anti-Soviet policies, but it also increased his suspicions about Truman, who after all presided over Churchill's powerful performance. The United States was, it seemed, at best conniving and at worst plotting with Churchill in this new anti-Soviet offensive.

By then, Stalin had still more indications of a toughening U.S. line: Byrnes's speech in New York on February 28; the support that both the United States and Britain gave the Iranian government's protest in the UN Security Council against Soviet actions; and the "long telegram" by George F. Kennan, picked up by Soviet intelligence in Washington, where it was widely circulated. Coupled with Churchill's open call for British–American military cooperation, it was more than enough to renew fears about the dangers of an British–American bloc against the U.S.S.R., which Kremlin leaders still hoped that "imperialist contradictions" would prevent. But Stalin fully understood the formidable strategic consequences that a combination of American economic and atomic power with the British empire's global military infrastructure would have. In their copies of the Fulton speech, both Stalin and Molotov underlined precisely those passages in which Churchill described the sinews of British–American power.

But if a challenge, Fulton was also an opportunity. Because of Churchill's well-known anti-Soviet record, which went back to the very beginning of the Soviet state, he was an ideal reminder of the external threat still emanating from the West that Stalin needed to rally his people around him. That is why, instead of silencing the "iron curtain" speech, which his control over the media would have allowed, Stalin chose to publicize and then criticize it in the Soviet press. After several critical reviews had appeared in the press, Stalin published his own answer to Churchill in *Pravda* on March 14. Kremlin records show that, as he usually did in important cases, Stalin wrote the "interview" entirely by himself (including the questions by a mythical "correspondent"). In this piece, Stalin rather skillfully depicted Churchill as a war-monger and an anachronistic Tory running against the tide of history. But Stalin did not issue a wholesale call to arms against this anti-Soviet crusade; the threat had to be serious enough to energize his people into needed vigilance, but manageable enough not to scare them into panic. So he ended the "interview" with optimistic assurances about the inevitable defeat of Churchill and "his friends" should they try to attack the Soviet Union and its allies.

Stalin's rejoinder set the tone for a new line of Soviet propaganda that was increasingly anti-Western and that began to emphasize the need to mobilize against "aggressive tendencies" in the West. As international relations became tenser, it seemed logical to tighten the domestic ideological screws. In April 1946, Stalin's new favorite, the Politburo member Andrei Zhdanov, following instructions from his boss, began to direct the party machinery toward "curing ills on the ideological front" and rejecting the notion that "people should have a rest after the war."

At the same time, Stalin carefully avoided linking Churchill's line with official U.S. policy. Giving almost friendly advice to the new American ambassador in Moscow, Walter Bedell Smith, he urged the United States not to pull anti-Soviet chestnuts out of the fire for Britain. Stalin still hoped to prevent a looming British–American alliance and to play the two imperialist countries off against each other. But his own actions undercut such hopes and tended to produce the opposite effect.

IRAN AND TURKEY

Two major crises in 1946, those over Iran and Turkey, worsened Soviet–American relations. Soviet interests in Iran were twofold: oil and security. Soviet policy-planners viewed this neighboring country as a potential launching pad for attack against the U.S.S.R. and its oil deposits around Baku; they were determined to use the wartime occupation of northern Iran and the local communist (Tudeh) party as basic tools to serve their interests after the war. And they worried about American intentions. Gromyko wrote an assessment in mid-1944: "U.S. aspirations to increase its influence in the Near and Middle East, particularly in Iran, would not be in the interest of the U.S.S.R."

On July 6, 1945, the Politburo decided to organize a separation movement in South Azerbaijan and other provinces of northern Iran, making use of ethnic Azeri and Kurds in those areas. In that part of Iran under Soviet occupation, the Tudeh party was reorganized into the Azerbaijan Democratic party (ADP), a broader, less visibly pro-Soviet organization led by communists. It is still not clear what Stalin was really after in this scheme: nominal independence of northern Iran under an ADP government (which would solve both security and oil problems); regional autonomy within the Iranian state (the separatists' proclaimed goal); or a national liberation movement that he could control and use as leverage to wrest oil concessions from Teheran. For its part, Teheran, encouraged by the U.S. embassy, refused to set up a joint oil company with a predominant Soviet interest before the complete withdrawal of all occupation forces.

In order to increase pressure on Iran and to gain time, Stalin delayed withdrawal of Soviet troops in violation of earlier agreements. When the Iranian government appealed to the UN Security Council, the Soviet delegation found itself isolated. In the face of opposition at the United Nations, especially by Britain and the United States, Stalin decided to accept a compromise offered by the Iranian prime minister during his visit to Moscow in February and March 1946. In return for the withdrawal of Soviet forces, Iran would sign an oil concession. The catch was that the concession would have to be approved by the Iranian parliament, the Majlis, after new elections. Stalin reluctantly delivered his part of the deal and did not intervene when later in the year Iranian forces brutally suppressed ADP separatists. In the end, the Soviet Union was double-crossed, for after a lot of foot-dragging, the Majlis rejected the oil concession in February 1947.

The crisis over Turkey developed along similar lines. In 1946, Stalin stepped up his war of nerves against Turkey by backing old territorial claims of Armenian and Georgian nationalists. Surviving circumstantial evidence suggests that he also built up a strong military presence along the Turkish border for the purpose of either blackmail or invasion. The latter was a gamble that even the chastised Molotov found too dangerous; he tried to talk his boss out of the build-up and later admitted that Stalin's demands were "an ill-timed, unrealistic thing." But according to Molotov, Stalin insisted: "Go ahead; push for joint ownership [of military bases on the straits]!"

Coming on the heels of the Iranian crisis, Stalin's campaign against Turkey met with firm resolve on the part of the U.S. and British governments, which began military preparations to defend the Turks. Soviet intelligence was bound to pick up those signals, which probably was the main reason why Stalin backed off in the fall of 1946. Molotov later recalled his relief: "It was good that we retreated in time, for otherwise it would have led to a joint aggression against us."

Stalin's conduct in Iran and Turkey revealed the same pattern: brutal pressure, reliance on force and covert methods, blackmail, and a last-minute retreat when faced with strong opposition or a risk of war. In both cases he ended up with the worst of both worlds. He failed to get what he wanted, and he got what he feared and tried to avoid: an increasingly united British–American bloc and the dissipation of Soviet influence in the region, a void that the United States rushed to fill. An even more lasting negative effect of Soviet actions in 1946 was crystallization of the belief in the West (on both elite and public levels) that the Soviet Union was bent on expansion and that it could be stopped only by preponderant force.

Was Stalin aware of the connection between his own actions and a growing resistance to them? Probably not. Much like his counterparts in the West, he tended to think that his rivals' basic motives were constant, thus not contingent on the other side's actions. Besides, he viewed rivalry as a normal part of a geopolitical "great game," a game in which one knocks at various doors, winning here and losing there without interrupting "business as usual," a game that he played much more cynically and eagerly than did leaders of the Western democracies.

Stalin's ability to separate his unsuccessful regional probing from other issues was evident in bargaining with his allies over the peace settlement in Europe. At sessions of the Council of Foreign Ministers in Paris and New York, as well as at the Paris Peace Conference, he gained what he considered to be essential and gave way in other matters. Hard-headed Soviet diplomacy was able to achieve its basic aim: peace treaties with former German satellites that helped to legitimate Soviet dominance in eastern Europe. Concerning another sensitive issue, the Kremlin circumvented Western insistence on the withdrawal of Soviet troops from Romania and Hungary by insisting that those troops were needed to secure communications lines to the Soviet zone in Austria, with which there was not yet a peace treaty (largely because of Soviet obduracy).

Stalin clearly did not want a major rupture with the Western powers, however, and on matters that he considered peripheral, such as the amount of reparations from Italy and the status of Trieste, he compromised. As he cabled Molotov (in Paris) on June 23, 1946, "I think we must not derail the conference because of the issue of Trieste." Accordingly, he permitted Trieste to be placed under international control instead of being incorporated into Yugoslavia, as the government of that communist-led country demanded—this despite Molotov's concern that the United States and Britain "consider Trieste as a beachhead . . . in the Balkans." In the face of firm opposition, Stalin also dropped his Mediterranean project, explaining in a cable to Molotov, who needed little consolation about this particular decision, that "the time is not yet ripe for us to clash over the fate of these territories and to quarrel over their future with the rest of the world."

THE MAJOR ISSUES: GERMANY AND EASTERN EUROPE

The key element of a comprehensive peace settlement—the fate of Germany—remained unresolved and became increasingly contentious. The Kremlin saw the U.S. decision to stop payment of reparations from the American zone to the Soviet one as a clear violation of agreements made at Potsdam and an indication that the United States was in Germany for the long haul. Soviet leaders were disturbed by clear signals that the United States and Britain intended to strengthen the economy in their zones of occupation at the expense of the Soviet zone, most notably by Secretary Byrnes's famous speech in Stuttgart in September 1946 about rebuilding the German economy and by the beginning stages of the consolidation of the American and British zones. Such steps would make it difficult, if not impossible, to create a united and pro-Soviet Germany.

That task was further complicated by internal contradictions in Soviet occupation policy. Heavy reparations, massive industrial dismantling, and brutal behavior by Red Army personnel tarnished the Soviet image and model in the eyes of most Germans. Yet Stalin was not ready to give up his maximum goal. Through the early part of 1947, he continued to instruct communists in the Soviet zone to proceed with "winning over" people in the western zones by promises from the new Socialist Unity party and by appeals to German national-patriotic sentiments. Talking in January 1947 with Wilhelm Pieck and Otto Grotewohl, leaders of the new party, Stalin said: "If we succeed in completing this first stage, that will be well and good. If we don't, we'll accept the consolidation of German administration in the Soviet zone." In other words, a separate East German state remained an option, but Stalin hoped for more and was unwilling to assume responsibility for solidifying Germany's division.

In eastern Europe, Soviet officials continued to push the development of "people's democracies." The policy called for breaking up large landed estates, nationalizing banking and industry, and strengthening local communist organizations—all while preserving a facade of democratic institutions and coalition governments. While "building socialism" remained Stalin's ultimate intention for the affected countries, that stage was presumably to be reached by varying "national ways" short of violent revolution and massive repression. Accordingly, Stalin even restrained his clients in Poland from suppressing their bourgeois opponents and in May 1946 warned Polish leaders not to alienate that country's Roman Catholic Church. The Polish road to socialism, he insisted, was to develop along democratic lines without resort to a dictatorship of the proletariat.

The Kremlin also continued to tolerate noncommunist leaders in Hungary and Czechoslovakia with the proviso that they loyally follow Moscow's lead in foreign policy. As long as governments in eastern Europe followed generally pro-Soviet policies, and as long as there were no serious attempts by the United States or Britain to undermine his influence, Stalin was confident that he could manage this vital security zone without blatantly violating the Yalta principles regarding "liberated" Europe.

Finland, which admittedly lay outside the main approaches to Russia, provided an unusual case of Soviet toleration. During a previously unreported meeting with a Finnish delegation in October 1945, Stalin referred to Soviet policy toward Finland as "generosity by calculation." He added, "When we treat neighboring countries well, they will respond in kind."

Behind the lingering degree of moderation in Soviet policy, however, a radical shift in the Soviet leadership's perception of the changing world scene was taking place. The United States was quickly replacing old European rivals as Russia's principal adversary, one bent on restoring traditional enemies such as Germany and Japan, encircling the Soviet Union with military bases around its periphery, and threatening the U.S.S.R. with its atomic monopoly. That the Baruch Plan, proposed by the United States in July 1946, would put the Soviet atomic program under strict international control immune from a veto by the UN Security Council, while preserving America's atomic lead, only confirmed these suspicions.

Newly declassified Soviet documents give many illustrations of this new perception among the Soviet hierarchy. Litvinov concluded one report about U.S. policy with the cautious warning that "the establishment of American control over the Iranian and Chinese armies as well as the acquisition of numerous naval and air-force bases in various parts of the world may be regarded as a potential interference." (Molotov found this statement entirely too tentative and crossed out the word "potential.") And during a closed discussion of Soviet foreign propaganda at a meeting of the CPSU's Central Committee in July 1946, high functionaries spoke earnestly about "a full-scale propaganda offensive" of "so-called allies" aimed at "mobilizing the western public for a future war against the U.S.S.R." Interestingly enough, the Soviet side felt itself to be on the defensive in this mounting ideological conflict. In summarizing the discussion, Alexei Kuznetsov, a secretary of the committee, said: "We have no real propaganda. . . . We are being pushed out from everywhere; they are advancing while we are on defensive, and even this defense we conduct badly, unskillfully."

A SPIRIT OF CONFRONTATION

Driven by events and by Stalin, Soviet officials increasingly emphasized the spirit of confrontation in their internal assessments of their former allies. They wrote about the "aggressive intentions of the atomic powers" and the "militarization of U.S. foreign policy." The standard doctrinal explanation for this shift in America's image and behavior emphasized the changing "correlation of political forces" within the United States, where "the Roosevelt trend" was being overpowered by a "new American reactionary trend, particularly after the Moscow conference of the three ministers," as Molotov reported to this staff after the Paris Peace Conference.

Perhaps the best example of this reassessment of former allies was the Novikov telegram, a long analytical report on U.S. foreign policy compiled on Molotov's instruction in the fall of 1946 by Nikolai Novikov, Soviet chargé d'affaires in Washington. In some ways, it was almost a mirror image (albeit a much less sophisticated one) of Kennan's famous "long telegram" from Moscow, the report that later served as the basis for the influential "X" article. Both dispatches depicted the other side as driven by an insatiable urge for world domination, as being a power that could be contained only by superior force. Novikov, worried about America's global reach, described the United States as trying to reduce Soviet influence in neighboring countries in order to hamper "the process of democratization" there and to create conditions "for the penetration of American capital into their economies." The report concluded that, to achieve global dominance, the United States was using the threat of war against the Soviet Union (see document 3).

At home, the tightening of the screws intensified. Stalin was only too ready to use growing international tensions as justification for his campaign to mobilize the country, a campaign that presaged even more intense rivalry with the West. In August 1946, the official campaign against "ideological relaxation" and "servility" before the West—the "Zhdanovshchina"—was launched with the punishment of many literary journals and individuals for "crimes" and "mistakes." In an angry tirade against "cosmopolitan" intellectuals, Stalin asserted: "You are walking on your tiptoes as if you were pupils and they [in the West] the mentors. It is wrong in its very essence." Couched as it was against intellectuals, the campaign was also a shrewd appeal to Soviet patriotism and national dignity that appealed to many ordinary folk. In essence, Stalin was trying to root out admiration for Western culture by fostering pride in the Soviet Union's ideology and social system and in its alleged cultural and moral superiority over the "rotten West." Also as part of the campaign, Stalin retracted wartime concessions to the Orthodox Church and had official propaganda once again emphasize Soviet patriotism instead of the Russian nationalism that had come to the fore during World War II.

The campaign entailed more direct, although perhaps less publicly obvious efforts to reduce Western influence in Soviet territory. These included practical measures such as curtailing the distribution of British–American propagandistic publications (permitted during the war), a drastic reduction in subscriptions to foreign newspapers and books, and tightening of controls over personal contacts with foreigners—to the point of placing a ban on marriages with them in 1947. The iron curtain between the U.S.S.R. and the rest of the world was indeed going down (see document 4).

The anti-Western ideological campaign served to deflect popular discontent with mounting economic problems at home. The fall of 1946 was a season of a severe famine, caused by a bad harvest and aggravated by corruption and inefficiency in the government bureaucracy. When the Kremlin reduced bread rations and raised food prices, it channeled the anxiety caused by these steps toward foreign and domestic enemies. Widespread rumors explained the new restrictions as a part of "war preparations" for future contingencies. By the end of 1946, the basic Cold War psychology, a vision of the world split into the two opposing systems, was taking hold of the Soviet mind-set. Those few people in Soviet officialdom who did not fully share this simple vision and who had growing misgivings about the Kremlin's tough line, people such as Litvinov and Maisky, were being forced from their positions. The climate of growing international tensions helped sustain a semblance of solidarity between the Soviet people and their "Vozhd" (leader) in the face of external threat.

Especially effective was the propaganda theme of "a thankless West" that had won the war by Soviet blood and now was denigrating its former ally. One can see Zhdanov's speech on November 6, 1946, celebrating the anniversary of the Bolshevik Revolution, as a particularly vivid illustration of this theme. As usual, Stalin himself edited speeches prepared for the occasion. Judging by his notes on the draft's margins, Stalin especially liked the following sarcastic passage, which he reinforced by adding the words "high moral qualities": "If you read the western press now, it is amazing how the Soviet people have changed. When our blood was pouring over the battlefields of war, the Soviet people were admired and praised all over the world for their courage, endurance, and high moral qualities. And now they are being blamed for everything, including for having a very bad national character."

Despite the growing and mutually nourished tensions, however, Soviet actions did not reveal serious concern about any looming Western aggression or preparations for a major war. Contrary to widespread assumptions in the West, demobilization reduced the size of the Red Army from 11,365,000 in 1945 to 2,874,000 by 1948, and the military budget of 1946–1947 was cut by almost 50 percent from its top war level to 73,700,000 rubles (or about half of the Pentagon's budget). By the end of 1946, Soviet troops were withdrawn from Manchuria and the Danish island of Bornholm, which some officials in the Soviet Ministry of Foreign Affairs had wanted to turn into their "Baltic Gibraltar." Documentation on Soviet military planning during this period is still too scarce for firm conclusions, but available evidence (i.e., the operational plan for Soviet troops in Germany approved in November 1946) indicates that contrary to American expectations, Soviet contingency plans did not call for offensive operations in western Europe but concentrated instead on holding the line of defense in Germany.

In some respects, Soviet propaganda, too, observed limits. It still spoke in terms of "a struggle of two trends" in world politics, of "Anglo–American reaction," without directly identifying either with the U.S. and British governments. Stalin carefully crossed out references to an "Anglo–American bloc" in his subordinates' drafts of public statements; he usually replaced them with the more neutral "England and the U.S.A." Through the time of his interview with Harold Stassen in April 1947, Stalin kept talking about peaceful coexistence between socialism and capitalism, carefully preserving his moderate image. Avoiding open confrontation, Stalin continued his tough bargaining over Germany and other unresolved issues. From his perspective, the Rubicon of the Cold War still lay ahead.

EFFECTS OF THE TRUMAN
DOCTRINE AND THE MARSHALL PLAN

The proclamation of the Truman Doctrine in March 1947 had no immediate impact on Soviet thinking and policy. The Kremlin was naturally concerned about the global overtones of the American crusade against a "totalitarian" threat, but the doctrine's practical meaning, assistance to Greece and Turkey, was neither surprising nor immediately challenging. Because both Greece and Turkey were by then in the Western sphere of influence, Truman's action simply confirmed the Soviet view that the United States was filling in the weak spots of the British Empire.

Accordingly, the Soviet government did not issue any protest or offer any other official reaction to Truman's speech. An editorial in *Pravda* depicted it as another manifestation of U.S. expansionism and confined itself to a guarded warning that the doctrine was "not conducive to the cause of peace and security." Soviet diplomats reporting from the United States were restrained in their analysis, which emphasized the tentative and controversial nature of a move that faced serious resistance in America itself. When Stalin met with Secretary of State George C. Marshall during the meeting of foreign ministers in Moscow in April, he ignored the subject completely, concentrating instead on Germany. And although the former allies remained deadlocked between the Soviet insistence on reparations and the Western desire for German economic unity, Stalin showed patience and cautious optimism, saying in conclusion that "compromises were possible on all main questions, including Germany's demilitarization, political structure, reparations, and economic unity."

Indeed, some new Soviet foreign policy initiatives during the first part of 1947 also indicated a potentially more cooperative approach, especially with regard to Korea and international control of atomic energy. Concerning the reunification of Korea, the Soviet side broke the logjam in Soviet–American talks by agreeing to speed up the work of the joint commission charged with establishing an interim government. On atomic energy, there was a shift from the previous propagandistic position of banning all atomic weapons to a more realistic proposal calling for the establishment of international control over their production.

It was at this juncture that, on June 5, 1947, the Marshall Plan was announced. The initial Soviet reaction was a mixture of interest, uncertainty, and suspicion as Soviet analysts tried to decipher the plan's real meaning. The most negative interpretation came from the recently promoted Ambassador Novikov in Washington, who described the American proposal as aimed at creating "a western European bloc against us." One leading Soviet economist and adviser to Stalin, Yevgeni Varga, was more balanced in his report to Molotov. He wrote that the plan was driven by American economic self-interest, which required a stimulation of European consumption of American goods in order to avoid a looming economic crisis. Although Varga warned that the United States would attempt to gain from these credits "the maximum political advantages," his analysis did not preclude Soviet participation in the plan provided that political conditions attached to it could be kept to a minimum.

Molotov (and probably Stalin) seemed to share this basic view that the Marshall Plan could be either a threat or a potential opportunity. Molotov was apparently encouraged by Marshall's suggestion that Europeans themselves should draw up aid programs for their countries. His final handwritten comment about the invitation for the U.S.S.R. to send delegates to a conference in Paris to discuss Marshall's proposal was, "We should prepare ourselves." Recalling Molotov's position, an aide later described it as "an attempt, if not to eliminate, then at least to minimize its negative aspects and insure that they would not impose any conditions on us. In a word, it should be something like Lend-Lease." The term "Lend-Lease" also figured in an informal briefing that officials of the Foreign Ministry conducted for the editors of *Pravda*.

With such hopes, the Soviet government decided to participate in initial discussions of Marshall's proposals at a conference in Paris and advised its clients in eastern Europe to do the same. The seriousness of the Soviet approach was indicated by the size of the delegation sent to Paris: over 100 persons, including many technical experts. The delegation, headed by Molotov, carried instructions to clarify the scope and conditions of the proposed aid program as well as to insist on its being organized on a country-by-country basis rather than requiring an all-European plan that, the Kremlin feared, would be dominated by the United States and become a nucleus for an anti-Soviet bloc. The instructions also forbade acceptance of other conditions "that might infringe upon the sovereignty and the economic independence" of the European countries and directed Soviet negotiators to oppose any use of German resources in the program unless approved by the Council of Foreign Ministers, in which Russia played a major role. Thus, the instructions revealed two basic Soviet apprehensions regarding the Marshall Plan: that it would steer eastern Europe into close economic ties with the West and enhance Germany's economic reintegration into the Western economy without satisfying major Soviet interests in the German settlement (see document 5).

Once in Paris, the Soviet delegation quickly realized that both of these fears were well founded. The first contacts with the heads of the British and French delegations convinced Molotov that they were scheming with Americans against the Soviet Union, for both men insisted on an all-European plan and on inclusion of German resources while discouraging Soviet efforts to clarify or modify the American proposal. In reports to Stalin on June 28 and 29, Molotov complained about British and French subservience to U.S. policy and about their eagerness "to use this opportunity to penetrate internal economies of the eastern European countries and especially to reroute the flows of European trade for their own interests."

That was indeed the heart of the matter. Incorporation of east European countries into an all-European plan of economic recovery would open their economies to Western capital and restore trade patterns between eastern and western Europe that had been disrupted by bilateral trade agreements between the Soviet Union and its clients after World War II. The Soviet leaders knew only too well that in an open-door competition their country was no match for the American economic juggernaut. They also knew that once this economic gravitation set in, the political one would soon follow. Once fleshed out, the Marshall Plan indeed became, in the Kremlin's view, a recipe for undermining the Soviet security zone in eastern Europe.

This view was reinforced on June 30, when Molotov received an urgent message originating from Soviet intelligence sources in London. Reporting on secret talks between Undersecretary of State William Clayton of the United States and members of the British cabinet, the message accurately relayed the gist of the British–American agreement: The Marshall Plan was to become a unified program for European economic reconstruction that should include Germany and be administered by a special agency under U.S. oversight. Molotov learned only later that U.S. and British officials had already decided to go forward with the Marshall Plan even without Soviet participation, while still hoping to lure eastern European counties, but he knew enough.

Alerted by the intelligence report, Molotov tried to fight back by emphasizing that the conference's original mandate "does not include drafting of an all-round program for European countries" and that "the German issue is subject to discussion by the four powers: Great Britain, France, the U.S.S.R. and the U.S.A." But given the British–American agreement behind the scenes, further Soviet participation in the conference looked increasingly futile. In his report to Stalin on July 1, Molotov summarized his generally pessimistic interpretation: "Both Britain and France are now in a difficult economic situation. . . . Their only hope is the United States, which demands . . . that they establish some kind of an all-European body to provide for U.S. interference in the economic and political affairs of European countries. Great Britain, and to some extent France, count on using this body to promote their own interests."

The next day "Mr. Nyet," as Molotov was becoming known, announced the Soviet government's refusal to participate in further discussions of the Marshall Plan. When Britain and France proceeded to invite interested countries to meet again on July 12 to set up a European recovery program, the Soviet side quickly decided not to participate and to force its clients in eastern Europe to follow its lead.

The question then became one of how to proceed. The Kremlin first considered trying to disrupt a second conference from the inside. It advised the Yugoslavs, who had already decided to boycott the conference, "to send your delegation there and give a good fight to America and its satellites, Britain and France, in order to prevent the Americans from unanimously pushing through their plan, and then to leave the conference, taking with you as many delegates from other countries as possible." Similar instructions were transmitted on July 5 through Soviet ambassadors to communist leaders of Poland, Czechoslovakia, Romania, Bulgaria, Hungary, Albania, and Finland. The temptation to harass and embarrass the "cunning West" was strong indeed.

But then the Kremlin sensed danger in such a scheme. There was no guarantee that some of the hard-pressed east Europeans, especially the Czechoslovaks and Poles, who had shown some vacillation, would not yield to the temptation of massive Western assistance. So after first advising all European countries in the Soviet orbit to delay their responses, Molotov soon rescinded his instructions of July 5. Soviet allies in eastern Europe were to stay home.

Some of those allies were not pleased. That was especially so in the case of Czechoslovkia, whose government had already voted unanimously in favor of participation. A Czechoslovak delegation, led by Prime Minister Klement Gottwald, a communist, was urgently summoned to Moscow for a chilly encounter with Stalin. The Kremlin's master first talked to Gottwald alone and then addressed the whole delegation with a warning: "Objectively, you are helping, whether you want it or not, . . . to isolate the Soviet Union. . . . Our people and we will not understand it. You need to rescind your decision, . . . to refuse to participate in this conference—and the sooner you do it, the better."

The guests' assurances of continuing loyalty and friendship were of no avail. When Foreign Minister Jan Masaryk and others started talking about their industries' dependence on the West and their dire economic situation, Stalin countered with an offer to increase trade with and economic assistance to Czechoslovakia. The Czechoslovaks had to submit, as did their Polish counterparts, who learned about "their" refusal to go to Paris before they announced it themselves. Stalin got his way, but at the high price of internal frustration and resentment among his client nations (which may have served a hidden purpose of the Marshall Plan's authors) (see document 6).

It was asserted both then and years later that given internal American political debate about the Marshall Plan, Stalin might have hurt it more by staying in it rather than by walking out. But even if Soviet diplomacy were sophisticated enough to play on nuances of the American political process, Stalin's strategic choice would likely have remained the same. The stakes—complete Soviet control over its own economy and over eastern Europe—seemed simply too high to afford such a gamble. "They were drawing us into their company but in a subordinate role," Molotov recalled long afterwards. "We would have certainly become dependent on them without getting anything substantial in return." It was more natural for Stalin to assume the worst about his adversaries' and clients' intentions—and thus to proceed with a sharper division of the continent—than to face the uncertainties of greater economic interdependence of European countries under a U.S.–sponsored recovery program.

In any case, the Marshall Plan, with all its implications, prompted another serious reassessment of Soviet thinking and policies. To Soviet leaders, it became clear that the Americans were bringing into the Soviet–American competition their most powerful weapon (along with the atomic bomb); they were transferring the game to a trade–economic chessboard, where the Soviet Union was least competitive. In the minds of the men in the Kremlin, who were accustomed to thinking about exploitation and class struggle in crude Marxist terms, the goal of European recovery could only mean the prospect of the restoration of a capitalist western Europe (including West

Germany) as a junior partner in the U.S.–led anti-Soviet bloc. Finally, all the worrisome pieces of postwar American policy fell into a single clear-cut image of the United States as a new "center of imperialist reaction" bent on world hegemony, with the U.S.S.R. and its allies being the main obstacles. The Truman Doctrine, the Marshall Plan, and even the Rio Pact became organic parts of a single global design. Soviet–American rivalry for global influence was now the name of the game for Soviet diplomats and military leaders, who saw the United States as mounting an offensive against the Kremlin's gains.

Now even Novikov's long report of 1946 was castigated within the Soviet Foreign Ministry for being "too soft" in its analysis of U.S. policies. As a clear signal, Novikov was summoned to Moscow and given a dishonorable discharge. The Soviet embassy's political report for 1947 depicted the United States, the "organizer and leading force of the imperialistic camp," as engaged in establishing "an anti-Soviet front in Europe," setting up Japan as "America's main stronghold in its struggle against communism in the Far East," and encouraging "pro-fascist forces" in eastern Europe. The report concluded that the United States had "completely broken away from Roosevelt's foreign and domestic policy" and stepped onto "an adventurous [i.e., risky] path of preparations for a new world war." In this framework, the doctrine of containment, publicized in the summer of 1947, looked to Soviet eyes more like a doctrine of "encircling" or "rolling back" than one of simply containing Soviet power. Revealingly, as one Soviet analyst later recalled, there was considerable pressure from above to translate "containment" as "strangulation" in preparing Kennan's "X" article, which appeared in July 1947, for Molotov and Stalin.

A new stage of Soviet–American confrontation also required a redefined image of Western capitalism, one different from the fairly benign and quasi-realistic interpretations of the mid-1940s. On the one hand, the rival system now had to appear more malevolent and dangerous, but on the other hand, more fragile and constrained, in order to leave hope for ultimate victory. Thus, Varga's 1945 book *Changes in the Economy of Capitalism* was, in the course of an orchestrated ideological campaign, now subjected to sharp criticism for being too optimistic about capitalism's potential for economic development and too naïve about its presumed ability to coexist with socialism.

The Marshall Plan and the diplomatic maneuvering around it also revealed the residual vulnerability of the Soviet Union's security zone in eastern Europe and increased the Kremlin's doubts about its new clients' ability to withstand similar temptations in the future. Not surprisingly, the

Soviet response was to try to frustrate Washington's "grand design" in western Europe while further consolidating its own sphere in the eastern part of the continent. To help achieve both aims, the Kremlin established, in September 1947, the Communist Information (Cominform) Bureau, reminiscent of the Comintern that had been dissolved in 1943, as a new agency to coordinate, under Russian control, the policies and activities of communists worldwide.

Even before the Marshall Plan, the Kremlin was becoming increasingly concerned about communist parties in both eastern and western Europe. In eastern Europe, the campaign to create "people's democracies" was stalling in the face of surviving noncommunist opposition and grave socioeconomic problems. A detailed inventory, conducted by the Foreign Policy Department of the CPSU's Central Committee in the summer of 1947 and based on a country-by-country analysis, showed that serious obstacles still stood in the way of building Soviet-style socialism in eastern Europe. The report spelled out several main criteria of progress: a significant degree of communist political control; increasing nationalization of industrial, transportation, and financial systems (together with progress in land reform); and a dependably pro-Soviet foreign policy. At the bottom of the list were Romania, Hungary, and especially Czechoslovakia, where "the prospects for the construction of a new democracy were worse than in any other country," mainly because of local communists' failure to consolidate power. The Czechs were also blamed for their vacillation over the Marshall Plan—"a gross political mistake and a manifestation of ill will with respect to the Soviet Union." So when Stalin had to deliver on his promise to expand trade with Czechoslovakia, he was none too generous. In the fall, he angrily turned down a draft trade treaty with that country (prepared by his Ministry of Foreign Trade) as too one-sided and as rewarding Prague—still called a "non-Soviet ally"—for playing games at the expense of the U.S.S.R.

Also in the spring and summer of 1947, communists in Poland, Bulgaria, Hungary, and Romania intensified campaigns against their democratic rivals, lobbying Moscow to give them a green light to suppress the opposition. With the Kremlin's consent, principal opposition leaders in Bulgaria and Romania were arrested in June and July on espionage charges (which had some basis in Romania) and their parties were banned. In Hungary, Prime Minister Imre Nagy, falsely linked to a conspiracy plot, fled the country and left his Smallholders party split and marginalized. Only in Czechoslovakia, with its democratic traditions and the absence of Soviet troops, were communists still reluctant to go against the rules of parliamentary democracy.

This time, in contrast to 1946, the Kremlin unleashed its communist clients against their rivals in order to tighten Moscow's control over its east European satellites. In all likelihood, the Soviet government even delayed the ratification of peace treaties with some countries so that Soviet occupation troops could ensure the success of these efforts. This shift in Soviet strategy was a response to both difficulties with the "people's democracy" line and especially diminishing returns of collaboration with the West, which lifted the external restraints on Soviet action in eastern Europe.

That the U.S. counteroffensive of 1947 also played an important role in the Soviet crack-down in eastern Europe was a connection that American intelligence understood. One report sent to the White House late in July 1947 observed that absent the Western initiatives, the U.S.S.R. "might have considered its control in [Hungary, Romania, and Bulgaria] sufficiently strong to permit early ratification of the treaties without jeopardizing its ultimate domination." It added that recent developments had "intensified Soviet determination to maintain its extraordinary powers of control over these countries."

In another situation, too, Stalin acted to make sure that east European countries coordinated their foreign policies with his. Early in August 1947, Josef Tito and Dimitrov announced their intention to conclude a Yugoslav–Bulgarian treaty of friendship, cooperation, and mutual assistance. Stalin was furious, for he had advised the two governments to postpone any such move until the Soviet Union had concluded a peace treaty with Bulgaria. In the face of Stalin's fury, the two governments backed down.

Stalin also used the conference of European communist parties in Czklarska Poremba, Poland, in September 1947, to tighten his grip over east European communist parties and to launch them on a new offensive. Andrei Zhdanov, who presided over the conference, delivered his sharpest criticism against the French and Italian communists, who under U.S. pressure had left coalition governments and gone into opposition, for their timidity in resisting the forces of reaction. The new strategy, Zhdanov said, was "to destroy the capitalist economy and to work systematically toward the unity of healthy national forces" against U.S. assistance. That new strategy implied radical means: general strikes, militant demonstrations, and even the building up of armed revolutionary underground movements.

This policy was almost a U-turn from Stalin's earlier line of restraining militant communism in western Europe in hopes of continued cooperation with Western leaders. With that hope now gone, Stalin was cynically turning Western communists into Soviet "fifth columns" ordered to destabilize western Europe and derail implementation of the Marshall Plan (see document 7). Perhaps inadvertently, Stalin thereby sacrificed prospects for the further growth of communism in western Europe because its militant anti–Marshall Plan campaign, so obviously directed by Moscow, led communist parties there into political isolation. Although clearly offensive in its form, Stalin's response to the Marshall Plan may be seen as desperate defense on the part of the weaker side, whose leaders understood that they had no real alternative to the U.S.–led rehabilitation program or even any effective means to sabotage it.

In eastern Europe, Soviet resources were much more formidable, and Moscow now used them to speed up the Sovietization of countries in its orbit. At the Cominform's opening conference, Zhdanov sharply criticized Czechoslovak and Polish communists for "excessive compromises" and "nationalist deviations" from the only correct (i.e., Soviet) model of building socialism. A radical revision of the concepts of "people's democracy" and "national ways to socialism" was now in full swing, with growing emphases on communist monopoly of political power, crash industrialization programs, class struggle, and the dictatorship of the proletariat. Any transgressions from this model were now considered to be "nationalistic deviations" betraying impermissible insubordination and hidden anti-Sovietism. Through the Cominform and other means, Moscow actively supported the most loyal pro-Soviet elements among east European communists in their efforts to remove moderate forces from their ranks. Thus, successful Sovietization of east European countries seemed to require the Bolshevization of local communist parties.

The concept of the "two camps" became the ideological underpinning of all these changes. Put forth in Zhdanov's main speech at Czklarska Poremba, the term was probably inserted by Stalin, who in turn may have borrowed it from a report by Varga in the summer of 1947. "Two camps" became a powerful metaphor of the times; it pictured the world split into two irreconcilable coalitions of countries caught in a deadly conflict in which there could be no neutrals. Thus, by the fall of 1947, the ideology, policy, and propaganda of the Soviet Union at (cold) war had become fully coordinated.

Soviet propaganda, now blatantly anti-American, openly identified "reaction" and "war-mongerism" with official Washington. A prelude to this campaign occurred in September, when a well-known Soviet writer, Boris Gorbatov, was secretly commissioned to write an insulting political pamphlet on Truman for a Moscow literary newspaper, in which the U.S. president was described as "a little man in short pants." U.S. Ambassador

Smith protested, only to be told by Molotov that the Soviet government had no control over its press (though even this statement had to be cleared with Stalin, whereupon the foreign minister reminded his boss about the Gorbatov commission). Another small but telling detail is that political caricatures in the Soviet press that had previously dealt only with generalized images of American "capitalists" began to depict President Truman and his fellow "cold warriors," while the Cold War itself was fleshed out in the image of an old witch with ugly, icy features.

At the same time, the last remaining channels of Western propaganda in the Soviet Union were being closed. A popular Russian-language magazine, *Amerika*, and its British counterpart were quietly taken out of public distribution late in 1947, and early in 1948 Soviet technicians began the jamming of Russian-language programs over Voice of America and the British Broadcasting Company. The iron curtain had come down all the way (see document 4).

CRISES OF 1948–1949 AND THE DEEP FREEZE

The Kremlin maintained, with some fine-tuning, the dual Cominform strategy—disruption in the West, consolidation in eastern Europe—into 1948. With regard to western Europe, the typically cautious Stalin continued a balancing act between trying to cripple implementation of the Marshall Plan and not provoking a feared direct American intervention in Italy and France. That danger was particularly acute in Italy, where hard-fought elections took place in 1948, in connection with which the possibility of a communist victory led to contingency planning for the introduction of American troops. Fearing such a scenario, the Kremlin advised Italian communists not to start an armed insurrection. Despite earlier calls to form armed underground movements, Molotov told them that an insurrection would be "entirely inappropriate" and could be resorted to only in response to a military attack by reactionary forces. The United States poured millions of dollars into the election campaign in support of noncommunist parties, and the Kremlin had to swallow electoral defeat in Italy. This setback put an end to high hopes for the "Euro-communism" of the 1940s.

HARSH CRACKDOWN IN EASTERN EUROPE

Losing ground in the West, the Kremlin redoubled its efforts to seal off and ensure its control of eastern Europe. Here, the weakest link remained

Czechoslovakia, where local communists were still sharing power with other parties. Faced with a prospect of defeat in upcoming parliamentary elections, they flirted with the idea of staging a preventive coup, but hesitated before taking the final step. The Kremlin sent Molotov's deputy, Valerian Zorin, to Prague as a troubleshooter, but instructed him not to meet with President Eduard Beneš. As the situation became tenser, Zorin reported to Moscow that "Gottwald still would like to avoid any tough measures against the reaction [noncommunists] although the latter has become quite brazen."

Contrary to traditional assumptions in the West, newly declassified documents show that Moscow neither gave any direct orders to Gottwald nor offered to move Soviet troops in Germany and Austria close to the Czechoslovak borders. They suggest, in fact, that it was Gottwald who, looking for face-saving "outside pressure," asked Zorin for the deployment of troops. Molotov's instructions to Zorin on February 22 were quite definite: "Proposals to move Soviet troops in Germany and Austria as well as to give Gottwald orders from Moscow we consider uncalled for." Obviously not wanting to trigger a Western reaction by showing its hand too openly, the Kremlin merely advised Gottwald "to stand more firmly, not to yield to the right, and not to hesitate." It was rightly assumed that Gottwald understood what was expected of him.

Using well-organized mass demonstrations as leverage, communists forced President Beneš to permit a restructuring of the cabinet before elections, thus creating a situation in which it could be packed with communists. Foreign Minister Masaryk died under mysterious circumstances, ostensibly (and officially) by committing suicide. In the next three months, the communist-dominated cabinet rewrote the country's constitution and conducted rigged parliamentary elections, which gave them an overwhelming majority. Anguished by these events, Beneš resigned, to be replaced by his nemesis, Gottwald. The new president and his party proceeded to purge noncommunists from the governmental bureaucracy and to emasculate their former partners in the National Front.

Czechoslovakia, described by visiting Polish communists only few months earlier as "the last state among people's democracies that American imperialism was still counting on," finally became a Soviet-type state. Now, Stalin could afford to be more generous with economic help for a loyal ally in dire straits. In other respects, too, the price of victory was high: The Kremlin's camouflage notwithstanding, events in Czechoslovakia, which became known as the "coup de Prague," frightened western European countries into closer ties with the United States and hastened the creation of the North Atlantic Treaty Organization (NATO).

Just as the "least reliable" "non-Soviet" ally was being transformed into a reliable Soviet one, the Kremlin's former favorite, communist Yugoslavia, was losing Moscow's trust. The cooling-off period in Soviet–Yugoslav relations, which began late in 1947, reflected changes on both sides: Tito's growing appetite for regional hegemony in the Balkans, on the one hand, and Stalin's diminishing tolerance of such wayward independence, on the other. To Stalin's great annoyance, Tito attempted to speed up the conclusion of a Yugoslav–Bulgarian treaty; to engage the Soviet Union more deeply in the civil war in Greece (which Stalin thought too risky a gamble); and finally, without the Kremlin's sanction, to introduce Yugoslav troops into Albania, which Tito wanted to incorporate. Disturbed by this challenge to his project of building a hierarchic Soviet bloc, Stalin decided to nip the incipient rebellion in the bud by teaching Tito (and potential imitators in eastern Europe) a sharp lesson in the dangers of insubordination.

Early in 1948, the Kremlin took several harsh steps. It rejected Belgrade's request for a loan and a trade treaty; recalled Soviet military advisers from Yugoslavia; and launched a series of accusations, both directly and through the Cominform, that the leaders of Yugoslavia were opportunistic, deviant, and anti-Soviet. Then, for a final humiliation, it summoned the Yugoslav leaders to the next meeting of the Cominform, which, as everyone knew, would be set up as a collective inquisition. Accustomed to having his way with "junior partners" in eastern Europe, Stalin seriously underestimated Yugoslavia's stubbornness. Tito refused to subject himself to the Cominform's whipping, and Moscow's relentless campaign of harassment and pressure failed to intimidate or split the tight Yugoslav leadership.

Tito's defiance led to a severe setback for the Kremlin. The absence of a common border and possible international repercussions severely restricted Stalin's military options against the dissident ally, and as the conflict escalated politically, it produced the first open split in the postwar international communist movement. Excommunicated from the latter, Yugoslavia turned to the West for military and economic assistance. Delighted and hopeful, the United States started a covert campaign to stimulate Tito-like defections in other east European countries.

Having failed in his immediate goal of subduing Belgrade, Stalin used this conflict to tighten his grip over his satellites still further. Local communist parties were purged of "Titoist elements" and "their agents," who were now equated with "fascists." The resulting witch-hunt atmosphere allowed some communist leaders to settle personal scores with party rivals by denouncing them as "Titoists" and "traitors." Although Stalin occasionally tried to restrain the blood-thirsty zeal of his henchmen, these vendettas served his purpose well because the blood of the victims tied the survivors to Moscow.

The Kremlin also took steps to speed up the political and economic integration of eastern Europe. It imposed almost identical treaties of "friendship, cooperation, and mutual assistance" on Romania, Bulgaria, Hungary, and Finland in 1948 (similar treaties had been concluded earlier with Poland, Yugoslavia, and Czechoslovakia). Each of them contained clauses calling for military cooperation in the event of attack by Germany and its allies. The Soviet government decided, after some vacillation, to continue to identify Germany as the principal threat not, as Molotov explained to his east European counterparts, because it failed to see other potential sources of aggression, but because it did not want to dramatize the situation and sought to emphasize the contrast between the "firm, self-confident tone" of the Soviet government and the "nervous tone" of governments in the West. Molotov evidently had in mind the Brussels Pact concluded by Great Britain, France, and the Benelux countries in March 1948, which included security guarantees against not only Germany, but also "other countries," presumably—and disturbingly—the U.S.S.R., as well. This pact, which had the blessing of the United States, caused serious concern in the Kremlin as a sign of hostile intentions.

Soviet strategy was to stay one step behind the West in solidifying the division of Germany and the continent as a whole. Because the United States had already moved to foster the economic integration of western Europe through the Marshall Plan, the Kremlin responded in December 1948 with the decision to set up a council to coordinate economic cooperation between the U.S.S.R. and five east European countries (with Yugoslavia excluded). The council's purpose was to create closer economic ties among member states and to provide a common front, a Soviet bloc, in the world economy, thus to discourage the West from using lack of coordination in eastern Europe for their own interests. The formal establishment of the Council for Mutual Economic Assistance (known both as CMEA and as Comecon) took place in Moscow a month later (in January 1949).

THE BERLIN BLOCKADE, NATO, AND OTHER ISSUES

The most important crisis of 1948 took place over the most crucial of Cold War issues: Germany. The evolution of U.S. policy reinforced Soviet suspicions of Western aims in Germany. As an internal memorandum on the subject that circulated in the Foreign Ministry early in October 1947 stressed, the Soviet Union was faced with "a real threat of the political dismemberment of

Germany and the inclusion of West Germany, with all its resources, in the western bloc, pulled together by the United States." Soviet diplomats made an effort to reverse this trend by proposing a peace treaty that would create "a united democratic Germany," but the initiative was rebuffed at a meeting of the Council of Foreign Ministers in London late in 1947.

Molotov boasted to Stalin that he "struck at the allies' weak spot" by pressing them on their alleged plans of zonal consolidation. But he was unable to disrupt those plans. France agreed to unify its occupation zone with the U.S. and British zones (Bizonia) to create Trizonia, and then, at a separate conference in London, the United States, Britain, France, and the Benelux countries took the decisive step of proposing a West German constituent assembly—that is, the establishment of a West German state. That development, coupled with ongoing preparations for the introduction of a new currency in the emerging Trizonia, was rightly perceived in Moscow as a complete break with the Yalta–Potsdam agreements on four-power control over Germany, especially since the conference in London was summoned without even informing the fourth party to the German settlement, the U.S.S.R.

In analyzing these events for the Kremlin, the Soviet Foreign Ministry concluded that "the western powers are transforming Germany into their stronghold and [intend to include] it in the newly formed military–political bloc, directed against the Soviet Union and the new democracies [in eastern Europe]." Desperate to forestall such developments, the Kremlin decided to counterattack by using the most tangible advantage it still held in Germany: control over the geographic space between the western zones and Berlin, which was located in the heart of the Soviet zone.

The Soviet leadership must have made the key decision early in March 1948, when Marshal Vasily Sokolovsky, the Soviet representative on the Allied Control Council, and Vladimir Semyenov, a political adviser in Berlin, were urgently summoned to Moscow. Following his return, Sokolovsky stalked from the Control Council's meeting on March 20, thus paralyzing that body. By April 1, a series of restrictions were introduced on the communication lines between Berlin and the western zones, and within days the Berlin blockade began in earnest. The Soviet argument for it was not without a certain logic: Since the London decisions ran counter to the Potsdam agreements and the allied control mechanism based on those agreements, the Western presence in Berlin lost its earlier justification, and the Soviet side had justification for closing its occupation zone.

What did Stalin expect from this high-stakes showdown? Was he trying to "kick them [the Western allies] out" of Berlin, as he told East German leaders in March, and as Truman believed? Or did he want, by weakening their position in Berlin, to force them into reversing the London decisions and reopening negotiations about a German settlement, as he repeatedly told Western contacts during subsequent meetings? The second version seems more likely, although had the Western powers decided to retreat, Stalin would certainly not have minded that outcome, either.

At first, prospects looked good from the Soviet side. Most observers assumed that West Berlin could not survive in isolation. "Our control-and-restrictive measures have dealt a strong blow to the prestige of the Americans and Britons in Germany," the chiefs of the Soviet Military Administration in Germany reported to Moscow on April 17. They added that (as they wanted to believe) the German population thought that "the Anglo-Americans have retreated before the Russians" and that "this testifies to the Russians' strength." With municipal elections looming in West Berlin, Soviet officials sought to discredit the Western powers by picturing them as helpless to resist the blockade. They hoped that fearful or resigned citizens of West Berlin would turn to Soviet authorities for the necessities of life.

But the tide soon began to turn. The Kremlin underestimated Western resolve and ingenuity. The massive airlift became a solution that Soviet officials could negate only by risking an open military conflict, which was not a part of their plan. While the stalemate continued, the Western powers proceeded with currency reform and with plans for creating a West German state. Stalin's increasing anger over and frustration at Western defiance found an outlet mainly in his handwritten remarks on documents placed before him. For example, in the margins of a translated diplomatic note from Paris, he penned these comments: "Scoundrels"; "It is all lies"; "It is not a blockade, but a defensive measure"; and "Ha-ha!" But in talks with the three Western ambassadors in August, Stalin was firm and in full control, insisting that their governments cancel or at least postpone implementation of the London decisions. The Western powers remained adamant, however, and after prolonged procrastination, Moscow finally had to retreat fully and to acknowledge their rights in Berlin.

Again, as with Turkey and Iran, Stalin's hardball tactics, which he pursued far too long, proved to be counterproductive. Instead of blocking the implementation of the Western plan for Germany, the Berlin blockade accelerated it. Moreover, the brutal pressure scared other west European countries into closer alliance with the United States. The road to NATO was now open. Stalin's worst fear, a U.S.–led Western bloc united against the Soviet Union, was coming into being, in large part thanks to his own inadvertent assistance. As Russian historians Vladislav Zubok and Constantine Pleshakov have noted, Stalin "did not want the Cold War but . . . did not know how to avoid it."

In 1948–1949, Soviet–American diplomacy almost came to a halt as propaganda and mutual recriminations replaced serious negotiations. Even the usual niceties of diplomatic discourse fell victim to the rancor. In May 1948, the U.S. State Department, concerned that Stalin might misread American intentions and overreact, sent the Kremlin a confidential message through Ambassador Smith that contained two basic points: (1) the United States would not accept any new Soviet encroachment "beyond the present limits" of communist power, but it had no plans for a military attack against the U.S.S.R., and (2) the current U.S. policy was not subject to change because of presidential elections or economic downturn, but "the door is always open for full discussion and the composing of our differences."

Molotov responded in appropriate diplomatic tones, but in reality the Kremlin was no more ready to enter that door than was the White House. Stalin jotted a sarcastic "Ha-ha!" by the quoted passage in Smith's note, and evidently decided both to embarrass the Americans and to use the incident for propaganda purposes. He had the text of the Smith–Molotov exchange published in the Soviet press without informing the American side ahead of time. Russian propaganda treated Smith's démarche as an example of U.S. hypocrisy mixed with the inability to come up with any constructive ideas for improving Soviet–American relations.

This blow-up was only part of an intensive propaganda campaign designed to discredit "Truman's hawks" in the upcoming presidential election. The Kremlin watched that election very closely, giving special attention to the Progressive party's candidate, Henry A. Wallace, who seemed to promise a real alternative to the administration's Cold War policies. Stalin evidently had high hopes that a strong showing by Wallace could conceivably become a catalyst for the resurrection of the "Roosevelt trend" in U.S. politics. Although Stalin advised Wallace that a visit to Moscow would be too risky (for Wallace's campaign), he approved of the idea of a public appeal in the form of an open letter. When Wallace's letter was published by the *New York Times* on May 12, less than a week after publication of the Smith–Molotov exchange, Stalin promptly responded with an open letter of his own, calling Wallace's a "very important document" that could provide a "fruitful basis . . . for coexistence" and for the "peaceful resolution of differences between the U.S.S.R. and the U.S.A."

The Wallace–Stalin exchange made a big splash around the world, but it made it easier for Truman and American conservatives to tag Wallace as a fellow traveler being used by Moscow. More importantly, Stalin's brutal action in Berlin and eastern Europe belied his own words about peace and co-existence and contributed to Truman's surprising victory in November. Moscow still confronted the same policies in Washington.

Within the Soviet Union itself, 1948 was a year of growing tensions and escalating repression. The anti-Western, xenophobic campaign reached new heights with a struggle against so-called cosmopolitans, mostly Jews in various professions. Thus, the Kremlin resurrected popular anti-Semitism both to weed out Western influence and to rally the Soviet mob against foreign enemies and their "domestic agents." Thousands of Jewish officials and intellectuals, including Molotov's wife, were sent to prison on fabricated espionage charges; some of them were "officially" executed (e.g., Molotov's orthodox deputy Solomon Lozovsky), and some secretly assassinated (e.g., the famous actor and theatre director Solomon Mikhoels).

Stalin's spy-and-enemy mania peaked as the Cold War became more frigid. His working assumption was that Western imperialism would now redouble its efforts to organize a "fifth column" within the Soviet bloc, as he himself was trying to do in the Western sphere, a fear that was not without some basis. The Kremlin knew about the reorganization of the U.S. intelligence community and its covert operations in Europe and Asia. Indeed, scholars are now learning that the scope of those operations was much wider than previously thought, for the Central Intelligence Agency (CIA) in fact got into the business of setting up emigré groups to serve as nuclei for future anti-Soviet revolts all over eastern Europe. "Such units," wrote Kennan, then a State Department liaison with the CIA, to one of his colleagues in the fall of 1948, "may represent a closer approximation of the absolute weapon than the atomic bomb," over which the United States still enjoyed a monopoly.

Such calculations would not have surprised Stalin. Moscow was monitoring the activities of anti-Soviet Russian immigrants in the United States and paying special attention to their frequent contacts with the U.S. government. The Kremlin was also aware that Washington was working with members of the old German intelligence network specializing in Soviet matters. Together, these developments left the Kremlin in no doubt that Americans were sheltering its most rabid enemies in order to use them against the U.S.S.R.

There were indeed a number of real spy cases in the early postwar years, but Stalin's response to this problem was way out of proportion. Early in March 1949, he dismissed even close subordinates such as Foreign Minister Molotov and Foreign Trade Minister Mikoyan from their cabinet posts for alleged lack of vigilance. His obsession with internal enemies was reflected in a speech before the CPSU's Central Committee on March 30, 1949 (recorded in fragments by the editor-in-chief of *Pravda*, Pyetr Pospelov): "Where is the main danger now? It comes from honest fools and blind. At the hands of such honest but blind people our country can perish. . . . Our enemies conduct their policy by these fools' hands."

By that time, Stalin was himself blinded by the crackdown on his intelligence network in the United States. Except for a rapidly shrinking British connection (mostly through Kim Philby, London's liaison with the CIA since the fall of 1949), the Truman White House became impenetrable to Soviet eyes. And although the general course of American policy looked more or less clear and settled, the details did not, and people in the Kremlin still hoped that some concessions on the key questions of Germany and the Western bloc might be forthcoming.

It may have been this combination of uncertainty and hope that pushed Stalin to one of his most intriguing moves in 1949. Documents from the Kremlin archives reveal that in January 1949, Stalin was seriously considering the idea of using Wallace, who had offered his mediation, as a secret channel between the Kremlin and the White House. According to Molotov's draft instructions to the Soviet ambassador in Washington, the main purpose of such a risky operation would be to find out "whether there is any tendency in the U.S. government toward improving relations with the U.S.S.R."

Stalin zigzagged on this project. He began by turning it down, then changed his mind and gave it a green light, only to reverse himself again in a few days after initial contacts in Washington. In an interview with American journalists, Stalin offered to meet with Truman to discuss ways to improve Soviet–American relations—a gesture then written off as a propaganda trick, but one now acquiring new meaning in the context of the Wallace mediation project. Overall, this abortive "peace feeler" betrays not only the Kremlin's ignorance about the realities of power in Washington, but also Stalin's desperate hope for some last-minute loosening of the U.S. position before the division of Germany became final and NATO was established. His secret diplomacy having failed, Stalin went on making efforts at least to forestall both of those developments.

Soviet agents tried to follow the process of secret negotiations over the North Atlantic Treaty. From the Soviet standpoint, the most troubling aspects of the emerging alliance were the leading role of the United States and the obvious intent to widen its geostrategic orbit by bringing Italy, Spain, and Portugal, as well as Scandinavian countries, into the alliance. Soviet analysts also emphasized the conspicuous facts that Germany was not named as a potential enemy and that no country from the Soviet bloc was asked to join the alliance—a combination that in Soviet eyes was sure proof of the treaty's anti-Soviet thrust. Also worrisome to the Kremlin were leaks in the Western press about a possible "secret protocol" to the treaty calling for "terminating" west European communist parties' activities in case of war or the immediate threat of it.

The first official Soviet reaction to the proposed North Atlantic Treaty was a statement issued by the Foreign Ministry on January 29, 1949. It protested that the draft treaty was directed against the U.S.S.R. and that it violated the UN Charter as well as the Soviet Union's wartime treaties with Britain and France. In February, the Kremlin approached the government of Norway, which has a long border with the U.S.S.R., with an offer for a nonaggression treaty. Moscow was greatly concerned about the prospect of Western military bases at the country's doorstep and wanted to lure Norway away from the emerging alliance. But Oslo declined the offer, while uttering assurances that it would remain Moscow's good neighbor even as a member of NATO.

Even less productive were the Kremlin's other preventive moves: threats to annul treaties with Britain and France, the instigation of mass anti–NATO demonstrations by west European communists, and the concentration of troops near Yugoslavia. If anything, these steps facilitated the concluding stage of treaty negotiations by accentuating the specter of a "Soviet threat." On March 31, only days before the treaty was to be signed, the Politburo solemnly reiterated and amplified the Foreign Ministry's statement. From that point on, Soviet policy, as earlier with the Marshall Plan, became one of trying to disrupt implementation of the treaty by staging an intensive anti–NATO campaign through the Cominform, local communist parties, and the newly created Soviet Peace Committee, a "public" organization created in August 1949 that became the nucleus for an extended network of similar front organizations all over the world.

The formation of NATO was a crucial development for the Soviet Union. It meant a military–political follow-up to the economic division of Europe started by the Marshall Plan and resulted in the institutionalization of a Western anti-Soviet bloc headed by the United States that the Kremlin had tried so hard but ineffectually to prevent. In addition, the openly confrontational configuration in Europe meant that the Soviet Union could not consider reducing its presence in eastern and central Europe, for that would be an unacceptable loss of face before an implacable enemy. Moscow saw as its only choices the firm retention of its control over its orbit or the resort to war and even more brutal repression should that control be directly challenged.

Despite this stark situation, Stalin still sought to forestall a final division of Germany. In part it was a matter of tactics; he still wanted to stay one step behind the West in order to avoid responsibility for the country's division. At a meeting in December 1948, he told East German leaders: "You do not want to act as the initiators of Germany's split and that is only natural. But if a separate West German government is formed, . . . a government should also be formed in Berlin." At the same time, Stalin still saw a united, neutral, and demilitarized German state as preferable to complete separation. In his view, the latter condition would be neither durable nor beneficial for the Soviet interests in the long run. A student of Bismarck's and Hitler's policies, Stalin was deeply impressed by German nationalism, which he thought was likely to overwhelm foreign occupation and to foment "German revanchism" once again. He probably also suspected that a much smaller and poorer East Germany would not be competitive against its more productive, U.S.–supported counterpart. Besides, separation would deprive the Soviet Union of its ultimate prize in Germany: access to the Ruhr region, the country's industrial heartland.

So even after the key decision to set up a West German state was reached on April 25, 1949, the Soviet government continued to fight back. It tried to hold off the final stage of this process and presented itself as the only champion of German unity. When Stalin detected a lack of resolve on the part of his new foreign minister, Andrei Vyshinsky, during a discussion of the German question at the Council of Foreign Ministers in May, he sent stern warnings about Western "machinations": "It looks as if you don't quite understand that the three powers' proposal boils down to their intent to merge the eastern zone with the western ones on their own terms, [which are] absolutely unacceptable to us; they want to swallow our zone and to tie us to their chariot in Germany, depriving us at the same time of those rights to reparations which we received in Potsdam." Because the Soviet counterproposal was not going through, Stalin instructed Vyshinsky "to emphasize the contrast between their separatist position and our proposals, aimed at creating a united, democratic, peace-loving German state."

Meanwhile, perhaps still hoping for the best but also preparing for the worst, Stalin continued with the covert, methodical Sovietization of the eastern zone. Documents from East German archives confirm that by the early 1949, the Socialist Unity party was fully transformed into a Bolshevik-type party and that internal security forces were beefed up under close Soviet guidance to monitor and subdue remaining opposition groups. Embryonic military units and training centers were set up, under the auspices of the (East) German "Directorate for the Interior," in the summer of 1948 on Stalin's personal orders. All these steps could serve dual purposes: They could provide the nucleus of a separate East German state or become the institutional bases for Soviet influence in a united Germany. When finally, in October 1949, the formation of the German Democratic Republic (G.D.R.) was announced, the new entity was called "provisional," which was meant, as Stalin told his East German clients, to "serve as a hint that the government has been formed [only] . . . until Germany is unified."

THE SOVIET A-BOMB, THE SINO–SOVIET TREATY, AND THE WAR IN KOREA

Between the ratification of the North Atlantic Treaty and the establishment of the G.D.R., the Western world was shaken by news of the first atomic explosion in the Soviet Union. The giant effort, aided by successful espionage, bore fruit several years earlier than Washington had expected (see document 8). Although the test in Semipalatinsk, Kazakhstan, took place on August 29, the Soviet side kept silent about it, and it was not until September 23 that President Truman publicly acknowledged the event. "Truman's announcement has produced an incredible uproar here," Vyshinsky gleefully reported to Stalin from his UN post in New York; "naturally, I am not going to make any comments on this."

Low-profile was indeed the Soviet way of spinning this awesome news, but the Kremlin certainly appreciated its significance and was greatly relieved by the end of America's atomic monopoly. In a closed ceremony at which he gave awards to key participants in the atomic project, Stalin said, "Had it taken another year or year and a half for us to develop the bomb, we would have probably 'tasted' it on ourselves." Nevertheless, having countered America's atomic ace, Stalin decided to downplay the matter publicly as much as possible. For one thing, he did not want to admit, even in retrospect, that the United States had indeed had this key strategic advantage over the Soviet Union for four long years—something that the Kremlin had kept hidden from Soviet citizens all that time. Besides, Soviet propaganda was constantly playing on the contrast between the "atomic blackmail" and "saber rattling" of "western imperialism" on the one hand, and the Kremlin's "strong nerves" and peaceful intentions, on the other.

That is why Stalin handled his own announcement in a low-key way. He personally drafted a press release as a semiofficial response to

Truman's announcement. The statement confirmed the explosion but described it as "peaceful" and asserted that the U.S.S.R. had "opened the secret of the atomic bomb by 1947." Stalin played his atomic camouflage game to the end, but made sure that the West got the message.

While the Kremlin attached great importance to the superweapon's symbolic and political use, Stalin and his commanders did not yet think in terms of atomic warfare. As long as Stalin was alive, these weapons were not assigned to troops or integrated into the country's military doctrine. In preparations for atomic war, the Soviet Union lagged well behind the United States.

In the fall of 1949, the Kremlin obtained another trump card in its struggle with the West—a powerful new ally in the East. As we have seen, Stalin did not rush to embrace the Chinese communists led by Mao Ze-dong. For two years after 1945, a period in which the outcome of the civil war in China was uncertain, Stalin tried to play the role of broker, in part because he did not trust Mao as a loyal communist and in part because he did not want to aggravate Soviet–American rivalry in China. At the same time, however, he prudently kept options open by maintaining contacts and covertly providing some military assistance to Mao. In 1948, all of these calculations began to change, especially as the tide of war turned and growing tension with the United States removed the main external restraint. Stalin started to reassess Mao and admitted to his inner circle that Moscow had underestimated China's revolutionary potential.

Still, he made his moves with a characteristic caution. Exchanges of visits between Soviet and Chinese communist officials took place at a high level in the spring and summer of 1949. Stalin was pleased by Mao's proposal for a partnership against Western imperialism, but it was only after the proclamation of the People's Republic of China, on October 1, that he finally agreed to Mao's repeated request to be received in Moscow.

The negotiations between the world's two mightiest communist potentates in Moscow in the winter of 1949–1950, now fully documented from both sides, were a remarkable exercise in high-stakes diplomacy. Although Stalin held the highest card thanks to the Soviet Union's greater industrial power and to the fact that its revolution was "older," Mao was the new ruler of a land much more populous than the U.S.S.R. Moreover, he enjoyed the prestige of having come to power largely unaided by "Big Brother" Russia and of being an anti-imperialist hero.

After tense moments and the threat of a stalemate, Stalin finally agreed to replace the Sino–Soviet Treaty of 1945 with a new one requested by Mao. Having overwhelmed Mao by this concession, Stalin was then able to insist on terms highly favorable to the Soviet side. The formation of the Sino–Soviet alliance, cemented by the Treaty of Friendship, Alliance, and Mutual Assistance signed on February 14, 1950, became a momentous event. It formed a bridge between the early Cold War and its subsequent development. Coupled with the Soviet atomic bomb, it changed the overall correlation of forces and encouraged Stalin to begin a new counteroffensive against the West.

With the division of Europe firmly solidified and China now governed by communists, Stalin was ready to take new risks in Asia. In April 1950, he finally gave the green light to North Korean leader Kim Il Sung, who had made repeated requests for Soviet backing of a military attack against South Korea. Stalin had several reasons for adopting such a policy. New circumstances, including what appeared to be a lack of U.S. commitment to South Korea's security, seemed to offer an opportunity to expand the area under his control and also to encourage revolutionaries in other parts of Asia. Moreover, the seizure of South Korea might reinforce communist China's isolation from the West, thus making that country more dependent on the U.S.S.R. But Stalin got a different war in Korea from the one he expected. As things turned out, Kim's large-scale attack across the thirty-eighth parallel in Korea on June 25, 1950, set the course for intensification of the Cold War and for massive militarization on both sides of the ideological divide.

CONCLUSION: STALIN'S COLD WAR STRATEGY IN RETROSPECT

It has been half a century since the beginning of the Cold War and about a decade since its sudden end. Yet despite recent research in newly opened archives, some basic questions about the Soviet road to the Cold War remain. Was Stalin's Soviet Union seeking security or expansion? Was Stalin a revolutionary romantic, a Russian/Soviet imperialist, a cynical practitioner of Realpolitik, or a megalomaniac craving power for power's sake? Furthermore, was he a genius, however evil, or an inept bungler who often ended up getting precisely what he sought to avoid? Such questions may have no definitive answers, but one can draw some tentative conclusions.

First, there was clearly some logic to what often looked like the madness of Soviet foreign policy. Its overriding goal was remarkably consistent throughout World War II and the Cold War: security through aggrandizement and consolidation of the Soviet sphere. The ways to that goal were varied and at times contradictory, from an amicable deal with Hitler on dividing the continent to a lethal war against Hitler's empire, and from alliance with Britain and the United States to Cold War against these former comrades in arms. The Bolsheviks in the Kremlin were entirely unscrupulous and free-wheeling in selecting policies to fit changing circumstances.

Whether they were guided primarily by Marxist ideology or by national security interests is largely an artificial distinction. Ideology was important as a prism through which Soviet leaders saw the world and which made them predisposed to see U.S. policies as expansionist and threatening. Thus, ideology contributed to suspicions and tensions as the Soviet–Marxist version of universalist vision clashed with the liberal exceptionalism of its American counterpart. Besides, in the Bolshevik mentality, ideology and national interests were blended into a single whole since for Stalin and his lieutenants preservation and expansion of the Soviet domain were necessary for promoting world revolution. "Whatever is good for the Soviet Union is good for the world revolution" was an unwritten rule for the men in the Kremlin, who saw no inherent contradiction between those two goals. But whenever there was a conflict between Soviet egotism and ideological interests, they would invariably choose the former over the latter. For Stalin and his circle, enhancing Soviet power, which also meant enhancing their own power, was, unsurprisingly, the first priority. To it they subordinated everything and everyone else, whether the Russian people, foreign communists, or former capitalist allies.

Much the same can be said about the elusive line between security and expansion. Here, however, Soviet concerns were hardly new. As empire builders from Romans to Britons illustrate, security through expansion was no Soviet invention. Even in America's case, as Walter Lippmann once said, seeking security and building an empire were two sides of the same coin. It is even debatable whether Soviet empire-builders were any more driven by ideological universalism than their American rivals, although for Americans ideology was more amorphous than for the Bolsheviks.

Both sides in the Cold War exhibited symmetry in their strategic thinking as well. After all, Soviet leaders had their own crude version of containment. In Marxist terms, Western capitalism was both hostile and inherently unstable. The task confronting the Kremlin, then, was to hold the line and exploit the capitalist enemy's difficulties until its internal contradictions would lead to a new cycle of depression, war, and revolution—developments that would, in the Soviet view, make possible another breakthrough for communism. The experience of Stalin's generation seemed to validate such expectations. World War I and the Russian Revolution paved the way for the emergence of the first socialist state, and then the Great Depression and World War II made possible the expansion of the Soviet system.

Indeed, in Moscow's view, the latter development was the major cause for the West's reversion to Cold War, but that price seemed justified. As Molotov later claimed, "We had to consolidate what we had conquered, to make our part of Germany socialist, to establish order in Czechoslovakia, Poland, Yugoslavia, etc., all of which were in a very fluid condition. So, we had to squeeze out the capitalist order—hence the Cold War."

Those policies affirmed, Molotov added another note of realism, however: "Naturally one has to observe limits. I think Stalin abided by them very well." One might well ask how differently relations between the Soviet Union and the West would have developed had Stalin avoided provocative acts in essentially peripheral areas, such as those in the cases of Turkey, Iran, Manchuria, and Korea. But seen overall, the Kremlin's boss was basically cautious in his waging of the Cold War; he sometimes came close to, but never crossed, the fatal line of direct military collision with the United States. In this sense, he was a fitting, one might even say responsible, partner-adversary for Western leaders who were pushing their own agenda and who, like Stalin, were concerned about the danger of the opponent's overreaction to unwanted pressure.

There was, nevertheless, a substantial and significant difference between the Soviet and American empires during the Cold War. It lay in the nature of imperial control and the methods used to build spheres of influence. The American empire was generally pluralistic and open, while the Soviet one was totalitarian and closed. To put it more colorfully, a Soviet "empire by rape" stood in contrast to an American "empire by seduction" (or as Geir Lundestad puts it, "by invitation" on the part of countries afraid of being raped). More than anything else, it was Soviet heavy-handedness that made its sphere, which covered much of the Eurasian landmass, unacceptable to the United States both for domestic and geopolitical reasons. It was also the legacy of that heavy-handedness that doomed the Soviet empire itself to rapid disintegration once its leaders disavowed the threat of military suppression against its satellites.

But Soviet policy options, far from being simply a matter of free choice, were always constrained by the weight of history, by lack of resources, and by the nature of the Stalinist system. The Soviet Union was, as John Lewis Gaddis persuasively suggests, essentially "a one-dimensional power" that lacked economic, cultural, and other "soft" power leverages. When confronting multidimensional American power, the U.S.S.R. had to maximize its main asset: military power. Moreover, Soviet leaders could not count on countries

in eastern Europe, where old enmities and anti-Russian feelings were histor-
ically strong, to be both fully independent and pro-Soviet. Finally, Soviet
leaders, accustomed to total control over their own subjects and knowing no
other way to organize society, could confidently deal only with puppets running familiar Soviet-type systems. In short, given their history, political system, and priorities, as well as challenges from the West, Soviet leaders could
hardly have done other than they did in creating their Cold War empire.

If such was indeed the inescapable logic of Soviet strategy, then one
must ask how effective Soviet leaders really were in pursuing their own
aims. For many years, observers have repeatedly made the case that by
frightening the West into united opposition to Soviet policy instead of engaging it in a more skillful game of give-and-take, one that might have undermined Western resolve, Stalin was his own worst enemy. As early as 1950
Kennan observed that it was primarily Soviet actions that made it possible
for "us [Americans] to pull ourselves together and to increase our strength"
when a different approach might "have had us . . . in a [grave] state of un-
preparedness."

Although Soviet understanding of American politics was too crude
for such fine-tuning, one can make the case that the men in the Kremlin
saw the stakes as too high to allow risky efforts—experiments, really—to
accommodate their rival. If even the United States, with its preponderant,
multidimensional power and margin of safety, could or would not adopt a
more accommodating policy (never mind the reasons why it would not),
then in the view of the Kremlin, a weaker Soviet Union could afford one
even less. For both sides, the premium was on toughness and on worst-case
scenarios, which together led to escalation of the conflict between them.

But would notably different U.S. policy have changed Soviet behavior?
The prevailing view in the West is that it would not have. We can never be
certain, however, for after the death of Roosevelt the United States never
really put accommodation to the test.

Perhaps one should ask the reverse question, too, one almost never
asked. What would the Soviet side have had to do to accommodate the
Americans and thus end the Cold War? American "terms of settlement"
were no secret to the Kremlin, for they were occasionally spelled out by Secretary of State Dean Acheson and other high-ranking U.S. officials: Soviet
withdrawal from central and eastern Europe, lifting the iron curtain, stopping
anti-American propaganda, and ending support for communists in other
parts of the world. In the view of the men then in the Kremlin, acquiescence
in such demands would have stripped the Soviet Union of its security belt
in Europe, betrayed what it leaders saw as its global mission, and exposed the

still young and battered system to destabilizing ideological "contamination" from abroad. Judging by the subsequent fate of the Soviet empire, those fears were not altogether unfounded. In short, for the Soviet side, these were terms of capitulation, not of reasonable accommodation. The Soviet Union was too strong to accept such terms—too strong to capitulate and too weak ultimately to win. Such was the essence of Stalin's Cold War predicament.

From another perspective, however, perhaps Stalin's greatest strategic blunder lay in engaging his country, so much in need of reform and rebuilding, in a global power struggle that could not be won. Did he, in considering the options available to him, make a fundamentally flawed choice? If so, it took almost fifty years of Cold War to demonstrate that point.

Documents

1

STALIN TO "POLITBURO FOUR" ([VYACHESLAV] MOLOTOV, [LAVRENTI] BERIA, [ANASTAS] MIKOYAN, AND [GEORGY] MALENKOV) CIPHERED [CODED] TELEGRAM, DECEMBER 9, 1945

Analyzing the international events for the period from the London conference of five ministers to the forthcoming conference of three ministers in Moscow, one can come to the following conclusions.

1. Thanks to our tenacity we won the struggle over the issues which had been discussed in London. The conference of the three ministers in Moscow signifies a retreat of the U.S.A. and England from their positions in London since this conference will now work without China's involvement on European questions and without France's involvement on questions concerning the Balkans.
2. We won the struggle in Bulgaria and Yugoslavia. The testimony to this are the results of elections in those countries. If we had stumbled on the issues regarding those countries and had not held on, then we would have definitely lost there.
3. At some point you [Molotov] gave in to pressure and intimidation on the part of the U.S., began to stumble, adopted the liberal course with regard to foreign correspondents, and let your government be pilloried by those correspondents in expectation that this would placate the U.S. and Britain. Of course, your calculation was naive. I feared that with this liberalism you would undercut our policy of tenacity and thereby let our state down. At that time the entire foreign press yelled that Russians were caving in and would make concessions. But an accident helped you and you returned in time to the policy of tenacity. It is obvious that in dealing with partners such as the U.S. and Britain, we cannot achieve anything serious if we begin to give in to intimidation or betray uncertainty. To get

anything serious from partners of this kind, we must arm ourselves with a policy of tenacity and steadfastness.

4. The same policy of tenacity and steadfastness should be our guide in our working toward the conference of three ministers.

2

A COMPILATION OF [WRITTEN] COMMENTS ON DRAFT TREATIES REGARDING DEMILITARIZATION AND DISARMAMENT OF GERMANY AND JAPAN PROPOSED BY [U.S. SECRETARY OF STATE JAMES] BYRNES, JUNE 8, 1946 (COMPILED BY COMRADES NOVIKOV AND ZARUBIN OF MFA [MINISTRY OF FOREIGN AFFAIRS], U.S.S.R.)

Enclosed in: Molotov to Stalin, 8 June 1946

[About] Draft Treaty regarding demilitarization and disarmament of Germany
    [Several] comrades . . . voiced their opposition to the proposed drafts giving a number of reasons. Analyzing those arguments one can draw the conclusion that in proposing this treaty the American government is pursuing the following goals:

1. To shorten the duration of Germany's occupation.
2. To disrupt the receipt of reparations from Germany by the Soviet Union.
3. To weaken controls over Germany.
4. To undermine the influence of the U.S.S.R. on issues related to Germany and other European countries.
5. To replace the task of real military and economic disarmament of Germany with the opposite goal of preserving Germany as a strong power.
6. To speed up Germany's reconstruction in order to use Germany against the Soviet Union.
7. To undo all the jointly arrived-at Allied decisions on Germany.

What follow are individual [written] statements by different comrades on each of these goals.

1. To shorten the duration of Germany's occupation.

a) The [proposed] treaty on disarmament and demilitarization of Germany is designed to dismantle the occupation of Germany (Com. [A. A.] Andreev).

b) The Soviet occupation serves not only to democratize a part of Germany, but also to weaken reactionary forces in its other parts; that is why Americans and the British seek to hasten its termination (Com. [M. I.] Kalinin).

c) Byrnes' proposal in reality leads to the termination of occupation, which was designed to bring about a real disarmament and liquidation of industry that can be used for war purposes (Com. [L. M.] Kaganovich). . . .

g) The Americans would like to end the occupation of Germany as soon as possible and to remove the armed forces of the U.S.S.R. from Germany, and then to demand a withdrawal of our troops from Poland, and ultimately from the Balkans (Com. [G. K.] Zhukov). . . .

2. To disrupt the receipt of reparations from Germany by the Soviet Union.

a) The American draft is designed to complicate the receipt of our reparations from Germany (Com. Andreev).

b) The draft treaty does not provide for the continuation of getting reparations from Germany, [thus] endangering the issue of vital importance to the U.S.S.R. (Com. [V. G.] Dekanozov). . . .

4. To undermine the influence of the U.S.S.R. on issues related to Germany and other European countries.

a) Byrnes' draft is calculated to push us out of Germany as soon as possible, whereby Americans want to get ahead and look kinder in German eyes in order to bring Germany to their side against us (Com. Andreev). . . .

c) Byrnes' move pursues the provocative goal of presenting us as "cold-hearted" and themselves as benign "peacemakers" (Com. Kaganovich).

d) Given the established practice of building blocs between the U.S., Great Britain, and other countries, the role of the Soviet Union in controlling Germany's demilitarization and disarmament will be jeopardized (Com. [N. M.] Shvernik). . . .

5. To replace the task of real military and economic disarmament of Germany with the opposite goal of preserving German as a strong power.

a) The proposal does not include the liquidation of all German industry which may be used for military production; it also fails to include the transfer of production capacity not needed for Germany's civilian industry to the U.S.S.R. and other Allies under the rubric of reparations (Com. Shvernik). . . .

c) The draft treaty bypasses a number of important decisions made at the Crimea and Berlin [Potsdam] conferences, including measures to decentralize . . . Germany's economic might (Com. [A. I.] Vyshinsky).

d) The measures proposed . . . deal only with control over disarmament without tackling all the issues of liquidation of or real control over German industry and of rooting out any Nazi and militaristic influence from the German people's life, as was provided for by the decisions of the Crimea conference (Com. [L. A.] Govorov).

e) In Germany there are still plenty of . . . specialists who would be ready, given the chance and weakened control over Germany, to begin restoring Germany as a state and as a military–industrial force (Com. N. N. Voronov). . . .

6. To speed up Germany's reconstruction in order to use Germany against the Soviet Union.

b) Fearful of consolidation of growing anti-fascist and anti-capitalist forces, the Americans and British are in haste to "normalize" conditions for the resurrection of a reactionary, bourgeois Germany in order to prevent the complete rooting out of fascism (Com. Kaganovich).

c) The withdrawal of Soviet and other troops from Germany is in the interest of England and the U.S.A. since it gives [their] capitalists freedom of action and provides an opportunity to strengthen reactionary elements in all of Germany through private channels (Com. Kalinin). . . .

e) Economic and political unification of Germany under American leadership would also mean a military revival of Germany and, in a few years, a German–British–American war against the U.S.S.R. (Com. [S. A.] Lozovsky). . . .

3

THE [NIKOLAI] NOVIKOV
REPORT ["TELEGRAM"]

Washington, 27 September 1946

[All underlining replicates that of Foreign Minister Vyacheslav Molotov.]

U.S. Foreign Policy in the Postwar Period.

The foreign policy of the United States, which reflects the imperialist tendencies of American monopolistic capital, is characterized in the postwar period by a striving <u>for world supremacy</u>. This is the real meaning of the many statements by President Truman and other representatives of American ruling circles: that the United States has the right to lead the world. All the forces of American diplomacy—the army, the air force, the navy, industry, and science—are enlisted in the service of this foreign policy. For this purpose broad plans for expansion have been developed and are being implemented through diplomacy and the establishment of a system of naval and air bases stretching far beyond the boundaries of the United States, through the arms race, and through the creation of ever newer types of weapons.

1. a) The foreign policy of the United States is conducted now <u>in a situation that differs greatly</u> from the one that existed in the prewar period. . . .

b) . . . Europe has come out of the war with a completely dislocated economy, and the economic devastation that occurred in the course of the war cannot be overcome in a short time. All of the countries of Europe and Asia are experiencing a colossal need for consumer goods, industrial and transportation equipment, etc. Such a situation provides American monopolistic capital with <u>prospects for enormous shipments of goods and the importation of capital</u> into these countries—a circumstance that would permit it to infiltrate their national economies. . . .

c) ... [W]e have [also] seen a failure of calculations on the part of U.S. circles which assumed that the Soviet Union would be destroyed in the war or would come out of it so weakened that it would be forced to go begging to the United States for economic assistance. Had that happened, they would have been able to dictate conditions permitting the United States to carry out its expansion in Europe and Asia without hindrance from the USSR.

In actuality, despite all of the economic difficulties of the postwar period connected with the enormous losses inflicted by the war and the German fascist occupation, the Soviet Union continues to remain economically independent of the outside world and is rebuilding its national economy with its own forces.

At the same time the USSR's international position is currently stronger than it was in the prewar period. Thanks to the historical victories of Soviet weapons, the Soviet armed forces are located on the territory of Germany and other formerly hostile countries, thus guaranteeing that these countries will not be used again for an attack on the USSR. . . .

Such a situation in Eastern and Southeastern Europe cannot help but be regarded by the American imperialists as an obstacle in the path of the expansionist policy of the United States.

2. a) The foreign policy of the United States is not determined at present by the circles in the Democratic party that (as was the case during Roosevelt's lifetime) strive to strengthen the cooperation of the three great powers that constituted the basis of the anti–Hitler coalition during the war. The ascendance to power of President Truman, a politically unstable person but with certain conservative tendencies, and the subsequent appointment of [James] Byrnes as Secretary of State meant a strengthening of the influence on U.S. foreign policy of the most reactionary circles of the Democratic party. . . .

b) At the same time, there has been a decline in the influence on foreign policy of those who follow Roosevelt's course for cooperation among peace-loving countries. Such persons in the government, in Congress, and in the leadership of the Democratic party are being pushed farther and farther into the background. The contradictions in the field of foreign policy existing between the followers of [Henry] Wallace and [Claude] Pepper, on the one hand, and the adherents of the reactionary "bi-partisan" policy, on the other, were manifested with great clarity recently in the speech by Wallace that led to his resignation from the post of Secretary of Commerce. . . .

3. Obvious indications of the U.S. effort to establish world dominance are also to be found in the increase in military potential in peacetime and in the establishment of a large number of naval and air bases both in the United States and beyond its borders.

In the summer of 1946, for the first time in the history of the country, Congress passed a law on the establishment of a peacetime army, not on a volunteer basis but on the basis of universal military service. The size of the army, which is supposed to amount to about one million persons as of July 1, 1947, was also increased significantly. The size of the navy at the conclusion of the war decreased quite insignificantly in comparison with wartime. At the present time, the American navy occupies first place in the world, leaving England's navy far behind, to say nothing of those of other countries. . . .

The establishment of American bases on islands that are often 10,000 to 12,000 kilometers from the territory of the United States and are on the other side of the Atlantic and Pacific oceans clearly indicates the offensive nature of the strategic concepts of the commands of the U.S. army and navy. . . .

All of these facts show clearly that a decisive role in the realization of plans for world dominance by the United States is played by its armed forces.

4. a) One of the stages in the achievement of dominance over the world by the United States is its understanding with England concerning the partial division of the world on the basis of mutual concessions. The basic lines of the secret agreement between the United States and England regarding the division of the world consist, as shown by facts, in their agreement on the inclusion of Japan and China in the sphere of influence of the United States in the Far East, while the United States, for its part, has agreed not to hinder England either in resolving the Indian problem or in strengthening its influence in Siam and Indonesia. . . .

5. a) If the division of the world in the Far East between the United States and England may be considered an accomplished fact, it cannot be said that an analogous situation exists in the basin of the Mediterranean Sea and in the countries adjacent to it. . . . The United States . . . is not interested in providing assistance and support to the British Empire in this vulnerable point, but rather in its own more thorough penetration of the Mediterranean basin and Near East, to which the United States is attracted by the area's natural resources, primarily oil. . . .

c) The irregular nature of relations between England and the United States in the Near East is manifested in part also in the great activity of the American naval fleet in the eastern part of the Mediterranean Sea. Such activity cannot help but be in conflict with the basic interests of the British Empire. . . .

It must be kept in mind, however, that [recent] incidents . . . and the great interest that U.S. diplomacy displays in the problem of the [Turkish] straits have a double meaning. On the one hand, they indicate that the United States has decided to consolidate its position in the Mediterranean basin. . . . On the other hand, these incidents constitute a political and military demonstration against the Soviet Union. The strengthening of U.S. positions in the Near East . . . will therefore signify the emergence of a new threat to the security of the southern regions of the Soviet Union. . . .

7. a) The "hard-line" policy with regard to the USSR announced by Byrnes after the rapprochement of the reactionary Democrats with the Republicans is at present the main obstacle on the road to cooperation of the Great Powers. It consists mainly of the fact that in the postwar period the United States no longer follows a policy of strengthening cooperation among the Big Three (or Four) but rather has striven to undermine the unity of these countries. The objective has been to impose the will of other countries on the Soviet Union. . . .

b) The present policy of the American government with regard to the USSR is also directed at limiting or dislodging the influence of the Soviet Union from neighboring countries. In implementing this policy in former enemy or Allied countries adjacent to the USSR, the United States attempts, at various international conferences or directly in these countries themselves, to support reactionary forces with the purpose of creating obstacles to the process of democratization of these countries. In so doing, it also attempts to secure positions for the penetration of American capital into their economies. Such a policy is intended to weaken and overthrow the democratic governments in power there, which are friendly toward the USSR, and replace them in the future with new governments that would obediently carry out a policy dictated from the United States. In this policy, the United States receives full support from English diplomacy.

c) One of the most important elements in the general policy of the United States, which is directed toward limiting the international role of the USSR in the postwar world, is the policy with regard to Germany. In Germany, the United States is taking measures to strengthen reactionary forces for the purpose of opposing democratic reconstruction. Furthermore, it displays special insistence on accompanying this policy with completely inadequate measures for the demilitarization of Germany.

The American occupation policy does not have the objective of eliminating the remnants of German Fascism and rebuilding German political life on a democratic basis, so that Germany might cease to exist as an aggressive force. . . . Instead, the United States is considering the possibility of terminating the Allied occupation of German territory before the main tasks of the occupation—the demilitarization and democratization of Germany—have been implemented. This would create the prerequisites for the revival of an imperialistic Germany, which the United States plans to use in a future war on its side. One cannot help seeing that such a policy has a clearly outlined <u>anti-Soviet edge</u> and constitutes a serious danger to the cause of peace.

d) The numerous and extremely hostile statements by American government, political, and military figures with regard to the Soviet Union and its foreign policy are very characteristic of the current relationship between the ruling circles of the United States and the USSR. These statements are echoed in an even more unrestrained tone by the overwhelming majority of the American press organs. <u>Talk about a "third war,"</u> meaning a war against the Soviet Union, and even a direct call for this war—with the threat of using the atomic bomb—such is the content of the statements on relations with the Soviet Union by reactionaries at public meetings and in the press. At the present time, preaching war against the Soviet Union is not a monopoly of the far-right, yellow American press represented by the newspaper associations of Hearst and McCormick. This anti-Soviet campaign also has been joined by the "reputable" and "respectable" organs of the conservative press, such as the *New York Times* and *New York Herald Tribune.* . . .

The basic goal of this anti-Soviet campaign of American "public opinion" is to exert political pressure on the Soviet Union and compel it to make concessions. Another, no less important goal of the campaign is the attempt <u>to create an atmosphere of war psychosis</u> among the masses, who are weary of war, thus making it easier for the U.S. government to carry out measures for the maintenance of high military potential. It was in this very atmosphere that the law on universal military service in peacetime was passed by Congress, that the huge military budget was adopted, and that plans are being worked out for the construction of an extensive system of naval and air bases.

e) Of course, all of these measures for maintaining a high military potential are not goals in themselves. They are only intended <u>to prepare the conditions for winning world supremacy</u> in a new war, the date for which, to be sure, cannot be determined now by anyone, but which is contemplated by the most bellicose circles of American imperialism.

Careful note should be taken of the fact that the preparation by the United States for a future war is being conducted with the prospect of <u>war against the Soviet Union</u>, which in the eyes of American imperialists is the main obstacle in the path of the United States to world domination. This is indicated by facts such as the tactical training of the American army for war with the Soviet Union as the future opponent, the siting of American strategic bases in regions from which it is possible to launch strikes on Soviet territory, intensified training and strengthening of Arctic regions as close approaches to the USSR, and attempts to prepare Germany and Japan to use those countries in a war against the USSR.

4

THE MINISTER OF STATE SECURITY APPEALS FOR MEASURES TO CLOSE DOWN BRITISH PROPAGANDA IN THE U.S.S.R.

2 November 1946

To Comrade A[ndrei] Zhdanov,

The MGB [Ministry of State Security] is receiving information about negative influence of the journal *Britansky Soyuznik* [*British Ally*], published in the Soviet Union, on some contingents of Soviet readers.

Systematically published in the pages of this journal are articles which directly or indirectly pursue one goal—to create an impression among Soviet readers about advantages of daily life, culture, and "democracy" in the "British Commonwealth" as compared to the Soviet Union. For example:

a) in a series of articles on the new system of social security . . . , a notion is being foisted upon readers about the well-being of English workers and the unremitting concern of the British government about them;

b) systematically published are articles depicting unprecedented flowering of science in British colonies, with special attention given to work of native scientists and the allegedly favorable conditions under which they work;

c) in all kinds of reports and short stories of outwardly innocent nature, British everyday life is being described in such a way and with such detail as to create among Soviet readers an impression of unusually high material level [standard of living] of an average Englishman;

d) a number of articles seek to justify British policy in Greece, Indonesia, Iran, Egypt, etc.;

e) the so-called weekly reviews of press and events published in every issue of the journal usually contain biased, falsified interpretation of international problems camouflaged by an outwardly objective presentation of "facts."

The journal systematically publishes detailed reports on statements of the leaders of the British government and some reactionary members of the Parliament containing distorted depictions of the Soviet government's foreign policy.

The journal *Britansky Soyuznik* has a circulation of fifty thousand copies and is widely disseminated in the Soviet Union. . . . A large percentage of the journal's circulation (10,300 copies) is distributed through retail sales and gets into hands of accidental readers.

Among the journal subscribers one can find teachers, professors, and writers.

Articles published in the journal are often assessed incorrectly by some readers and in a number of cases some of them, referring to the journal's information, actually contribute to dissemination of the British propaganda in their surroundings. Thus, a faculty member of the Peat Institute, V. Rakovsky, using "facts" from *Britansky Soyuznik*, stated that bourgeois–democratic regimes have a number of advantages over socialism, and that natives in the British colonies live well and have no hostility toward Englishmen. In his words, the allies' military equipment and their successes in the last war were superior to the Soviet ones. . . .

There have been cases in which some military personnel sent letters to the journal editors expressing their warmest gratitude for the publication of "the indispensably valuable material that helps to really appraise our ally."

Such uncritical attitude toward *Britansky Soyuznik* is explained in part by some readers' conviction that this journal is being censored by proper Soviet authorities and that therefore its materials are objective. The journal readers are also disoriented by the absence of a reference to the journal's being an organ of the British Foreign Office; that is why they mistake it for a Soviet publication.

Probably it would be expedient to charge the Department of Propaganda and Agitation of the Central Committee with consideration of the problem of *Britansky Soyuznik* and with mapping out practical measures to suppress the influence of this harmful journal on Soviet readers and restrict its distribution through retail sale.

Requesting your instructions,

V[ictor]Abakumov

Sent to: Stalin, Zhdanov

5

INSTRUCTIONS FOR THE SOVIET DELEGATION TO THE MEETING OF FOREIGN MINISTERS IN PARIS, JUNE 25, 1947

1. The Soviet delegation's preliminary task is to obtain from the French and British foreign ministers information on the nature and conditions of the proposed economic assistance to Europe. The delegation should clarify in particular the questions about scale, forms, and terms of this assistance.

2. The delegation should also request from the French and British delegations information on British–French talks in Paris on June 17–18, and in particular should ask to be familiarized with their experts' documentation.

3. Since the delegation can hardly expect to get satisfactory information from the French and British ministers on the nature and conditions of American assistance to Europe, the delegation should propose that the ministers send a request to the U.S. government about American economic aid and credits (i.e., their size, interest, time limits, etc.), as well as about whether European countries can be confident of Congressional approval of the aid proposed by the administration.

4. The Soviet delegation must be guided by the presumption that the matter of American economic assistance to Europe is to be handled not through compiling a [common] economic program for European countries, but through identifying their economic requirements and needs for American assistance (in credits and goods) and compiling individual requests on a country-by-country basis. In following this line the delegation should not allow the ministers' meeting to concentrate on investigating and inspecting European countries' resources. Such attempts are to be rejected on the

grounds that the meeting's main purpose is to identify the needs of European countries and the readiness of the U.S.A. to satisfy them, but not to compile economic plans for European countries.

5. When the discussion gets to the point of identifying European countries' needs (requests) for American assistance and thereby to the problem of enlarging the number of countries involved, the Soviet delegation should propose to give priority to those European countries which were subject to German occupation and which contributed to the cause of victory. In case French and British delegations insist on including other European countries in this discussion, the Soviet delegation may give consent to their participation with the proviso that former enemy countries—Italy, Romania, Bulgaria, Hungary, Austria, and Finland—are invited only for consultation.

6. When discussing specific proposals related to American aid to Europe, the Soviet delegation should object to those conditions of this aid that might infringe upon the sovereignty and the economic independence of European countries.

7. At the discussions the delegation should object to attempts to use German economic resources for the needs of European countries as well as attempts to provide U.S. economic assistance to Germany since the German question can be discussed only by the Council of Foreign Ministers and not by this meeting.

6

RECORD OF I[OSEF] V[ISSARIONIVICH] STALIN'S CONVERSATION WITH THE CZECHOSLOVAK GOVERNMENT DELEGATION ON THE ISSUE OF THEIR POSITION REGARDING THE MARSHALL PLAN AND THE PROSPECTS FOR ECONOMIC COOPERATION WITH THE U.S.S.R.

Moscow, 9 July 1947

SECRET

Present: Comrade I. V. Stalin, Comrade V. M. Molotov, Prime Minister of [the] Czechoslovak Republic [K.] Gottwald, Minister of Foreign Affairs [J.] Masaryk, Minister of Justice [P.] Drtina, General Secretary of the Ministry of Foreign Affairs of the Czechoslovak Republic Gendrih [Heidrich?], and Czechoslovak Ambassador Gorak [Horák].

Comrade Stalin asks Gottwald, what questions do you have for us?

Gottwald responds that they would like to discuss three main questions:

1. participation at the Paris Conference on July 12, 1947,
2. the Czechoslovak Republic's treaty with France,
3. trade negotiations between the Czechoslovak delegation and the [Soviet] Ministry of Foreign Trade.

Comrade Stalin asks Gottwald which question they would like to begin with.

Gottwald responds that they would prefer to begin with the first question.

Comrade Stalin says that approximately two or three days after comrade V. M. Molotov returned from Paris, the Yugoslavs asked us what should they do—whether to take part in the conference on July 12 in Paris, or not. They expressed their opinion that they were thinking about refusing to participate in that conference. Later on Romania and Bulgaria addressed us with the same question. Initially, we thought that we should recommend that they go to that conference and then ruin it. We were convinced, on the basis of the materials that we received from our ambassadors, that under the cover of credit assistance to Europe they were organizing something like a western bloc against the Soviet Union. Then we made a firm decision and announced our opinion to everybody that we are against participation in this conference. . . .

We were surprised that you decided to participate in this conference. For us, this issue is the issue of friendship between the Soviet Union and the Czechoslovak Republic. Objectively, you are helping, whether you want it or not, . . . to isolate the Soviet Union. Look what is happening. All the countries which have friendly relations with us are not going to participate in this conference, while Czechoslovakia, which also enjoys friendly relations with us, will. Therefore, they will decide that the friendship between the Czechoslovak Republic and the Soviet Union is not all that solid, if it was so easy to put Czechoslovakia on the side of isolating the Soviet Union, against the Soviet Union. This would be seen as a victory over the Soviet Union. Our people and we will not understand this. You need to rescind your decision, you need to refuse to participate in this conference—and the sooner you do it, the better.

Masaryk asks Comrade Stalin to take into account that the Czechoslovak government was aware of the dependence of the Czechoslovak industry on the West. Representatives of industry believed it was expedient to participate in the conference, so that they would not miss an opportunity to get credits. At the same time, the Polish delegation arrived in Prague and told us that they decided to participate in the conference in Paris. As a result, the decision of the Czechoslovak government to participate in the conference in Paris on July 12, 1947 was taken unanimously by all political parties.

Then Masaryk continues that he was not going to deny the responsibility that he was also in favor of participating in the conference. However, he was asking [Stalin] to take into account that by making this decision, neither he nor the government of the Czechoslovak Republic wanted to do anything bad against the Soviet Union. In conclusion, Masaryk asks Comrade Stalin and Comrade Molotov to help to make their situation easier.

Comrade Molotov notes to Masaryk that even the fact of your participation in the conference by itself would be against the Soviet Union.

Masaryk responds that he, the government, all the parties, and the entire Czechoslovak people do not want to do, and will not do, anything against the Soviet Union.

Comrade Stalin says that we never doubted and do not doubt your friendship toward us, but objectively it looks different in reality.

Drtina says that he, on his [own] behalf and on behalf of all members of the party to which he belongs, states that if our decision is against the Soviet Union, then my party does not want to, and will not do it. My party will not do anything which would give any reason to interpret our actions as being against the Soviet Union. At the same time, Drtina is asking [Stalin] to take into account that the Czechoslovak Republic . . . depends on western countries for up to 60 percent of its exports and imports.

Comrade Stalin notes that Czechoslovakia has a passive trade balance with the West, and that Czechoslovakia has to export its currency to the West.

Drtina says that he has in mind the volume of import and export, and that the people of the Czechoslovak Republics [*sic*] believe that if we do not participate in that conference, then we would not get the credits, and, therefore, we would lower the living standards of our population because the trade between the Czechoslovak Republic and the Soviet Union has sharply decreased in 1947. Drtina finishes his comments with the request to help them get out of the existing situation, to increase trade with Czechoslovakia.

Comrade Stalin says that we need some goods which we can get from Czechoslovakia, for example, pipes for petroleum industry, rails for narrow railroad cars, and so on, and we can help Czechoslovakia, i.e. we could sign a trade treaty which would be beneficial for both sides.

Gottwald says that Czechoslovakia exports a lot of consumer and textile goods to the West, and the Soviet Union, so far, has not been buying them.

Comrade Stalin says, why, we will.

Gottwald asks Comrade Stalin and Comrade Molotov to write it down in the communique, so that the others would see what the Soviet Union is willing to give them as a result of this visit of the Czechoslovak delegation.

Masaryk and Drtina ask Comrade Stalin and Comrade Molotov to help them to formulate their refusal to participate in the conference in Paris.

Comrade Stalin says that they need to see how the Bulgarians formulated their refusal, to consult among themselves, and to draft needed formulations of the reasons for the refusal. . . .

Gottwald says that he has several smaller questions, and that he will write to Comrade Stalin about them.

Comrade Stalin agrees.

In concluding the conversation, Comrade Stalin reminds Gottwald and all members of the Czechoslovak delegation that it is necessary to refuse to participate in the conference in Paris today, i.e. July 10, 1947 [the conference having lasted beyond midnight].

Masaryk says that they will discuss this question tomorrow [presumably, for Masaryk, the 10th], and only toward evening would they be able to send their opinion to the government.

Comrade Stalin says that they would need to do it immediately.

The delegation thanks Comrade Stalin and Comrade Molotov for the reception and for the needed advice, and promises to do everything as they agreed to do.

Recorded by BODROV

7

RECORD OF THE MEETING OF COMRADE I[OSEF] V[ISSARIONIVICH] STALIN WITH THE SECRETARY OF THE CENTRAL COMMITTEE OF THE FRENCH COMMUNIST PARTY [MAURICE] THOREZ

Moscow, 18 November 1947

[Also] Present: Molotov, Suslov.

[Thorez begins the conversation with an expression of respect and gratitude to Comrade Stalin on behalf of all members of French Communist Party (FCP) and the Central Committee (CC) of the FCP.]

Com[rade] Stalin asks jocularly if Thorez is thanking him for the fact that in Warsaw [at the meeting of the Cominform in September 1947] the French communists were berated. . . .

Thorez responds that the Communist Party of France is all too grateful for having been told about its shortcomings. . . .

Thorez says that the estimate of the situation presented at the conference of nine communist parties is being brilliantly corroborated in France. In particular, the interference of the Americans in the country is increasing, economic difficulties are worsening, class struggle is growing more acute. The French Communist Party, according to the instructions of the conference of the nine, is waging a struggle in defense of the country's independence and is fighting alone against the entire coalition of reactionary forces. At the last municipal elections the [FCP] managed to preserve and even partially increase the number of its voters. . . .

Com. Stalin says that the struggle against the Marshall Plan should not be put forward too crudely. The [noncommunist] socialists will say that the communists are against accepting loans from Americans. The answer should be: no, not against. Communists are for loans, but on such conditions that will not harm national sovereignty. Communists are against the enslaving conditions that impinge upon the independence of France. This is how the Communists should formulate the issue. . . .

Thorez says that, [at] the conference of the nine communist parties, ... representatives of some fraternal communist parties sometimes subjected the FCP to unfair criticism. For instance, in particular the Yugoslav comrades reproached the [FCP] for having joined the resistance struggle all too late and for not ensuring the people's power at the moment of France's liberation. Thorez says that, in his opinion, this criticism is not justified. In order to gain a chance to correctly inform the party masses of France and not to disorient them, Thorez would like to know the opinion of Com. Stalin on this issue. ... The fact that the [FCP] failed to seize power during the liberation of the country in August 1944 is explained by [several] reasons of an international nature. The [FCP] at that time directed its efforts to advocate the speediest opening of the second front, intensification of the war and bringing closer a victory over Germany. The [FCP] was in the rearguard of American and British armed forces.

Com. Stalin says that it would be completely different story had the Red Army been positioned in France. ...

Com. Stalin says that the French communists could not [have] seize[d] power at that time. Even had they seized it, they would have lost it then, because of the presence of Anglo–American troops in the country.

... Com. Stalin says that the Yugoslav comrades ... owe much to the fact that their country was liberated by the Red Army. Had Churchill delayed opening the second front in northern France by a year, the Red Army would have come to France. Com. Stalin says that we [in Moscow] toyed with the idea of reaching Paris. ...

Com. Stalin says that, of course, the Anglo-Americans could not afford such a scandal, that the Red Army should liberate Paris while they sat on the shores of Africa.

Thorez says that he can assure Com. Stalin that the French people would have enthusiastically received the Red Army.

Com. Stalin observes that then it would have been quite a different picture. ... [Then Stalin inquires if the French communists have stockpiles of arms. Do they consider it necessary to have them?]

Thorez responds that the CC of the [FCP] authorized two comrades ... to deal specifically with this issue. ... They conduct work among old guerrillas, create organizations of paramilitary nature. The [FCP] managed to conceal a whole number of depots with armaments and ammunition.

Com. Stalin says that one must have armaments and organization if one does not want to become disarmed before the enemy. Communists could be attacked and then they should fight back. There can be all kinds of situations. Com. Stalin says that we [the Soviet Union] have arms and we can give them, if it becomes necessary. . . .

8

REPORT BY L. P. BERIA AND I. V. KURCHATOV TO I. V. STALIN ON PRELIMINARY DATA RECEIVED DURING THE ATOMIC BOMB TEST

The testing area 30 August 1949
(170 km west Top Secret
of Semipalatinsk) (Special Importance)
To Comrade Stalin I.V.

This is to report to you that due to the efforts of many Soviet scientists, designers, engineers, managers, and workers of our industry over four years of strenuous work, your assignment to create a Soviet atomic bomb has been fulfilled.

The creation of the A–bomb in our country has been achieved thanks to your daily attention, care, and help in [finding the] solution of this problem.

Being reported are preliminary data on the results of the test of the first copy of plutonium-charged A–bomb that was designed and built by the First Chief Directorate of the U.S.S.R. Council of Ministers under scientific guidance of Academician Kurchatov and the bomb's chief designer, corresponding member of the U.S.S.R. Academy of Sciences, Professor Khariton:

On August 29, 1949 at 4 A.M. Moscow time (7 A.M. local time), in a remote steppe region of the Kazakh Soviet Socialist Republic 170 km west of Semipalatinsk, at the specially constructed and equipped testing ground, there was obtained the explosion of the U.S.S.R.'s first atomic bomb, [one with] exceptional destructive and striking power.

The atomic explosion was recorded with special instruments as well as through personal observation of a large group of scientists, military and other experts, including members of the Special Committee, Comrades Beria, Kurchatov, Pervukhin, Zavenyagin and Makhnev, who took a direct part in the test.

Among experts there was Physicist Mesheryakov, who was one of our observers at the Bikini atomic bomb test.

I. OBSERVATION OF THE ATOMIC EXPLOSION

The phenomenon observed by all the participants leaves no doubt that the explosion was really an atomic one since it was accompanied by all the characteristics of a full-fledged atomic explosion including:

a) formation of the shock-wave of enormous destructive power;
b) formation of intense emission of light [modern term: thermal radiation] which had huge incendiary and destructive power non-existent in usual explosives;
c) formation of intensive initial nuclear radiation (of neutron and gamma-rays) possessing specific destructive effects and characteristic only of atomic explosions.

The characteristic features of the explosion of August 29 recorded by scientists and military observers were the following:

1. Precisely at the designated time at the bomb installation site (on the 30 meters high steel tower at the testing ground center) there occurred an atomic burst many times brighter than the sun.
   In ¾ of a second the burst took the shape of a hemisphere expanding to dimensions of 400-500 meters in diameter.
2. Concurrently with the light burst there formed an explosion cloud reaching in 2-3 minutes several km in height and breaking into the usual rain clouds that covered the sky during the test.
3. The light burst was followed by the emergence of an atomic explosion shock-wave of enormous power.

The explosion fireball and shock-wave thunder were observed by the experts and witnesses over a distance of 60-70 km away from the explosion site. . . .

CONCLUSIONS

Scientific-technical data received during the first 36 hours after the explosion demonstrate that the A-bomb design . . . has the following characteristics:

a) the explosion yield is equivalent to a simultaneous explosion of no less than 10,000 tons of TNT;

b) the shock–wave caused the complete destruction of industrial installa-
tions and brick houses within a radius of 1,500 m (i.e., 7 square km, or
700 hectares) and complete destruction of wooden buildings within a radius of 3 km (i.e., 12-30 square km . . .);

c) the bomb has . . . radioactive effect on living organisms, creating a zone
of lethal danger to humans within a radius of 1,200 m from the epicen-
ter (i.e., 5 square km . . .) and a not yet fully researched but clearly haz-
ardous zone of no less than 1,500 m (i.e., 7 square km . . .). . . .

The full report on the test results will be submitted to you in 1 to 1.5
months.

For the English translation of Stalin's order of August 20, 1945, setting up
the Special Committee, see *Cold War International History Project Bulletin*, no.
6–7: 269–270, which can now be supplemented by publication in English
of point thirteen (previously classified and now released for the cited volume on the U.S.S.R. Atomic Project (p. 13):

> 13. To charge Com. Beria with organizing intelligence work abroad in or-
> der to obtain more comprehensive technical/economic information on ura-
> nium industry and A-bombs; to put Com. Beria in charge of all intelligence
> work in this field conducted by intelligence agencies (NKGB [i.e., People's
> Commissariat of State Security], RUKA [i.e., Red Army Intelligence Direc-
> torate], and others).

ACKNOWLEDGMENTS

CITATIONS FOR DOCUMENTS ACCOMPANYING
SECTION 1, THE AMERICAN PERSPECTIVE

1. "The Atlantic Charter," *The Public Papers and Addresses of Franklin D. Roosevelt, 1941*, comp. Samuel I. Rosenman (New York: Harper, 1950), pp. 314–315.
2. "Comments on the Yalta Conference," John Foster Dulles papers (box 27, Vandenberg file), Selig G. Mudd Manuscript Library, Princeton University Archives.
3. "Kennan's Long Telegram," *Containment: Documents on American Policy and Strategy, 1945–1950*, ed. Thomas H. Etzold and John Lewis Gaddis (New York: Columbia University Press, 1978), pp. 50–63.
4. "Byrnes's Speech," *Vital Speeches*, 15 September 1946, pp. 706–709.
5. "Hoover's Speech," *Vital Speeches*, 15 October 1946, pp. 10–11.
6. "Wallace's Speech," *Vital Speeches*, 1 October 1946, pp. 738–741.
7. "Truman's Speech," *Public Papers of the Presidents of the United States: Harry S. Truman 1947* (Washington, D.C.: U.S. Government Printing Office, 1963), pp. 176–180.

CITATIONS FOR DOCUMENTS ACCOMPANYING
SECTION 2, THE RUSSIAN PERSPECTIVE

(Note: Basic translations were made as indicated; C. Earl Edmondson provided editorial assistance in the translation of documents 1, 2, 4, 5, and 8.)

1. "Stalin to 'Politburo Four,'" Archive of the President of the Russian Federation (APRF), fond 45, opis 1, delo 771, listy 2–3. Trans. Vladimir Pechatnov and Vladislav Zubok (note: unpublished archival material).

2. "A Compilation of Comments on Draft Treaties," *SSSR i German-skii Vopros*, vol. 2, *3 May 1945–3 August 1946*, comp. G. Kynin and J. Laufer (Moscow: Mezhdunarodnye Otnoshenya, 2000), pp. 575–579. Trans. Vladimir Pechatnov.

3. "The Novikov Report," in *Origins of the Cold War: The Novikov, Kennan, and Roberts "Long Telegrams" of 1946*, rev. ed., ed. Kenneth M. Jensen, trans. John Glad (Washington, D.C.: U.S. Institute of Peace, 1991), pp. 3–16.

4. "Minister of State Security Appeals . . . to Close Down British Propaganda," Russian State Archive of Sociopolitical History (RGASPI), fond 17, opis 125, delo 436, listy 27–29. Trans. Vladimir Pechatnov (note: unpublished archival material).

5. "Instructions for the Soviet Delegation to the Meeting of Foreign Ministers," G. Takhnenko, "Anatomia odnogo politicheskogo reshenia [The Anatomy of One Political Decision]," *Mezhdunarodnaya Zhizn* [*International Life*], no. 5 (1992): 123–124. Trans. Vladimir Pechatnov.

6. "Record of . . . Stalin's Conversation with the Czechoslovak Government Delegation," in *Stalin and the Cold War, 1945–1953: A Cold War International History Project Document Reader*, comp. and ed. Christian F. Ostermann et al., in conjunction with a conference conducted at Yale University, 23–26 September 1999, pp. 392–394. Trans. Svetlana Savranskaya (with minor changes by the authors for the purpose of clarification). Original source: G. P. Murashko et al., eds., *Vostochnaia Evropa*, vol. 1, pp. 672–675 (APRF, f. 45, op. 1, d. 393, l. 101-OS).

7. "Record of Meeting of . . . Stalin with . . . Thorez," in *Stalin and the Cold War, 1945–1953: A Cold War International History Project Document Reader*, comp. and ed. Christian F. Ostermann et al., in conjunction with a conference conducted at Yale University, 23–26 September 1999, pp. 403–407. Trans. Vladislav Zubok (with minor changes by the authors for the purpose of clarification). Original source: Mikhail Narinskii, "Torez, 1944–1947: Noviie materiali," *Novaia i noveishaia istoriia*, no. 1 (January–February 1996): 26–30 (APRF, f. 45, op. 1, d. 392, pp. 83–106).

8. "Report . . . to . . . Stalin on . . . Atomic Bomb Test" [Document N8], in *Atomnyi Proect SSSR: Dokumenty i Materialy* [*U.S.S.R.*

Atomic Project: Documents and Materials], vol. 2, bk. 1, *Atomic Bomb, 1945–1954*, ed. L. D. Ryabev (Moscow: RF Ministry of Atomic Energy, RFNC–VNIEF, 1999), pp. 639–643. Trans. Vladimir Pechatnov.

SELECTED READINGS

PRIMARY SOURCES

Acheson, Dean G. *Present at the Creation: My Years at the State Department.* New York: Norton, 1969.

Djilas, Milovan. *Conversations with Stalin.* Trans. Michael B. Petrovich. New York: Harcourt, Brace, 1962.

Etzold, Thomas H., and John Lewis Gaddis, eds. *Containment: Documents on American Policy and Strategy, 1945–1950.* New York: Columbia University Press, 1978.

Harriman, W. Averell, and Elie Abel. *Special Envoy to Churchill and Stalin, 1941–1946.* New York: Random House, 1975.

Kennan, George F. *Memoirs: 1925–1950.* Boston: Little, Brown, 1967.

Koenker, Diane, and Ronald Bachman, eds. *Revelations from the Russian Archives: Documents in English Translation.* Washington, D.C.: U.S. Library of Congress, 1997.

Procacci, Giuliano, et al., eds. *The Cominform: Minutes of the Three Conferences 1947/1948/1949.* Milan: Fondazione Giangiacomo Feltrinelli, 1994.

Resis, Albert, ed. *Molotov Remembers: Inside Kremlin Politics: Conversations with Felix Chuev.* Chicago: Ivan R. Dee, 1993.

Truman, Harry S. *Memoirs.* Vol. 1, *Year of Decisions.* Garden City, N.Y.: Doubleday, 1955.

SECONDARY SOURCES

Cohen, Warren I., ed. *The Cambridge History of American Foreign Relations.* Vol. 4, *America in the Age of Soviet Power, 1945–1991.* New York: Cambridge University Press, 1993.

Dallek, Robert. *Franklin D. Roosevelt and American Foreign Policy, 1932–1945.* New York: Oxford University Press, 1979.

Divine, Robert. *Second Chance: The Triumph of Internationalism in America during World War II.* New York: Atheneum, 1967.

Donovan, Robert J. *Conflict and Crisis: The Presidency of Harry S. Truman, 1945–1948.* New York: Norton, 1977.

Dunn, Dennis J. *Caught between Roosevelt and Stalin: America's Ambassadors to Moscow.* Lexington: University Press of Kentucky, 1998.

Fawcett, Louise. *Iran and the Cold War: The Azerbaijan Crisis of 1946.* New York: Cambridge University Press, 1992.

Filene, Peter G. *Americans and the Soviet Experiment, 1917–1933.* Cambridge, Mass.: Harvard University Press, 1967.

Fousek, John. *To Lead the Free World: American Nationalism and the Cultural Roots of the Cold War.* Chapel Hill: University of North Carolina Press, 2000.

Gaddis, John Lewis. *Russia, the Soviet Union and the United States: An Interpretive History.* 2nd ed. New York: McGraw-Hill, 1990.

———. *Strategies of Containment: A Critical Appraisal of Postwar American National Security Policy.* New York: Oxford University Press, 1982.

———. *The United States and the Origins of the Cold War, 1941–1947.* New York: Columbia University Press, 1972.

———. *We Now Know: Rethinking Cold War History.* New York: Oxford University Press, 1997.

Goncharov, Sergei N., John W. Lewis, and Xue Litai. *Uncertain Partners: Stalin, Mao, and the Korean War.* Stanford, Calif.: Stanford University Press, 1993.

Gori, Francesco, and Silvio Pons, eds. *The Soviet Union and Europe in the Cold War, 1945–1953.* New York: St. Martin's, 1996.

Hamby, Alonzo. *Man of the People: A Life of Harry S. Truman.* New York: Oxford University Press, 1995.

Harbutt, Fraser J. *The Iron Curtain: Churchill, America, and the Origins of the Cold War.* New York: Oxford University Press, 1986.

Haynes, John Earl. *Red Scare or Red Menace? American Communism and Anticommunism in the Cold War Era.* Chicago: Ivan R. Dee, 1996.

Haynes, John Earl, and Harvey Klehr. *Verona: Decoding Soviet Espionage in America.* New Haven, Conn.: Yale University Press, 1999.

Heale, M. J. *American Anticommunism: Combating the Enemy Within, 1830–1970.* Baltimore, Md.: Johns Hopkins University Press, 1990.

Hess, Gary. *The United States' Emergence As a Southeast Asian Power, 1940–1950.* New York: Columbia University Press, 1987.

Hogan, Michael J. *The Marshall Plan: America, Britain, and the Reconstruction of Europe, 1947–1952.* New York: Cambridge University Press, 1987.

Holloway, David. *Stalin and the Bomb: The Soviet Union and Atomic Energy, 1939–1956.* New Haven, Conn.: Yale University Press, 1994.

Klehr, Harvey, John Earl Haynes, and Fridrikh Igorevich Firsov. *The Secret World of American Communism.* New Haven, Conn.: Yale University Press, 1995.

Kimball, Warren F. *The Juggler: Franklin Roosevelt As Wartime Statesman.* Princeton, N.J.: Princeton University Press, 1991.

Kuniholm, Bruce R. *The Origins of the Cold War in the Near East.* Princeton, N.J.: Princeton University Press, 1980.

Larson, Deborah Welch. *Origins of Containment: A Psychological Explanation.* Princeton, N.J.: Princeton University Press, 1985.

Leffler, Melvyn P. *A Preponderance of Power: National Security, the Truman Administration, and the Cold War.* Stanford, Calif.: Stanford University Press, 1992.

Leffler, Melvyn P., and David S. Painter, eds. *Origins of the Cold War: An International History.* London: Routledge, 1994.

Levering, Ralph B. *American Opinion and the Russian Alliance, 1939–1945.* Chapel Hill: University of North Carolina Press, 1976.

———. *The Cold War: A Post–Cold War History.* Arlington Heights, Ill.: Harlan Davidson, 1994.

Lucas, Scott. *Freedom's War: The American Crusade against the Soviet Union.* New York: New York University Press, 1999.

Lundestad, Geir. *The American "Empire" and Other Studies of U.S. Foreign Policy in Comparative Perspective.* Oxford: Oxford University Press, 1991.

Maddux, Thomas. *Years of Estrangement: American Relations with the Soviet Union, 1933–1941.* Tallahassee: University Presses of Florida, 1980.

Mastny, Vojtech. *The Cold War and Soviet Insecurity: The Stalin Years.* New York: Oxford University Press, 1996.

Mayers, David. *George Kennan and the Dilemmas of U.S. Foreign Policy.* New York: Oxford University Press, 1988.

Messer, Robert. *The End of an Alliance: James F. Byrnes, Roosevelt, Truman, and the Origins of the Cold War.* Chapel Hill: University of North Carolina Press, 1982.

Miscamble, Wilson D. *George F. Kennan and the Making of American Foreign Policy, 1947–1950.* Princeton, N.J.: Princeton University Press, 1992.

Naimark, Norman M. *The Russians in Germany: A History of the Soviet Zone of Occupation, 1945–1949.* Cambridge, Mass.: Harvard University Press, 1995.

Naimark, Norman M., and Leonid Gibianskii, eds. *The Establishment of Communist Regimes in Eastern Europe, 1944–1949.* Boulder, Colo.: Westview, 1997.

Ninkovich, Frank. *The Wilsonian Century: U.S. Foreign Policy since 1900.* Chicago: University of Chicago Press, 1999.

Paterson, Thomas G. *Cold War Critics: Alternatives to American Foreign Policy in the Truman Years.* Chicago: Quadrangle, 1971.

———, ed. *On Every Front: The Making and Unmaking of the Cold War.* New York: Norton, 1992.

Pechatnov, Vladimir O. " 'The Allies Are Pressing on You to Break Your Will . . .': Foreign Policy Correspondence between Stalin, Molotov and Other Politburo Members (September 1945–December 1946)." Cold War International History Project, Working Paper No. 26. Washington, D.C.: Woodrow Wilson International Center for Scholars, 1999.

Sherwin, Martin J. *A World Destroyed: Hiroshima and the Origins of the Nuclear Arms Race.* New York: Vintage, 1987.

Smith, Tony. *America's Mission: The United States and the Worldwide Struggle for Democracy in the Twentieth Century*. Princeton, N.J.: Princeton University Press, 1994.

Stueck, William Whitney, Jr. *The Road to Confrontation: American Policy toward China and Korea, 1947–1950*. Chapel Hill: University of North Carolina Press, 1981.

Tanenhaus, Sam. *Whitaker Chambers: A Biography*. New York: Random House, 1998.

Taubman, William. *Stalin's American Policy: From Entente to Détente to Cold War*. New York: Norton, 1982.

Walker, J. Samuel. *Henry A. Wallace and American Foreign Policy*. Westport, Conn.: Greenwood, 1976.

Weinstein, Allen, and Alexander Vassiliev. *The Haunted Wood: Soviet Espionage in America—The Stalin Era*. New York: Random House, 1999.

Westad, Odd Arne. *Cold War and Revolution: Soviet–American Rivalry and the Origins of the Chinese Civil War, 1944–1946*. New York: Columbia University Press, 1993.

———, ed. *Reviewing the Cold War: Approaches, Interpretations, Theory*. London: Frank Cass, 2000.

Woods, Randall B., and Howard Jones. *Dawning of the Cold War: The United States' Quest for Order*. Athens: University of Georgia Press, 1991.

Yergin, Daniel. *Shattered Peace: The Origins of the Cold War*. Boston: Houghton Mifflin, 1977.

Zubkova, Elena. *Russia after the War: Hopes, Illusions and Disappointment, 1945–1957*. Armonk, N.Y.: Sharpe, 1998.

Zubok, Vladislav, and Constantine Pleshakov. *Inside the Kremlin's Cold War: From Stalin to Khrushchev*. Cambridge, Mass.: Harvard University Press, 1996.

INDEX

Abakumov, Victor, 166
Acheson, Dean, 40, 44, 50, 52, 150
African American opinion, 40, 45. *See also* National Association for the Advancement of Colored People, U.S.; White, Walter
Albania, 128, 135
Allied Control Council. *See* Germany
Alperowitz, Gar, 34
American Federation of Labor, 9, 10, 22. *See also* labor unions, U.S.
American Legion, 10, 46
American people: charitable giving to Russia by, 1; sacrifices in defense of freedom, 62. *See also* public opinion, U.S.
Americans for Democratic Action, 58
Amerika, 134
Andreev, A. A., 157–58
anticommunism, U.S., 3–6, 10, 44–48, 58, 61. *See also* public opinion, U.S.
Armenia, 103
Asia, 42–44, 50–51, 56, 60, 62, 90, 98, 103, 106, 112, 162. *See also specific countries*
Association of Catholic Trade Unionists, U.S., 46
Atlantic Charter, 14, 16, 26, 27, 65–66
Atlee, Clement, 55

atomic energy: failed U.S. efforts to achieve international control, 35–36; U.S.S.R. and, 121–22
Atomic Energy Commission. *See* United Nations
atomic weapons, 10, 21, 78; Soviet spying on secret bomb-building project, 10, 33, 93, 145, 178; Stalin and, 93–94, 105, 107, 145–46; tested, in U.S., 56; tested, in U.S.S.R., 145, 176–78; Truman's decision to build hydrogen bombs, 57; use of in war against Japan, 34, 105; U.S.S.R. and, 107, 125–26, 176–78
Austria, 25, 48, 53, 120, 168

Balkans. *See* Europe, southeastern
Benelux countries, 137–38
Beneš, Eduard, 135
Bentley, Elizabeth, 38
Beria, Lavrenti, 107, 116, 155, 176, 178
Berle, Adolf A., Jr., 10
Berlin, 26, 49, 103, 141; Soviet blockade of, 54–56, 138–39
Bessarabia, 89
Bevin, Ernest, 36, 92, 107–08
Black Sea, 103
Bolshevism (Leninist-Bolshevism), 88–89, 148

books, U.S., 18, 76
Bornholm, Danish island of, 124
Bretton Woods Conference, 38; U.S.S.R. and, 95, 115
Britansky Soyuznik [British Ally], 165–66; alluded to, 134
British Broadcasting Company, jammed in U.S.S.R., 134
Browder, Earl, 9, 13, 21, 32
Brussels Pact, 137
Budenz, Louis, 45
Bukovina, northern, 89
Bulgaria, 35–36, 42, 82, 91, 94, 104, 106–07, 112, 128, 131–32, 136–37, 155, 168
business organizations, U.S., 2, 10–11
Byrnes, James F., 27, 34, 39, 40, 47–48, 52, 60, 112, 157; at London Conference (1945), 35, 107–08; at Moscow Conference (1945), 36; Novikov mentions, 161, 163; at Potsdam Conference, 33; speech criticizing Soviet expansionism in February 1946, 37, 116; speech in Stuttgart, Germany, in September 1946, 41–42, 74–75, 120

Canada, 3, 38, 55, 56
Catholic World, 22, 45
Catholics. *See* Roman Catholic Church; Roman Catholics, Europe
Central Intelligence Agency, U.S.: covert operations, 141–42
Chamber of Commerce, U.S., 10
Chambers, Whittaker, 10
Changes in the Economy of Capitalism, 130
Charlotte Observer, 45
Chiang Kai-shek, 43–44
Chicago Tribune, 12
Chile, 50
China, 14, 40, 43–44, 48, 50, 56, 57, 95; excluded from postwar discussions on Europe, 113, 155; seen in West's

sphere by U.S.S.R., 91–92, 162; U.S.S.R. and civil war in, 111–12, 146–47
Churchill, Winston: criticizes Soviet violations of Yalta agreements, 28; decisions on Poland at Yalta criticized, 67–68; delivers "iron curtain" speech, 39–40, 116; distrusted by Soviet leaders, 93; efforts to improve Polish–Russian relations, 19–20; issues Atlantic Charter with FDR, 14, 65; meets FDR at Quebec, 21; mentioned, 97, 115, 117; military strategy during World War II, 15–16; "percentage deal," 96; quoted on Poland, 94; at Teheran Conference, 17; at Yalta Conference, 27, 98
civil liberties, U.S., 6
civic organizations, U.S., 2
Clay, Lucius, 54
Clayton, William, 52, 54, 127
Colby, Bainbridge, 6
Cold War: begins from U.S. perspective in late 1945 and early 1946, 34–35; dating the origins of, 2; depicted in U.S.S.R. as icy witch, 134; economic costs of Cold War policies in U.S., 62; Molotov on, 149; Stalin on, 85. *See also* anticommunism, U.S.; public opinion, U.S.; Stalin, Josef; Truman, Harry S.; Union of Soviet Socialist Republics; U.S. foreign policy; Wilsonian ideals in U.S. foreign policy
Collier's magazine, 11
Communist Information Bureau (Cominform), 6, 131–33, 136, 143
Communist International (Comintern), 5, 86–87, 98
Communist party, U.S., 2–3, 7, 13, 18, 21, 32, 46, 59; goals of, 4, 76–77; involvement in spying for U.S.S.R., 9–10. *See also* communists, U.S.

Communist party, U.S.S.R., 5; Central Committee of, 87, 122, 131, 142, 166; Politburo of, 99, 112–13, 116, 143

Communists: Canada, 38; Czechoslovakia, 133, 135; Europe, eastern, 131–32, 136; Europe, western, 52, 79, 131–33, 143; France, 97, 132, 173–75; Germany, 109, 121, 144; Iran, 118; Italy, 97, 132, 134; Latin America, 79; Poland, 111, 121, 131, 133, 135; U.S., 4–5, 12, 21–22, 32, 38, 44, 46, 48, 58, 61–62, 76–77, 79; U.S.S.R., 86–87, 148; Yugoslavia, 174. *See also* Communist party, U.S.; Communist party, U.S.S.R.

Congress, U.S., 1, 4, 7–8, 11, 17, 26, 30, 36, 38, 40, 46, 50–51, 53, 59, 61, 81, 83; Novikov on, 161–62

"cordon sanitaire," 89–90, 107

Congress of Industrial Organizations, U.S., 9, 11, 13, 22, 46, 59. *See also* labor unions, U.S.

containment policy, U.S., 48–49, 130

Costa Rica, 49

Council for Mutual Economic Assistance (CMEA, COMECON), 137

Council of Foreign Ministers 33, 41, 56; Conferences, at London (1945), 35–36, 107–11, 155; —, at London (1947), 138; —, at Moscow (1945), 36, 113–14, 155; —, at Moscow (1947), 125; —, at New York (1946), 119; —, at Paris (1946), 119

Crimean War, 103

Crowley, Leo, 31

Currie, Lauchlin, 10

Czechoslovakia, 53, 89, 96, 111, 121, 128–29, 131, 149; "coup de Prague" (1948), 135

Daughters of the American Revolution, 10

Davies, John Paton, 43

Declaration of the United Nations, 14–15

Declaration on Liberated Europe, 27, 98

Dekanozov, V. G., 158

Democratic party, U.S., 2, 8, 11, 15, 19, 22, 26, 44–46, 51, 58, 67; Novikov on, 161

Detroit Polish News, 28

Dewey, Thomas A., 21

Dies, Martin, 11

Dimitrov, Georgy, 104, 132

Djilas, Milovan, 97

Dodecanese Islands, 91

Drtina, P., 170–71

Dubinsky, David, 58

Duclos, Jacques, 32

Dulles, John Foster, 18, 35

Dumbarton Oaks Conference, 67

eastern Europe. *See* Europe, eastern

elections, U.S.: 1940, 12; 1944, 17, 19, 21–22; 1946, 46–47, 58, 80; 1948, 51, 59, 80

empires: American, 148–49; British, 111, 117, 125, 148, 162; —, alluded to, 92; Roman, 148; Soviet, 148–51

Eritrea, 91

espionage by the U.S.S.R. and U.S. communists, 9–10, 38, 42, 93–94, 107, 127, 142, 145, 178

Estonia, 12

Ethiopia, 7

Europe, eastern: of concern to U.S.S.R., 90–92, 96, 99, 103, 106, 113, 119–20, 127–34, 136–37, 141, 143, 150, 161; focus of Vandenberg speech (1945), 25–26; future of discussed at Teheran, 17; issue in U.S.-Soviet relations, 30, 32, 35, 41, 45–47, 49, 52–53, 79, 94. *See also* "cordon sanitaire"; "people's democracies"; spheres of influence; *specific countries*

Europe, southeastern (Balkans), 96, 104, 106–08, 112–13, 120, 136, 161. *See also specific countries*

Europe, western, 25, 41, 44, 49–56, 60, 79, 91. *See also specific countries*

European Recovery Program, 52–53. *See also* Marshall Plan

Executive Order No. 9835, U.S., 58

Far East. *See* Asia

Far Eastern Advisory Commission, 113–14

Farm Journal and Farmer's Wife, 22

farm organizations, U.S., 2

fascism, 77, 94–95

fascists, U.S., 58

Federal Bureau of Investigation, U.S., 10, 38, 59

"fifth columns," 132, 141

Finland, 5, 12, 96, 104, 121, 128, 137, 168

Foreign Affairs, 48

Four Policemen, 14; Stalin on, 95–96

Fousek, John, 3

France, 4–5, 13, 41, 49, 52–54, 57, 61, 113, 128, 137–38, 143, 155

Gaddis, John Lewis, 34, 149

Gallup polls, U.S., 13, 18–19, 27, 40, 55, 59

Georgia, 103

German–Russian nonaggression pact. *See* Molotov–Ribbentrop Pact

Germany: in 1930s, 7–8, 24; Allied Control Council for, 33, 108, 138; Byrnes states America's postwar policy toward, 41–42, 74–75; contested by West and U.S.S.R., 120–21, 125, 137–39, 142–44; demilitarization (disarmament) of, 108–09, 157–59, 163; East Prussia, 104; in era of World War I, 4–5; future of discussed at Teheran Conference, 17; future of discussed at Yalta Conference, 26–27; to be held in check, 95–96, 99, 108–10; as issue at Potsdam Conference, 33, 104; mentioned, 98, 103, 149, 163–64, 168; Ruhr region of, 104, 144; Soviet claims against, 91; Soviet occupation zone of, 94, 109–10, 120, 138–39, 144, 149; Soviet worries about, 92, 127, 157–59, 168; as topic in Vandenberg speech, 26; in World War II, 1, 3, 12–13, 16, 18, 20, 60–61, 92. *See also* Stalin, Josef, and Germany; Union of Soviet Socialist Republics, and Germany

Germany, east, 25, 40, 54–56, 121; German Democratic Republic (G.D.R.), 144–45

Germany, west, 40–41, 49, 54–56, 129–30, 138–39, 144

globalism, 61

Gorbatov, Boris, 133–34

Gottwald, Klement, 128–29, 135, 169, 171

Govorov, L. A., 159

Grand Alliance, 13

Great Depression, U.S., 3, 7

Great Britain (Britain; England; U.K.): as ally of U.S., 3, 13, 15, 22, 39, 61 81; ends aid to Greece and Turkey, 50; and Marshall Plan, 127–28; mentioned, 116, 137–38, 143, 155, 162; opposes postwar Soviet expansionism, 24–25, 106, 118–19; opposes second front in 1942, 16; opposes Soviet blockade of West Berlin, 54; opposition to communist revolution in U.S.S.R. in, 4, 78; postwar policy toward Germany, 41–42; Soviet expectations of, 96, 100; wartime policy toward Iran, 37. *See also* Atlee, Clement; Bevin, Ernest; *Britansky Soyuznik*; Churchill, Winston; Stalin, Josef, on Western allies and relations with them; Union of Soviet Socialist Republics, and hopes for British–American discord

Greece, 49–52, 54, 81–83, 97, 113, 125

Green, William, 22
Gromyko, Andrei, 95, 99–100, 104, 107, 118
Gromyko–Stettinius correspondence, 104, 108
Grotewohl, Otto, 121

Hamby, Alonzo L., 28
Harriman, Averell, 20, 30–31, 101, 111–12
Haynes, John Earl, 9
Heale, M. J., 3
Henderson, Leon, 58
Hiroshima, 33, 57, 105
Hitler, Adolf, 7, 11–14, 29, 103, 147
Hoffman, Paul, 53
Hogan, Michael J., 53
Hoover, J. Edgar, portrays Canadian and U.S. communists as threat to America, 38, 46–48, 76–77
Hopkins, Harry, 31–32, 102, 105
House Committee on Un-American Activities, U.S., 11
Hull, Cordell, 16
Humphrey, Hubert, 58
Hungary, 5, 48, 91, 104, 120–21, 131–32, 137, 168

India, 92
Indonesia, 162
International Monetary Fund, 38, 115
Iran, 36–37, 42, 91, 99, 118–19, 139, 149
iron curtain, 116, 123, 134, 150
isolationism, in U.S., 7, 14, 24, 60, 105
Italy, 5, 7, 25, 45, 49, 52–53, 67, 97, 107, 120, 134, 142, 168; colonies of, 103–04

Januszewski, Frank, 28, 67–68
Japan: as America's enemy in World War II, 3, 16, 19, 26, 31–32, 42, 60, 62; America's postwar policy toward, 24, 40, 43; atomic bombs dropped on

Japanese cities, 34; of concern to U.S.S.R., 90, 92, 96, 98–99, 105–06, 108, 111–12, 121, 130, 162, 169; expansionism in 1930s, 7–8, 13; Hokkaido, issue of Soviet landing on, 106; opposes Russia's communist government, 4. *See also* Far Eastern Advisory Commission; Kurile Islands; Sakhalin Island; Stalin, Josef, and Japan
Jenkins, Philip, 45
Jews, U.S., 45
Jones, Howard, 29

Kaganovich, L. M., 158–59
Kalinin, M. I., 158–59
Kennan, George F.: as aide to Averell Harriman during the war, 21; describes postwar U.S. policy as "containment," 48; expresses distaste for the Soviet dictatorship, 8; "long telegram" about U.S.S.R., 38–39, 69–73, 116, 122; quoted, 141, 150; "X" article read in U.S.S.R., 130
Kennedy, John F., 86
Khariton, Yuli, 105, 176
Khrushchev, Nikita, 106
Kiel Canal, 91
Kim Il Sung, 147
Klehr, Harvey, 9
Korea, 42–43, 57, 106, 125, 147, 149
Korean War, 62, 147
Kurchatov, I. V., 176
Kurile Islands, 90, 106
Kuznetsov, Alexei, 122

labor unions, U.S., 2, 6; changing role and communist penetration in 1930s, 7, 10; declining communist influence in, 48, 58–59; efforts to expel communist union leaders, 13; opposition to communist leadership of, 44, 76; support for Democrats in 1944 election, 22; unpopular postwar

strikes, 35. *See also* American
Federation of Labor; Congress of
Industrial Organizations; United Auto
Workers Union, U.S.
Lansing, Robert, 5
Latin America, 49–50, 79, 91
Latvia, 12
Lawrence, David, 27
League of Nations, 4–5, 16, 74
Leahy, William, 27, 34, 36
Leffler, Melvyn P., 23
Lend–Lease Act, 13
Lend–Lease aid to U.S.S.R., 16, 30–31,
96, 102
Lenin, Vladimir, 2, 4–5, 89, 94
Libya (*also* Tripolitania), 91–92, 108
Life magazine, 3, 39
Lippmann, Walter, 148
Lithuania, 12
Litvinov, Maxim, 91, 93, 95, 99, 104, 122,
124; Litvinov commission, 103–04
Lozovsky, Solomon, 90, 100, 109, 141,
159
Lublin committee, 20, 27, 32, 94, 98, 102.
See also Poland
Luce, Henry, 3, 26, 44
Lundestad, Geir, 149

MacArthur, Douglas, 43
Maclean, Donald, 42
magazines, U.S., 3, 11, 18, 22, 27, 32, 36,
39, 45, 76
Maisky, Ivan, 15, 91, 95–96, 100, 111,
113, 124
Malenkov, Georgy, 116, 155
Manchuria, 7, 48, 92, 106, 112, 124, 149
Mao Zedong, 43, 56, 146
Mark, Eduard, 38
Marshall, George C., 16, 43–44, 52–53,
125
Marshall Plan, 49, 50, 52–54, 56, 126–27,
137, 143. *See also* Molotov, Vyacheslav,
and Marshall Plan; Stalin, Josef, on

Marshall Plan; Union of Soviet
Socialist Republics, and Marshall Plan
Martin, Edward, 46
Masaryk, Jan, 129, 135, 170–72
Mazzone, Vito, 45
McIntyre, Marvin, 10
Mediterranean Sea, 99, 103–04, 108, 120,
162
Middle (Near) East, 44, 50, 60, 79, 81, 83,
162–63
Mikhoels, Solomon, 141
Mikolajczyk, Stanislaw, 19–21
Mikoyan, Anastas, 115, 141, 155
Ministry of Foreign Affairs, U.S.S.R., 91,
124, 137–38, 143
Ministry of Foreign Trade, U.S.S.R., 131
Molotov, Vyacheslav: and Brussels Pact,
137; and cessation of Lend–Lease,
102; chastised by Stalin, 108–09,
115–16; at conference with Czech
delegation, 169–70; and "coup de
Prague," 135; dismissed from office,
141; and Italian communists, 134;
and London Conference (1945),
107–10; and London Conference
(1947), 138; and Marshall Plan,
126–29; mentioned, 16, 23, 30–31,
35, 41–42, 90–91, 93, 98, 111, 122,
140, 155, 157, 160, 173; and Moscow
Conference (1945), 113–14; and
Paris Conference (1946), 120, 122;
and Poland, 97; and Potsdam
Conference, 104–05; quoted on
Cold War, 149; quoted on Russia's
record, 92–93; scolded by Truman,
102; and Turkish straits, 119; and
Yalta Conference, 99
Molotov–Ribbentrop (Soviet–German
Nonaggression) Pact (1939), 11, 89,
98
Montreaux Convention (1936), 42, 98,
103
Moscow Conference (1943), 16, 67

movies, U.S., 9, 18, 76
Munich Conference (1938), 14, 89
Murray, Philip, 46

Nagasaki, 33, 57
Nagy, Imre, 131
National Association for the
    Advancement of Colored People,
    U.S., 58
National Association of Manufacturers,
    U.S., 10
National Congress of American–Soviet
    Friendship, U.S., 18
National Labor Relations Board, U.S., 10,
    59
National Socialist (Nazi) party, 11
Nazi sympathizers, U.S., 61
New York Herald Tribune, 12, 164
New York Times, 38, 140, 164
news media, U.S., 3–4, 18–19, 44, 48–49,
    79. *See also* magazines, U.S.; movies,
    U.S.; newspapers, U.S.; newsreels,
    U.S.; radio, U.S.
news media, U.S.S.R., 3. *See also Pravda*
newspapers, U.S., 1, 12, 18, 27–28, 38, 45,
    76
newsreels, U.S., 3, 18
Newsweek, 36
Niebuhr, Reinhold, 45, 58
Ninkovich, Frank, 60
Nitze, Paul, 57
North Atlantic Treaty Organization
    (NATO), 50, 55–56, 135, 139. *See also*
    Union of Soviet Socialist Republics,
    and formation of NATO
Norway, 25, 143
Novikov, Nikolai, 122, 126, 130
Novikov telegram, 122–23, 130, 160–64
NSC-68, U.S., 49, 56–57, 61

Office of Strategic Services (OSS), U.S.,
    93, 98
Outer Mongolia, 106

Palestine, 91
Peace Committee, U.S.S.R., 143
Pearl Harbor, 7, 13–14, 29, 60
"people's democracies," 97, 121, 131–33
Pepper, Claude, 161
Perkins, Frances, 17
Persian Gulf, 91
Philby, Kim, 142
Pieck, Wilhelm, 121
Pleshakov, Constantine, 140
Poland: American views of postwar
    Poland, 35, 45, 48, 82; borders shifted
    westward, 98, 104; as issue during
    World War II, 17, 19–20, 22, 26–28,
    31–32, 35, 67–68, 92, 94; and Marshall
    Plan, 128–29; mentioned, 110, 131,
    149; Roman Catholics in, 97, 121;
    Soviet dominance over, 121, 137;
    Soviet plans for, 96–97; in World War
    II, 12, 20. *See also* Lublin committee;
    Polish government-in-exile
Polish Americans: concerns during World
    War II about Poland's future, 15, 17,
    21, 26, 28, 32, 67–68; FDR's relations
    with, 19, 21, 94
Polish government-in-exile, 19–20, 28,
    94, 102
Pope Pius XI, 10
Popular Front, 9, 32, 45, 58
Portugal, 142
Pospelov, Pyetr, 142
Potsdam Conference, 33–34, 93, 103–05;
    agreements mentioned, 110, 120, 138,
    159
Pravda, 112, 125–26, 142
Progressive party (1948), U.S., 58, 140
propaganda, U.S.S.R., 111, 117, 122, 124,
    133–34, 140–41, 145–46
Protestant churches, U.S., 5, 18
Protestants, U.S., 21, 26, 45, 51
public opinion, U.S.: declining trust in
    U.S.S.R. in fall 1945, 36; dislike of
    Stalin's violations of human rights, 25;

on foreign policy in 1930s, 7–8; importance of in U.S. political process, 2–3; initial views of Yalta Conference, 27–28; overall attitudes toward U.S.S.R. and domestic communists, 2, 4; popularity of anticommunist provision of Taft–Hartley Act, 59; regret in late 1945 that U.S.–Soviet relations were becoming tense, 35; response to U.S.S.R.'s blockade of Berlin in 1948, 54–55; strong opposition to U.S.S.R. and domestic communists in 1946–1947, 44, 48–49; support for anti-Russian stance in 1946, 40; support for internationalist foreign policy in 1944–1945, 23; support for proclamations reflecting Wilsonian ideals, 14; support for Truman Doctrine speech, 51; on U.S.S.R. and American communists in the 1920s, 6; on U.S.S.R. and domestic communists between 1939 and 1941, 11, 13; views about postwar Germany, 17, 74–75; wartime poll results on postwar U.S.–Soviet cooperation, 18–19; wartime support for new international organization, 16. *See also* American people; Gallup polls; Wilsonian ideals in U.S. foreign policy

Quebec Conference (1944), 21

radio, U.S., 1, 18, 27, 76
Reagan, Ronald, 30, 51, 58
Red Army, 92, 96–97, 99, 103, 109, 120, 124, 174
Red Scare of 1919–1920, 5–6
Red Scare of 1939–1941, 13
religious organizations, U.S., 2. *See also* Jews, U.S.; Protestant Churches, U.S.; Protestants, U.S.; Roman Catholic Church, U.S.; Roman Catholics, U.S.

reparations, sought by U.S.S.R., 27, 91, 104, 114, 120, 125, 157–58
Republican party: in 1944 election, 22; attitudes toward U.S.S.R. and domestic communists from 1917 to 1933, 8; efforts to ensure loyalty of federal employees, 59; mentioned 2–3, 6, 48; Novikov on, 163; opposition to Wilson's proposals for peace, 4; as possible guarantor of Poland's freedom, 68; postwar views of communists, 45–46; postwar views of situation in China, 44; response to Marshall Plan, 53; response to Truman Doctrine speech, 50; significance of Vandenberg's speech in 1945, 26; use and effectiveness of communist issue in 1946 election, 46–47, 51; use of communist issue in late 1930s, 11
Reuther, Walter, 58
Rio Pact, 130
Roman Catholic Church, 10, 12, 15, 19, 45
Roman Catholics: Europe, 45; Poland, 97, 121; U.S., 21–22, 26, 32–33, 44–46, 48, 51; U.S.S.R., 45
Romania, 28, 35–36, 42, 48, 82, 91, 94, 96, 104, 106–07, 113, 120, 128, 131–32, 137, 168
Roosevelt, Eleanor, 45, 58
Roosevelt, Franklin D.: in 1944 election, 22; appeals to Stalin in regard to Poland, 22, 28; Bern Incident and, 99; with Churchill at Quebec, 21; concerns about postwar era, 14–15; contrasted with Truman on policy toward U.S.S.R., 30; criticized by Stalin, 93–94; criticizes U.S.S.R. in 1940, 12; death of mourned in U.S.S.R., 101; desire for early second front, 16; efforts to improve Polish–Russian relations, 19–20; failure to act against domestic

communists criticized, 61; foreign policies toward U.S.S.R. evaluated, 60; "juggler" in wartime foreign policy, 15–16; loses confidence in Ambassador Standley, 1; mentioned, 31, 51, 65, 95, 161; with Molotov in 1942, 16; overall policies as president in 1930s, 7; pessimistic about Poland's future at end of Yalta Conference, 27; policies toward U.S.S.R. and domestic communists in 1930s, 7–8; policy toward Poland criticized, 27–28, 67; sees U.S.S.R. as potential ally in 1940–1941, 13; shows lack of interest in Soviet espionage, 10; with Stalin and Churchill at Teheran, 16–17, 101; Stalin's view that he was all-powerful during wartime, 18; at Teheran Conference, 101; Wilsonian ideals in January 1945 radio address, 23; Wilsonian language in December 1943 radio address, 18; at Yalta Conference, 26, 98. *See also* Union of Soviet Socialist Republics, "Roosevelt trend" valued in

Russia. *See* Union of Soviet Socialist Republics

Russian Orthodox Church, 87, 123

Russian Revolution (1917), 4–5, 88–89, 148

Russian War Relief, 1, 16

Russo–Japanese War (1904–1905), 90

Sakhalin Island, 90

Saturday Evening Post, 22

Scandinavia, 142

Schlesinger, Arthur, Jr., 45, 58

second front issue, 15–16, 93, 97–98, 174

Security Council. *See* United Nations

Semyenov, Vladimir, 138

Shvernik, N. M., 158

Smith, Walter Bedell, 117, 134, 140

Smith Act, 13

Socialist Unity party, Germany, 109, 120

socialists, Europe, 4

socialists, U.S., 4

Sokolovsky, Vasily, 138

Somalia, 91

South, U.S., 26

Soviet Union. *See* Union of Soviet Socialist Republics

Spain, 142

spheres of influence, 92–93, 96–97, 99, 104, 106, 112–13, 119–20, 125, 129–31, 141, 147–50, 162–63

spying. *See* espionage by U.S.S.R. and U.S. communists

Stalin, Josef: American views of, 12, 40; aware of history, 88, 92, 103; and Berlin blockade, 55–56, 138–41; and China, 111–12, 146–47; confers with Czech delegation, 128–29, 169–72; and control of subordinates, 115–16, 123–24, 141; on "correlation of forces," 94, 96, 98, 147; and crackdown in eastern Europe (1947ff.), 134–37, 141; desire for early second front, 15–16; on economic development, 90, 114–15; and Germany, 99, 108–09, 121, 125, 144–45; goals for postwar world, 16, 89, 93, 99; and Henry A. Wallace (1948), 140, 142; instructs "Politburo Four" (1945), 113, 155–56; and Japan, 99, 105–06, 108; on Marshall Plan, 52–53, 129, 132–33, 173; meets Maurice Thorez, 97–98, 173–75; meets with Hopkins in May 1945, 31–32, 102; mentioned, 25–26, 28, 30, 39; and militant policies, 132–34; misconceptions about U.S. political system, 18, 142; nonaggression pact with Hitler, 11, 89, 98; policies on Poland criticized, 67; at Potsdam Conference, 33–34, 93, 103–05; quoted on Cold War, 85; role in Cold

War assessed, 147–51; and security of U.S.S.R., 91–92, 100; shaping influences on, 88–89; on Soviet system, 87, 114; speech in February 1946, 38, 114; at Teheran Conference, 17; upset at abrupt cut-off of Lend–Lease aid, 31, 102; U.S. policies toward in 1930s, 8; wartime policy toward Poland, 19–20, 22; on Western allies and relations with them, 92–99, 101–02, 110–13, 116–17, 119–21, 123–25, 155–56; at Yalta, 27, 98–99. *See also* atomic weapons; Union of Soviet Socialist Republics

Standley, William C., 1–2, 16

Stassen, Harold, 125

State Department, U.S., 9, 23, 50, 57, 140

Stettinius, Edward, 104. *See also* Gromyko–Stettinius correspondence

Stimson, Henry, 30

straits, Turkish (Bosporus; Dardanelles), 91–92, 98, 103–04, 162

Sweden, 96

Taft, Robert, 53

Taft–Hartley Act, 59

Taubman, William, 100

Teheran Conference, 16–18, 26, 67, 101

Thorez, Maurice, 97, 173–75

Time magazine, 3, 26, 39

Tito, Josef, 56, 132, 136

Tocqueville, Alexis de, 62

Trans-Caucasus region, 103

Treasury Department, U.S., 10

Trieste, 120

Tripolitania. *See* Libya

Trotsky, Leon, 5

Truman, Harry S.: agrees with Churchill's "iron curtain" speech, 39; announces test of atomic bomb in U.S.S.R., 145; characterized, 28–29; decides U.S. should build hydrogen bombs, 57; demands of U.S.S.R., 106; develops

negative views of Byrnes, 36; fires Henry Wallace, 47; foreign policies evaluated, 60–61; issues executive order directed at communists in federal government, 58–59; mentioned, 111, 115, 138, 140–41; pledges support to Turkey, 42; policy toward U.S.S.R. during early months in office, 30–32; policy toward U.S.S.R. in 1946, 40; at Potsdam Conference, 33–34, 93, 105; privately expresses anti-Soviet views in 1946, 36–37, 48; privately predicts communist victory in China, 44; reads Kennan's "long telegram," 39; reasons for using atomic weapons against Japan, 34; recognizes Poland's government, 32; responds to Berlin blockade, 54–55; ridiculed in Soviet press, 133; Soviet views of, 101–02, 111, 160–61; supports international control of atomic energy, 35; Truman Doctrine speech, 50–51, 81–83; views of U.S.S.R. and U.S.–Soviet relations, 28–30

Truman Doctrine speech, 30, 51, 58, 60, 125

Turkey, 36, 40, 42, 49–52, 54, 81, 83, 96, 99, 103, 118–19, 125, 139, 149. *See also* straits, Turkish

Ukraine, 89

Union of Soviet Socialist Republics (U.S.S.R.; Russia; Soviet Union; Kremlin; Moscow): agreement at Yalta on western border adjoining Poland, 27; anti-Semitism, 141; anti-Western ideological campaign in, 123–24; and Berlin Blockade, 54–56, 138–39; communist ideas and practices in, 3, 5; concept of "two camps," 124, 133; concern over borders and security, 88–93, 98–100, 103–04, 106–07,

109–10, 112–13, 121, 130, 147–48, 163–64; concerns about the Atlantic Charter and Declaration of the United Nations, 14–15; control of U.S. Communist party, 4, 8; depicted in Kennan's "long telegram," 38–39, 69–73; depicted in NSC-68, 57; espionage in the U.S. and Canada, 9–10, 38, 33, 58–59; foreign policy of compared with U.S. foreign policy, 25; and formation of NATO, 142–44; hopes for aid for reconstruction, 95–96, 100, 126; hopes for being sole land power in postwar Europe, 100–01; hopes for British–American discord, 100, 104, 117, 162; hopes for postwar cooperation with West, 94–96, 111, 114, 125; ill-founded assumptions about relations with West, 100–01; invasion of Finland, 12; lack of understanding about U.S., 129, 150; leaders' views of U.S. policies, 92, 100–01, 105–06, 109, 111, 121–23, 128–30, 155, 157–59, 160–64; and Marshall Plan, 52–53, 126–33, 167–68; and Mediterranean Sea, 99, 103–04, 108; mentioned, 61; opposition to international control of atomic weapons, 35; as part of Grand Alliance, 13; peace treaties with former German satellites, issue of, 104, 107, 119–20, 132; planning for postwar era, 90–93; policy toward Iran, 37, 99, 118–19; postwar economic policy, 114–15; postwar military planning, 114, 124; postwar opinion in, 86–88; postwar policy toward Germany, 41–42, 110, 120–21, 137–38, 144–45, 157–59; postwar policy toward Korea, 42–43, 125, 147; postwar policy toward Turkey, 42, 99, 103, 118–19; repression of Catholics in, 45; response to Hiroshima, 105–06; responses to U.S. proposal about treaty on Germany,

108–10, 157–59; "Roosevelt trend" valued, 101, 111, 130, 140; Russian nationalism vs. Soviet patriotism, 87, 123; seen in U.S. as expansionist and uncooperative after 1945, 24; support for communist revolutions, 6; and Truman Doctrine, 125, 130. *See also* atomic energy; atomic weapons; "cordon sanitaire"; propaganda, U.S.S.R.; reparations, sought by U.S.S.R.; spheres of influence; Stalin, Josef

United Auto Workers Union, U.S., 13

United Nations, 14, 19, 26, 35, 40, 56, 79, 82, 95, 99, 118, 144; Atomic Energy Commission of, 36, 114; Security Council of, 37, 118, 122

U.S. foreign policy: compared with Soviet foreign policy, 25; economic motives in, 25, 52; influence of Japanese attack on Pearl Harbor on, 7, 60; overall influences on, 2–3. *See also* anticommunism, U.S.; Cold War; containment policy, U.S.; public opinion, U.S.; Roosevelt, Franklin D.; Truman, Harry S.; Union of Soviet Socialist Republics, leaders' view of U.S. policies; Wilson, Woodrow; Wilsonian ideals in U.S. foreign policy; *specific countries*

United States, core principles of, 3

Vandenberg, Arthur, 26, 28, 37, 51, 53, 67

Varga, Yevgeni, 126, 130, 133

Veterans of Foreign Wars, U.S., 10

Vietnam, 44, 50, 57, 61

Voice of America, jammed in U.S.S.R., 134

Voronov, N. N., 159

Voroshilov, Kliment, 91

Vyshinsky, Andrei, 144–45, 159

Wallace, Henry, 47–48, 58–59, 78–80,

140, 142, 161
Walsh, Edmund, 33
War Department, U.S., 23
Warsaw uprising (1944), 20, 94
western Europe. *See* Europe, western
White, Walter, 58
Wilson, Woodrow, 4–5, 6, 23. *See also*
    Wilsonian ideals in U.S. foreign policy
Wilsonian ideals in U.S. foreign policy,
    11, 14–15, 18, 22–26, 29, 43, 60, 106.
    See also Roosevelt, Franklin D.;
    Truman, Harry S.; U.S. foreign policy
Winchell, Walter, 10
Woods, Randall, B., 29
World Bank, 38
World War I, 3–4, 148. *See also* Wilson,
    Woodrow
World War II, 3, 6, 149; cost of to

U.S.S.R., 86, 92; lessons of in
    U.S.S.R., 88–90. *See also* atomic
    weapons; Pearl Harbor; Union of
    Soviet Socialist Republics

Yalta Conference (1945), 26–28, 31,
    67–68, 82, 98–99, 113; agreements
    mentioned, 110, 121, 138, 159
Yergin, Daniel, 34
Yugoslavia, 56–57, 112, 132, 136–37, 143,
    155. *See also* Tito, Josef

Zhdanov, Andrei, 117, 124, 132–33,
    165–66
"Zhdanovshchina," 123
Zhukov, Georgy, 110–11, 158
Zorin, Valerian, 135

ABOUT THE AUTHORS

Ralph B. Levering teaches U.S. diplomatic history at Davidson College in North Carolina. He is the author of *American Opinion and the Russian Alliance, 1939–1945* (1976), *The Public and American Foreign Policy, 1918–1978* (1978), and *The Cold War: A Post–Cold War History* (1994). He is the coauthor of *The Kennedy Crises: The Press, the Presidency, and Foreign Policy* (1983) and *Citizen Action for Global Change: The Neptune Group and Law of the Sea* (1999).

Vladimir O. Pechatnov is the chair of the Department of European and American Studies at Moscow State Institute of International Relations (MGIMO). His areas of research include U.S. political history and the history of Soviet–American relations. He is the author of *The Democratic Party of the United States: Electorate and Policy* (1981), *Hamilton and Jefferson* (1984), and *Walter Lippmann and the Ways of America* (1994). He has also published widely on the history of the early Cold War. He was a research fellow at the Institute of USA and Canada Studies under the Russian Academy of Sciences, served at the Soviet/Russian embassy in Washington, was a fellow at the Woodrow Wilson International Center for Scholars, and participates in the Cold War International History Project.

Verena Botzenhart-Viehe grew up in Germany in the 1950s, at the height of the Cold War. She now teaches history and geography at Westminster College in Pennsylvania. Her research and writing have focused on the American occupation of Germany, German–American culture clashes, and American ambassadors to Germany. She has written entries for the *Dictionary of International Statesmen* (1992) and *Notable Ambassadors* (1998). She is currently working on the representation of the Cold War in Ohio news-papers.

C. Earl Edmondson is the chair of the Department of History at David-son College in North Carolina. His teaching and research interests are fo-cussed on central Europe, Russia, and international relations in the twenti-eth century. He is the author of *The Heimwehr and Austrian Politics, 1918–1936* (1978), several entries in the *American National Biography* (1999), and numerous book reviews. He has studied abroad on various occasions, participated in a faculty exchange at the Moscow State Institute of Interna-tional Relations in September 2000, and attended the initial conference of the Russian International Studies Association in Moscow in April 2001.